ENGLISH HERITAGE

# Great Witcombe Roman Villa, Gloucestershire

A report on excavations by Ernest Greenfield
1960 - 1973

## Peter Leach

with

Lynne Bevan and Trevor Pearson

and with contributions by

J. Bayley, L. Bevan, S. Butcher, S. Cottam, J. Davies, B. Dickinson, J.G. Evans, T. Finney, J. Henderson, M. Henig, R. Jones, J. Price, J. Timby, D. Williams.

illustrations by

M. Breedon, N. Dodds and T. Pearson

BAR British Series 266
1998

Published in 2016 by
BAR Publishing, Oxford

BAR British Series 266

*Great Witcombe Roman Villa, Gloucestershire*

ISBN 978 0 86054 879 9

© English Heritage and the Publisher 1998

The authors' moral rights under the 1988 UK Copyright,
Designs and Patents Act are hereby expressly asserted.

All rights reserved. No part of this work may be copied, reproduced, stored,
sold, distributed, scanned, saved in any form of digital format or transmitted
in any form digitally, without the written permission of the Publisher.

BAR Publishing is the trading name of British Archaeological Reports (Oxford) Ltd.
British Archaeological Reports was first incorporated in 1974 to publish the BAR
Series, International and British. In 1992 Hadrian Books Ltd became part of the BAR
group. This volume was originally published by Archaeopress in conjunction with
British Archaeological Reports (Oxford) Ltd / Hadrian Books Ltd, the Series principal
publisher, in 1998. This present volume is published by BAR Publishing, 2016.

Printed in England

PUBLISHING

BAR titles are available from:

          BAR Publishing
          122 Banbury Rd, Oxford, OX2 7BP, UK
EMAIL   info@barpublishing.com
PHONE  +44 (0)1865 310431
FAX     +44 (0)1865 316916
          www.barpublishing.com

# CONTENTS

| | |
|---|---|
| SUMMARY | v |
| PREFACE AND ACKNOWLEDGEMENTS | vii |
| 1: INTRODUCTION AND METHODS OF ANALYSIS | 1 |

2: SITE NARRATIVE
Introduction

| | |
|---|---|
| 2.1: The South West Range (Lower Bath Suite) | 5 |
| 2.2: The North West Range (Upper Bath Suite) and Exteriors | 11 |
| 2.3: The Central Range | 14 |
| 2.4: The North Exteriors | 18 |
| 2.5: The North East Range | 20 |
| 2.6: The South East Range | 31 |
| 2.7: East and South East Exteriors | 40 |
| 2.8: The South Courtyard | 41 |
| Appendix: Index of phased contexts and features | 46 |

3: THE FINDS
Introduction by *P. Leach*

3.1: PREHISTORIC
Flint and stone by *L. Bevan*

| | |
|---|---|
| Pottery by *P. Leach* | 49 |

3.2: ROMAN
3.2.1.: Vessels

| | |
|---|---|
| Romano-British coarse pottery by *P. Leach*, Samian by *B. Dickinson*, Amphora by *D Williams*, Mortaria by *J. Timby* | 51 |
| Lids by *L. Bevan* | 69 |
| Glass by *J. Price and S. Cottam* | 73 |

3.2.2: PERSONAL OBJECTS

| | |
|---|---|
| Brooches by *S Butcher* | 82 |
| Glass beads by *J. Price and S. Cottam* | 83 |
| Jet beads by *L. Bevan* | 84 |
| Pendants by *L. Bevan* | |
| Bracelets (shale and copper alloy) by *L. Bevan* | 86 |
| Pins (copper.alloy, jet and bone) by *L. Bevan* | |
| Finger rings by *M. Henig* (silver); by *L. Bevan* (copper alloy); by *J. Price and S. Cottam* (glass) | 90 |
| Toilet accessories by. *L. Bevan* | |
| Buckles and buttons by *L. Bevan* | 91 |
| Gaming counters by *L. Bevan* (bone & pottery); by *J. Price and S. Cottam* (glass) | |
| Hobnails and shoe fittings by *L. Bevan* | 93 |
| 3.2.3.: COINS by *J. Davies* | 94 |

3.2.4.: BUILDING MATERIALS, FIXTURES AND FITTINGS

| | |
|---|---|
| Building stone by *L. Bevan* | 97 |
| Ceramic tile and brick by. *L. Bevan* | |
| Plaster and mortar by *P. Leach* | 101 |
| Window glass by *J. Price and S. Cottam* | 105 |
| Door furniture by *L. Bevan* | |
| Nails and miscellaneous iron fittings by *L. Bevan* | 106 |

### 3.2.5.: DOMESTIC TOOLS, UTENSILS, FITTINGS
Whetstones by *L. Bevan*
Querns and millstones by *L. Bevan*
Rubbers and pounders by *L. Bevan*
Knives and handles by *L. Bevan*
Projectile heads by *L. Bevan*
Iron tools, utensils and implements by *L. Bevan* ............ 109
Spindlewhorls by *L. Bevan*
Miscellaneous fittings and furnishings by *L. Bevan* ............ 116

### 3.2.6.: INDUSTRIAL BY-PRODUCTS
Slags and waste by *T. Finney* ............ 118
Metal and boneworking waste by *L. Bevan* ............ 120

### 3.2.7.: ENVIRONMENTAL
Animal bone and shell identified by *R. Jones and J.G. Evans*
Human remains by *J. Henderson* ............ 121
Carbonised plant remains by *A.M. Lab.*
Coal *by P. Leach* ............ 122

### 4.0 REVIEW AND DISCUSSION
4.1: Dating ............ 123
4.2: Function and reconstruction ............ 124
4.3: Status and economy ............ 129
4.4: Context ............ 133

CONSOLIDATED BIBLIOGRAPHY ............ 137

## LIST OF TEXT FIGURES

| | | |
|---|---|---|
| Fig. 1 | Site location, the Lower Severn region | viii |
| Fig. 2 | Locality and setting | x |
| Fig. 3 | The villa building and its environs | 3 |
| Fig. 4 | Building plan, rooms and excavated areas | 4 |
| Fig. 5 | South West Range, plan of principal areas and features | 6 |
| Fig. 6 | North West and Central Ranges and exteriors, plan of principal areas and Features | 12 |
| Fig. 7 | Central Range and South Courtyard, principal North-South section (composite) | 16 |
| Fig. 8 | North East Range and exteriors, plan of principal areas and features | 19 |
| Fig. 9 | South East Range and exteriors, plan of principal areas and features | 32 |
| Fig. 10 | South Courtyard, plan of principal areas and features | 42 |
| Fig. 11 | Prehistoric stone and flint | 50 |
| Fig. 12 | Roman pottery; Fabric A1 | 55 |
| Fig. 13 | Roman pottery; Fabric A1 | 57 |
| Fig. 14 | Roman pottery; Fabric B1 | 58 |
| Fig. 15 | Roman pottery; Fabric B3 | 61 |
| Fig. 16 | Roman pottery; Fabric D1 | 64 |
| Fig. 17 | Roman pottery; Fabrics D1 & D4 | 65 |
| Fig. 18 | Decorated samian (Fabric E) | 62 |
| Fig. 19 | Roman pottery; chronological representation of fabric types by eves. (%) | 67 |
| Fig. 20 | Roman pottery; chronological representation of form types by eves. (%) | 70 |
| Fig. 21 | Sources of Roman pottery at Witcombe | 72 |
| Fig. 22 | Roman vessel glass, numbered from catalogue | 79 |
| Fig. 23 | Brooches, beads and pendant | 85 |
| Fig. 24 | Copper alloy bracelets | 87 |
| Fig. 25 | Shale bracelets, bone pins and finger rings | 90 |
| Fig. 26 | Rings, toilet implements, dress accessories and counters | 92 |
| Fig. 27 | Roman coins; representation by coin issue periods (after Reece 1972) | 94 |
| Fig. 28 | Column shaft, bases and capitals | 98 |
| Fig. 29 | Column bases and architectural fragments, stone and marble | 99 |
| Fig. 30 | Stone tiles and architectural fragment | 100 |
| Fig. 31 | Clay roof tile and incised box tiles | 102 |
| Fig. 32 | Incised clay box tiles | 103 |
| Fig. 33 | Incised clay box tiles | 104 |
| Fig. 34 | Keys, lock and iron building fixtures | 107 |
| Fig. 35 | Iron Building fittings and fixtures | 108 |
| Fig. 36 | Whetstones, rubber and quernstones | 110 |
| Fig. 37 | Quern and millstones | 111 |
| Fig. 38 | Iron knives and blades | 113 |
| Fig. 39 | Knife handles, projectile heads and iron tools | 114 |
| Fig. 40 | Iron tools and utensils | 115 |
| Fig. 41 | Spindlewhorls, furnishings and handles | 117 |
| Fig. 42 | Villa layout, Periods 2 and 3 | 125 |
| Fig. 43 | Great Witcombe Villa in the 4th century, an isometric reconstruction view from the south | 127 |

## LIST OF PLATES

*NB. All photographic scales displayed are imperial (feet and inches)*

| | | |
|---|---|---|
| Pl. 1 | The remains as currently displayed; view from the North West Range towards the east. | |
| Pl. 2 | The remains as currently displayed; view from the North East Range towards Witcombe Wood. | vi |
| Pl. 3 | Stone column fragments reused in the hypocaust below Room 5, Lower Bath Suite. | |
| Pl. 4 | Room 7a cold bath and foundations distorted by subsidence, Lower Bath Suite | |
| Pl. 5 | Foundations and drain F5 within Room 8a, Lower Bath suite. | 7 |
| Pl. 6 | General view east of foundations to Rooms 11b, 9 and 8a, and drains F.3 and F.4, Lower Bath Suite. | 9 |
| Pl. 7 | Tile *pilae*, Room 9 hypocaust, Lower Bath Suite. View south west. | |

| | | |
|---|---|---|
| Pl. 8 | Foundations and hypocaust, Room 11b hot bath, Lower Bath Suite; view north east. | 10 |
| Pl. 9 | Drain F.2 exiting from beneath Room 11b, Lower Bath Suite; view north. | |
| Pl. 10 | Rooms 15 and 15a during excavation, Central Range; view south west. | 13 |
| Pl. 11 | Rooms 15 and 15a excavated, Central Range; view south west. | |
| Pl. 12 | Rooms 15 and 15a excavated, Central Range; view east. | 15 |
| Pl. 13 | Portico foundations, Room 32, Central Range; view south west. | |
| Pl. 14 | Drain F2 north of Rooms 15 and 15a, Central Range; view south west. | 17 |
| Pl. 15 | Period 3 cobbled track 888 and 890 approaching the villa from the north east, Area 71; view south west. | 21 |
| Pl. 16 | Rooms 42 and 43 fully excavated, North East Range; view south east. | 22 |
| Pl. 17 | View south west from Room 35 across the North East Range | 23 |
| Pl. 18 | Oven structure F22 with remains of the latest-phase hearth 686, Room 34, North East Range; view south west. | 25 |
| Pl. 19 | Second-phase hearth 690/691 in oven F22, Room 34, North East Range; view west. | 26 |
| Pl. 20 | Third-phase hearth 687/688 in oven F22, Room 34, North East Range; view south west. | 27 |
| Pl. 21 | View south east across Rooms 53, 34, 35 and 51, North East Range. | 28 |
| Pl. 22 | Drain F19 exiting Room 35, with Iron Age ditch 708 upper right, North East Range; view south east. | 29 |
| Pl. 23 | Drain F23 with re-used quernstone beneath corridor Room 51, North East Range; view north east. | 30 |
| Pl. 24 | Drains F52 and F53 below Room 27, view south east from Room 23-25 buttresses, South East Range. | |
| Pl. 25 | Remains of Period 4 floor 817 with re-used paving material in Room 27, South East Range; view east. | 33 |
| Pl. 26 | Part of drain F85 re-using clay imbrex roof tiles, Room 29, South East Range; view north west. | |
| Pl. 27 | Remains of "corn drying oven" F54 in Room 29, South East Range; view east. | 35 |
| Pl. 28 | Aisle plinths 3, 4 and 5 between Rooms 26 and 28, drain F49b left, South East Range; view south west. | 37 |
| Pl. 29 | View west across Rooms 31, 28, 26 and 27 to Rooms 19-25, South East Range. | 38 |
| Pl. 30 | Remains of Room 30 distorted through subsidence, South East Range; view south west. | 39 |
| Pl. 31 | Part of drain F72 re-using clay tegula and decorated flue tiles, South Courtyard; view north west. | 43 |

## LIST OF TABLES

| | | |
|---|---|---|
| Table 1 | Index of pottery fabric types | 51 |
| Table 2 | Roman pottery form series | 52 |
| Table 3 | Roman pottery, quantification by eves. per fabric type and period | 68 |
| Table 4 | Roman pottery, quantification of forms by eves. per fabric type | 71 |
| Table 5 | Chronological distribution of coins (issue periods 1-16, Reece 1972) | 95 |
| Table 6 | Summary of industrial debris per context | 118 |
| Table 7 | Quantities of debris types by weight | |
| Table 8 | XRF analysis of selected samples | 119 |

## SUMMARY

The Roman villa at Great Witcombe, Gloucestershire was discovered in 1818 and largely cleared by Samuel Lysons and its then owner Sir William Hicks. Since being taken into guardianship as an Ancient Monument the site has been re-excavated by Elsie Clifford (1938-9), and most recently by Ernest Greenfield (1960-73), whose work forms the basis of this publication. The villa was apparently founded on a virgin hillside site to exploit extensive southern and eastern views and a copious water supply, and built to a grand and unified design in the first decades of the 3rd century. Further expansion during the later 3rd and 4th centuries resulted in a sumptuous country house of courtyard plan, which included several mosaic pavements, two suites of baths and a prominent colonnaded central gallery and portico. A radical change of use after $c$ AD 380 preceded a final phase of occupation, which probably continued into the 5th century before eventual abandonment of the site. It is suggested that the villa belonged to the descendants of a veteran, settled on an estate established here at the foundation of the *colonia* at Gloucester. Investigation of the site has been almost wholly confined to the villa building and its immediate surroundings, although the position of at least one other large stone building is known in the vicinity.

*Plate 1* The remains as currently displayed; view from the North West Range towards the east.

*Plate 2* The remains as currently displayed; view from the North East Range towards Witcombe Wood.

# PREFACE AND ACKNOWLEDGEMENTS

Discoveries and remains preserved in and around the Cotswold Hills epitomise many of the most characteristic elements of the civil province of Roman Britain (Fig.1). Among these are the villas, many of which were buildings of considerable architectural pretension and frequently graced with heated rooms, bath suites, and mosaic paved floors, along with other manifestations of a Graeco-Roman inspired lifestyle. Woodchester and Chedworth are two of the most renowned establishments of this class in Britain, much of the latter being displayed as a public monument. The only other villa in Gloucestershire whose remains are accessible to the public, Great Witcombe, is far less famed, though evidently a site of equivalent status to many of the greatest houses of the province and occupying an outstanding position. Its relative obscurity today is due principally to the virtual absence of any detailed interpretation or publication of the site and its remains.

Despite the relative wealth and high concentration of villas in the Cotswold region (RCHM 1976) very few have been subjected to detailed excavation of a scale or quality which has led to adequate publication. Honourable exceptions include Barnsley Park (Webster 1981; Webster and Smith 1982; Webster *et al* 1985), The Ditches (Trow 1987), and Frocester Court (Gracie 1970; Gracie and Price 1980, and forthcoming). With the addition of Great Witcombe to this list it must be recognised that the history of previous work there and the quality of surviving data (as presented in this volume) will detract somewhat from its value in expanding the database for the study of these establishments and their context in Romano-British society. Nevertheless, in bringing together this account, with its focus the most recent campaigns of excavation by Ernest Greenfield in the 1960s and early 70s, it is hoped that both the importance and potential of Great Witcombe will be brought to the fore.

Following a preliminary campaign by Elsie Clifford just prior to World War II (Clifford 1955), Greenfield was employed to continue excavation at Great Witcombe as a prelude to the display of the villa remains as a monument in the care of the State. Necessarily, this imposed conditions upon the scope of potential research, although a relatively thorough investigation of the main building and its immediate context seems to have been achieved. Questions of origin and the development and operation of the building seem to have been largely resolved, the latter much assisted by an exercise in reconstruction prompted by Greenfield's results (Neal 1977). The data published now can undoubtedly contribute to more broadly based research themes relating to the character and development of the Romano-British rural economy, locally and further afield, and the place of villas such as this within it.

However, it is perhaps also pertinent to suggest some more immediate avenues of research whereby this presentation of data, and thus the value and importance of Great Witcombe itself, might be enhanced. As this report demonstrates, our by now relatively detailed knowledge of the building is hardly matched by corresponding detail relating to its setting. Excepting the building discovered by Hicks below the villa to the south east (Clifford 1955, 13-15, and fig.3), there is little clue to the arrangement of supporting facilities, other structures or enclosures in the immediate locality. To redress this lack most effectively a programme of geophysical prospection employing both resistivity and magnetometer survey should be instituted. Using the latest equipment and analytical processing programmes the quality of data from such surveys can be very high. This has been well demonstrated by recent work at Chedworth (Tabor 1996), and with particular force at the Wroxeter Roman town site (Gaffney and Linford 1998). Apart from the buildings of Coopers Hill Farm, Great Witcombe is currently surrounded by pasture fields, which are eminently suitable for such surveys. The targeting of areas to the south east around the second building and to the north where there is potential for Iron Age settlement, should be the priority, though more extensive coverage by less intensive survey would also be desirable. Such an approach provides the opportunity to obtain relatively high quality information over an extensive area, without the necessity of invasive and more costly excavation, although the latter should also be used judiciously and on a small scale as a proving or testing device for survey results. Conditions for the recovery of geophysical survey data are likely to be good here and could transform our knowledge and understanding of the villa and its environs.

This report attempts to provide as full an analysis of the surviving remains and records as possible following the retirement and subsequent death of Great Witcombe's latest excavator.

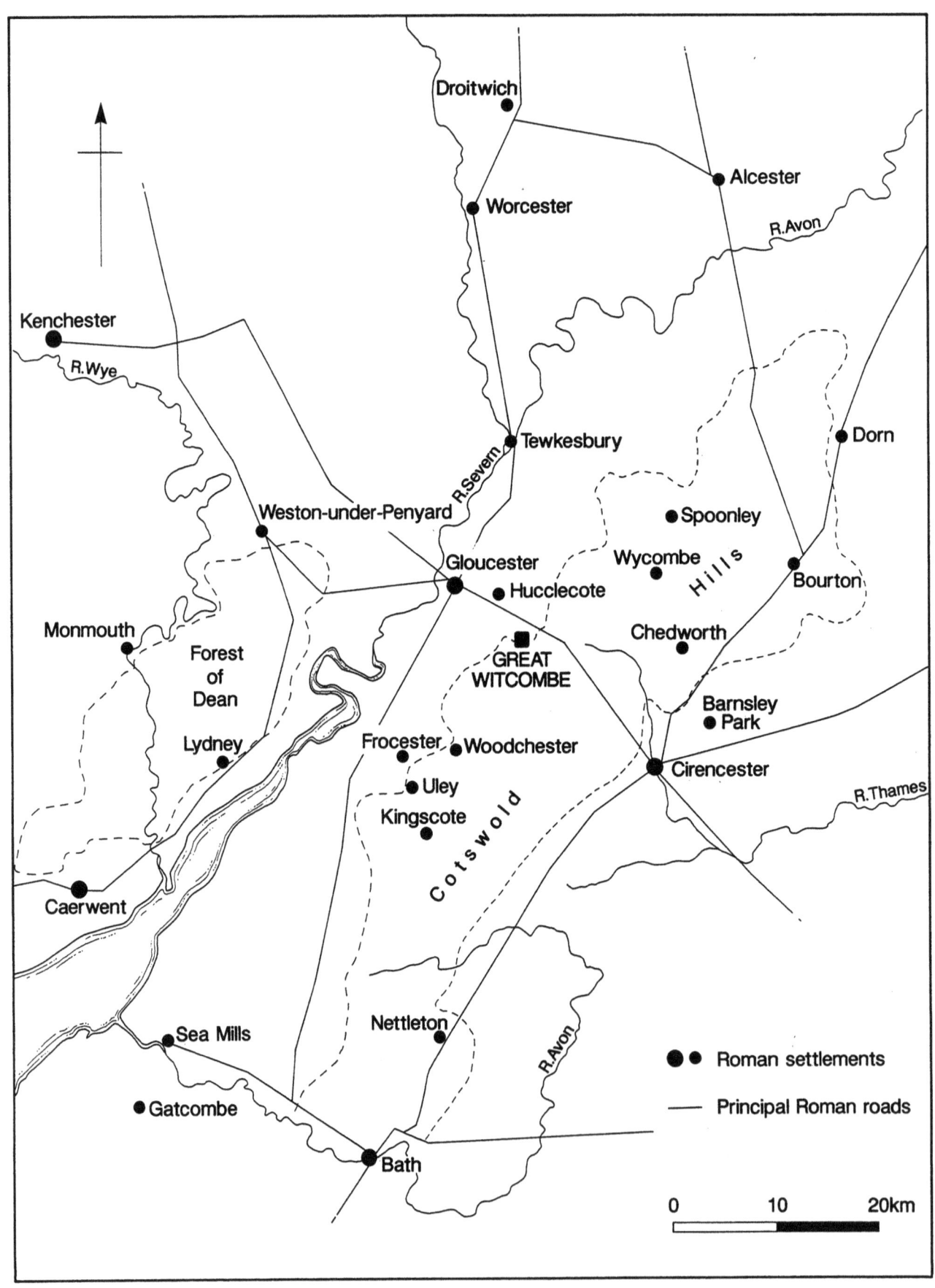

*Figure 1* Site location, the Lower Severn region

Regrettably it was not possible to enhance this analysis through the addition of personal experience or insights from Ernest Greenfield himself. Equally, it has not proved possible to acknowledge personally the efforts or support of those involved with the original excavation campaigns.

A project enabling analysis and publication of the works undertaken by Greenfield was commissioned by English Heritage through the Field Archaeology Unit of the University of Birmingham (BUFAU), commencing in 1986. At that time, lacking an adequately detailed research design, funding was insufficient to bring the project to completion by early in 1988. This was subsequently remedied and the report was finalised in 1994-5. I am grateful to successive Inspectors of Ancient Monuments at English Heritage for liason and support; initially Ian Stewart and Francis Kelly, and subsequently Glyn Coppack.

The preparation of this report would not have been possible without the input of many colleagues in BUFAU and of the specialist contributors, the majority of whom are acknowledged on the title page and by their contributions within this publication. An especial debt of gratitude is owed to Trevor Pearson and Agostino Fovaro (MA research student), assisted by Valerie Price, for their ordering and preliminary analysis of the primary field archive. In addition to her specific contributions, Lynne Bevan provided valuable assistance in co-ordinating the finds section of the report. Responsibility for the illustrations has been shared between Trevor Pearson, Mark Breedon and Nigel Dodds. With the exception of Plates 1 and 2 (by Peter Leach), all the photographs were taken by Ernest Greenfield. Secretarial and administrative support was provided by Ann Humphries, Jackie Pearson and Simon Buteux, and internal editing undertaken by Peter Ellis. The archive of finds and both the primary and secondary records generated by Greenfield's excavation are in the care of English Heritage, as are the conserved remains of the villa building whose site can still be visited and enjoyed.

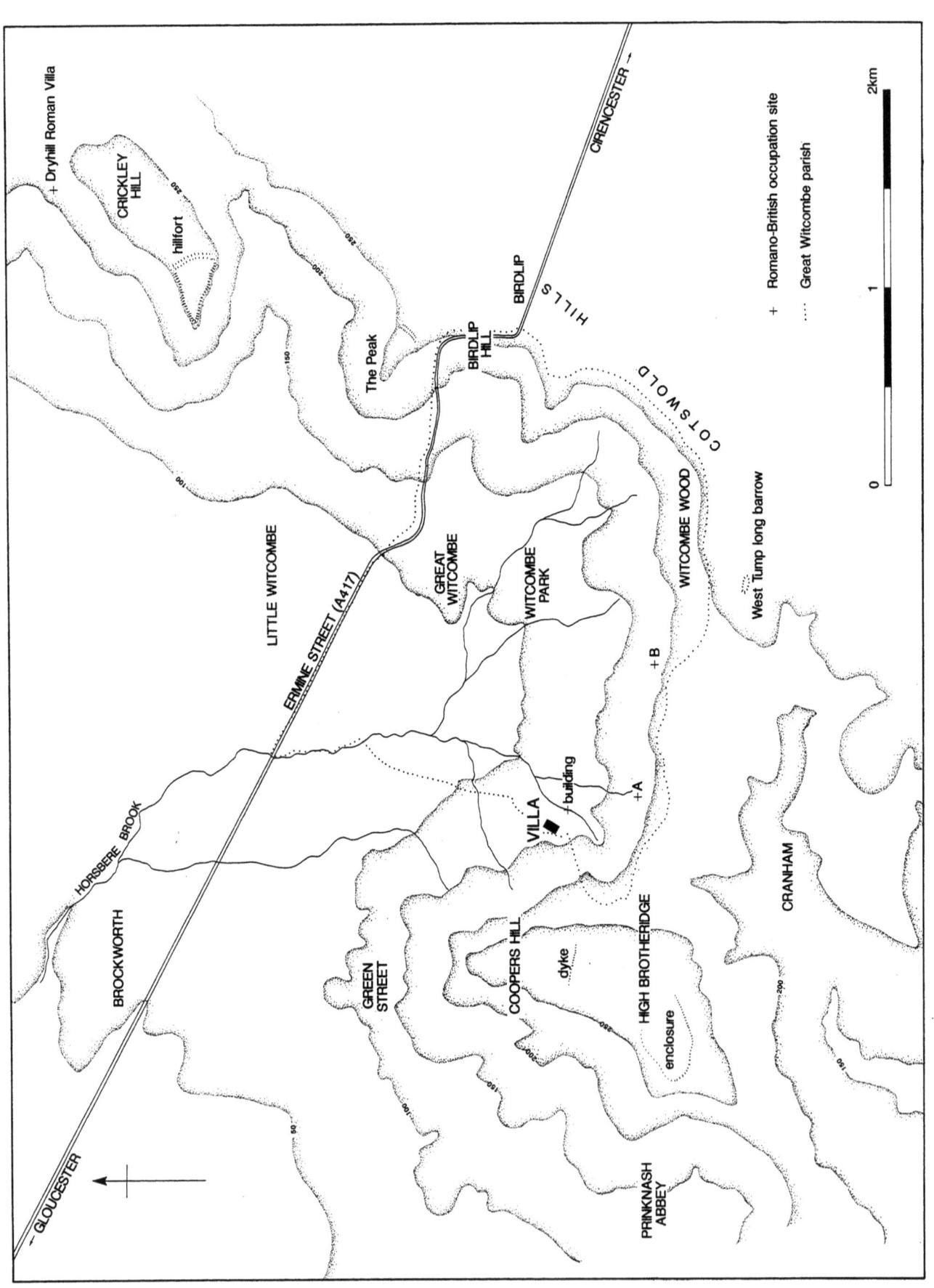

*Figure 2 Locality and setting*

# Chapter 1

# INTRODUCTION AND METHODS OF ANALYSIS

The Roman Villa at Great Witcombe (SO 899143) occupies a fine hillside position, at *c* 140m AOD, facing south east within a wide north-facing combe in the Cotswold Hills escarpment between Coopers Hill and Crickley Hill, some 5 miles to the southeast of Gloucester (Fig. 2). It is located upon a series of shallow terraces on the Upper Lias clay, close to its junction with the overlying Cotswold Sands, above which again rises the steep scarp slope of the Inferior Oolite. Springs emerging at the junction between the sands and Lias clay, combined with the moderate slope, give the site a certain instability. Their presence was almost certainly a factor in the choice of this location, although the splendid views across the combe eastwards and also up the Severn Vale to the north (Plates 1 and 2), were surely paramount (RCHM 1976).

The villa was discovered in 1818 by labourers removing an ash tree in a field belonging to Sir William Hicks of Witcombe Park. Almost immediately, excavations were then undertaken by Samuel Lysons, and continued by Hicks in 1819 following Lysons' death, to reveal virtually the entire plan of the villa buildings (Lysons 1819). A separate building was uncovered by Hicks c 100m down slope beside the stream to the south east, but is no longer visible (Fig. 3). Sometime later, but probably quite soon after the excavation, two buildings were erected over portions of the lower (SW) bath house range (Rooms 5 and 6, and 10 and 11) to preserve *in situ* the mosaic pavements found there. The main site was eventually given by the Hicks-Beach family in 1919 as a monument in guardianship to HM Office of Works (subsequently English Heritage), in whose care it remains to this day. In 1938, Mrs Elsie Clifford was commissioned to undertake a re-excavation of the site prior to consolidation of the exposed fabric. In the event she was only able to examine most of the west wing, before the outbreak of World War II in 1939 (Clifford, 1955). It was not until the 1960s that the work of re-excavation and clearance could continue, this time under the direction of the late Ernest Greenfield.

Greenfield's involvement at Witcombe began in 1960 with the excavation and recording of a drainage trench cut approximately north-south across the site. Although badly located relative to surviving structures, this excavation served to demonstrate the potential for deposits and new features which had survived previous clearance. Thereafter, in 14 seasons of work ending in 1973, all three ranges of the villa were re-excavated, along with their immediate exteriors and the whole of the southern courtyard. This seems to have involved a small team working for an average of 5-6 weeks per season during the summer months, and under the direct supervision of Ernest Greenfield. The location of the excavated areas can be reconstructed with reference to Interim Reports (existing only between 1960 and 1966), and the archive of site notebooks and plans made by the excavator (Fig. 4). In addition to uncovering the whole of the main villa structure again, a series of test pits were excavated by hand to the south and south east in 1966 and 1965 (the latter also relocating the building found in 1820, Fig. 3), and in 1961 further east around the combe at two localities where surface finds of Roman material were recorded (sites A and B, Fig. 2).

The prime purpose of this report is to provide an account and interpretation of the results obtained by Ernest Greenfield; it was not the intention to attempt a complete reinterpretation of the site involving all the material and records of previous excavations, although that data was extensively drawn upon, and this account is thus effectively now the most comprehensive review and interpretation of the villa's remains. By today's standards of archaeological site recording the excavation archive is fairly basic and of variable quality. Descriptions of deposits were very brief and no running numerical system was devised for the site structural record as a whole. Structural features newly identified by Greenfield were numbered sequentially, but with little more definitive description. Those identified by earlier excavators were not normally described or numbered, except in the case of rooms; following or extending the sequence originally devised by Lysons. The sparse records relating to walls and their respective relationships is particularly unfortunate, since much of the potential for additional analysis of the villa structure is now obscured by subsequent restoration work or hidden below ground. A good photographic archive was kept, but the few detailed site plans and sections and a lack of wall elevations further limit structural analysis as well as the detail of published plans in this report. The record of finds discovered during Greenfield's work is much better, frequently supplementing the often meagre graphic and stratigraphic records. All retained finds were given a unique find number, prefixed by the letter W for the site. Except in the case of coarse pottery, a secondary numbered sequence related to their material or class identity: thus coins C1-C225, or stone objects ST1-ST728; which are referenced to a site or deposit locality. This permits a fair degree of site distribution plotting, although excepting some coins, the exact position of most individual finds was not surveyed.

**Finds**: By far the largest body of data were the finds, the bulk of which were relocated and sorted for further identification. Specialist reports were commissioned for the majority, and their contributions are included later in this report. As mentioned above, the finds and their location in the course of excavation were relatively well recorded, and are thus of assistance in devising a scheme of chronological phasing for the site and its stratigraphy. In the course of excavation finds were collected and bagged together from one location - often a layer within a room or other site sub-division. The finds were subsequently identifiable by their bag and unique find number, although the latter was sometimes applied to a small group of material such as a collection of pottery or animal bone found together; and more specifically by the numbered material or class prefix (for stone, glass, iron, samian pottery, etc.) as mentioned previously. Finds were thus recorded on site (in notebooks) primarily by a running numerical sequence of bag numbers, applied throughout the 14 seasons of excavation and referenced to a site location. As far as is known, all identified finds were kept; with the exception of pottery (see report) and probably ceramic tile, only selective samples of which were retained. The overall distributions and significance of all the finds recovered during Greenfield's seasons is considered further in the concluding section to this report.

**Stratigraphy**: To overcome the lack of a coherent sequential system of context identification a new sequence of context numbering was devised, commencing with the number 501. These numbers were equated where possible to deposits recognised during the excavations and numbered by Greenfield according to room or open area locations. This has permitted the association together of additional information derived from drawings, photographs, and above all from the finds record. A concordance of new context numbers with the original site context records is deposited with the excavation archive, although in some instances new numbers had to be assigned where no original numerical reference to certain contexts, though evidently encountered in excavation, could be found. The new assigned context numbers provide the basis for discussion and interpretation of the site structure and a sequence of phased events.

**Phasing**: The creation of a comprehensive chronological system to embrace the full sequence of events represented in the archaeological record at Witcombe is hampered somewhat by the effect of previous work on the site. Notably, this has involved almost wholesale clearance with minimal record by Lysons and Hicks, and subsequent excavation to reveal and preserve major structural elements, rather than to disentangle their sequence through dismemberment. Greenfield's records of the remaining stratigraphy relate only to that remnant preserved mainly around the exteriors of the main building ranges, and only rarely undisturbed within rooms. He appears to have attempted a structural phasing of the villa based upon his own data, as evidenced by an overall site plan drawn up in 1974 (archive), but not elaborated upon further. An overall phasing scheme for Witcombe has been devised from Greenfield's data, with the support of information recorded by previous excavators. This proposes five major period divisions, though in all probability a simplification of what must have been a more complex sequence of events. The finds are perhaps the clearest testimony to a greater complexity, spanning a period from the late 1st to the end of the 4th century AD.

PERIOD 1: Pre Villa; prehistoric and early Roman features and deposits, including early ground surfaces; sometimes associated with datable finds. Few coherent structures. Prehistoric - mid 2nd century AD.

PERIOD 2: Villa Phase I; first major building layout comprising two equal sized suites of rooms aligned NW-SE - the East and West Wings, and linked by a long gallery of three rooms with a rectangular dining room opening off to the north - the Central Range. A separate bath house to the south west may also be of this phase. Early 3rd? century unitary plan; evidence of construction date poor and imprecise. Continues in this form through 3rd century, with some modifications?

PERIOD 3: Villa Phase II; major building modifications; south west extentions to W. Wing bath suite, octagonal dining room - Central Range, E. Wing additional rooms and S.E. Range aisled building. Later 3rd century reconstruction?, but some modifications probably 4th century.

PERIOD 4: Post-Villa Occupation?/Desertion; possible change of building use represented by late 4th century (from *c* AD 380) and later occupation? (4a). Post-Roman desertion and dereliction; medieval- early 19th century (4b).

PERIOD 5: Early 19th century - Modern; Lysons and Hicks' excavations and backfill (1818-19); subsequent consolidation, drainage or disturbances, including Clifford's 1938-9 excavations; modern turf/topsoil.

As will be apparent from the more detailed narrative of evidence recorded in certain rooms or areas around the villa buildings (below), there are hints of further potential sub-division in this system, notably within Periods 2 and 3; while Period 4 should probably be split. Nevertheless, the scheme proposed offers a basic framework around which the surviving and recorded excavation data can be ordered, to present a history and chronology for the Great Witcombe villa buildings.

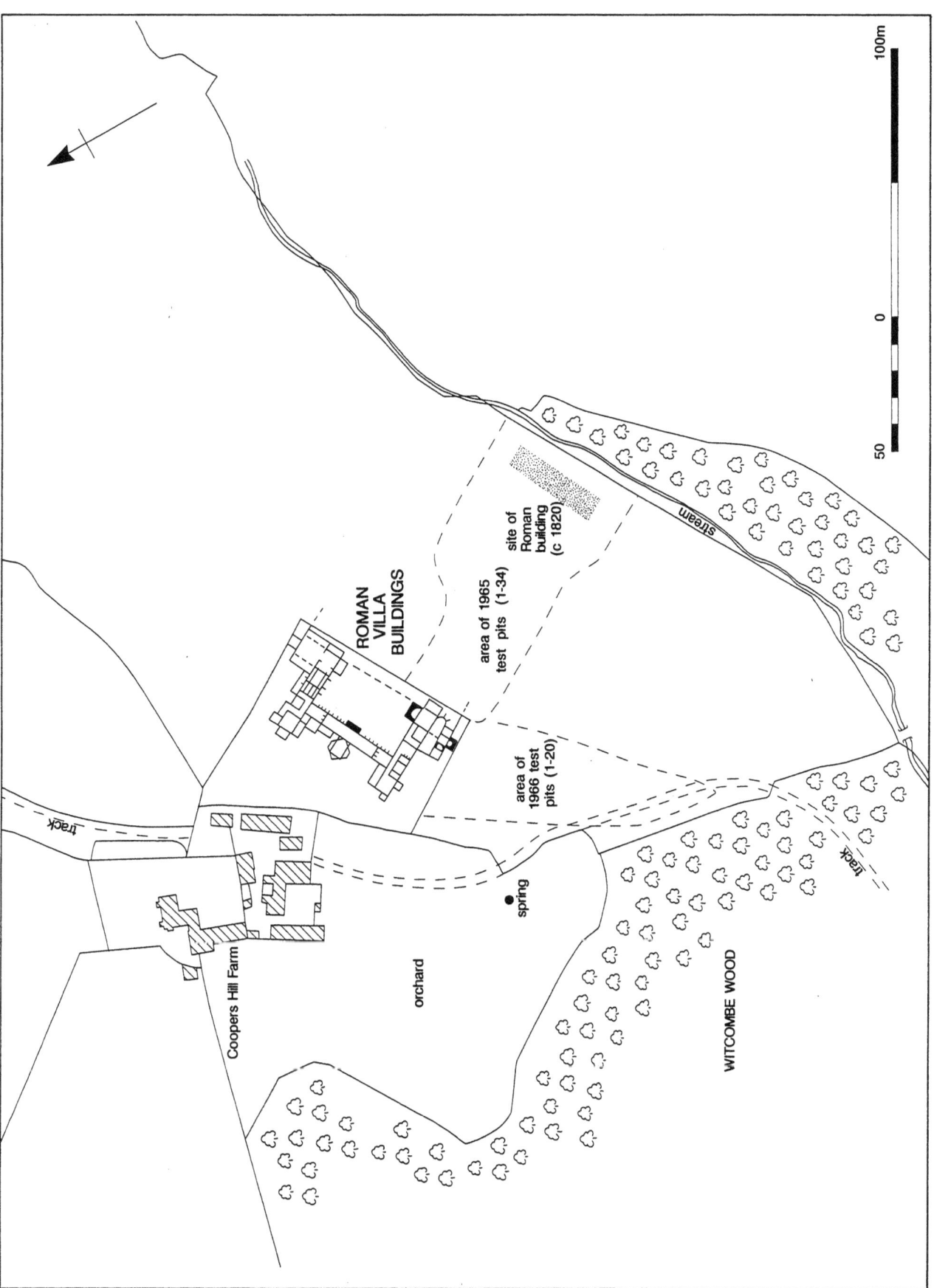

*Figure 3* The villa building and its environs

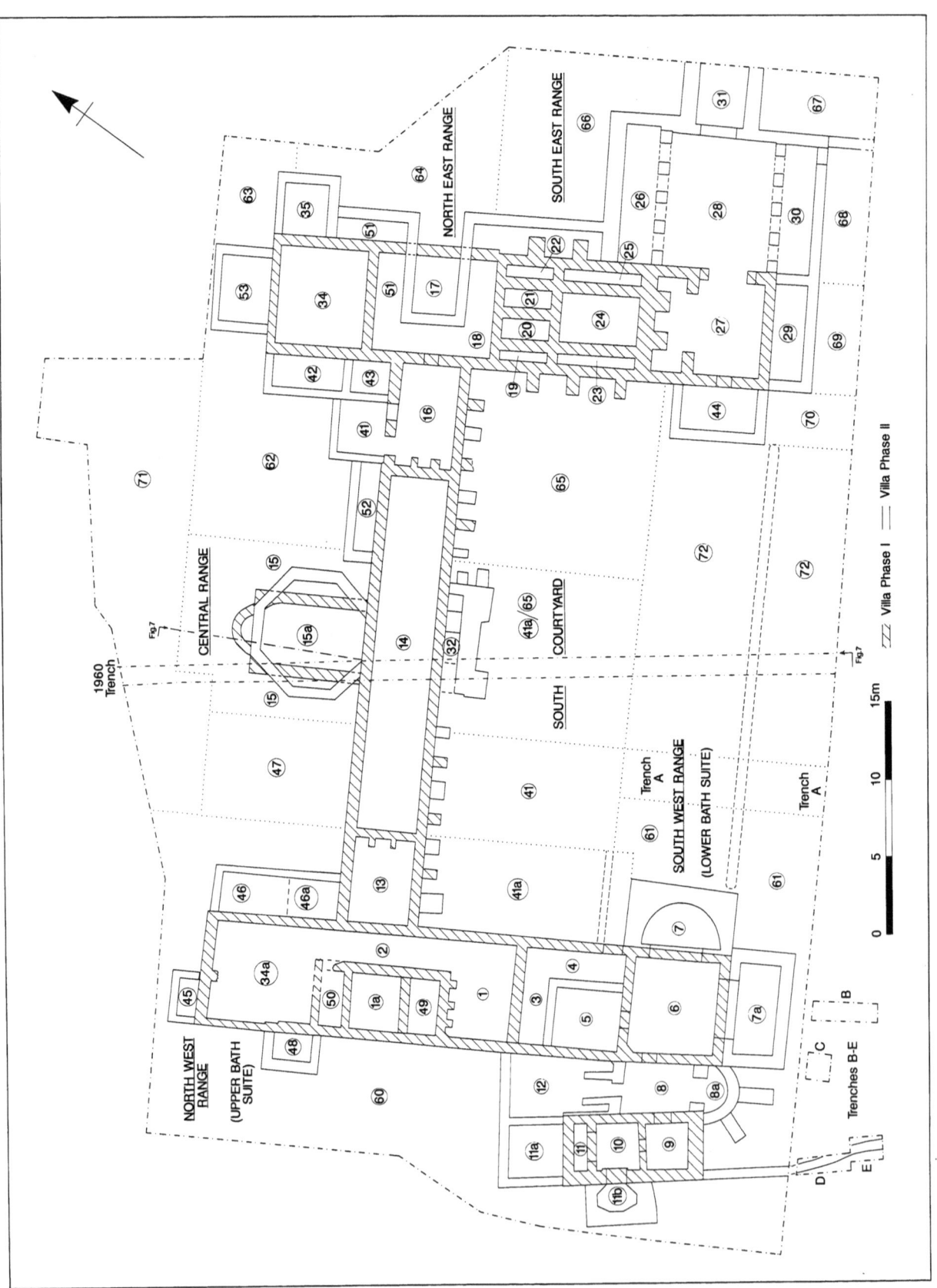

*Figure 4  Building plan, rooms and excavated areas (after Lysons, Clifford and Greenfield)*

Chapter 2

# SITE NARRATIVE

## Introduction

In the circumstances of previous excavation and recording, a geographically ordered account of the site and relevant surviving evidence from each area is felt to be most appropriate. Although this form of presentation normally takes precedence over a chronological account of the site and its components, periodization is applied wherever possible to the interpretation of specific features and contexts; and an overview of the villa remains and their evidence for the development and chronology of the site is given in the final section (4) of this report. The villa buildings and their exteriors are considered in a clockwise sequence, commencing at the south west (Fig. 4). Although not conforming strictly to the cardinal points, these are defined as follows: West Wing - S.W. Range and Exteriors, N.W. Range and Exteriors; Central Range and N. Exteriors; East Wing - N.E. Range, S.E. Range, E.and S.E. Exteriors; South Courtyard. A phased index of all recorded features (Greenfield) and new or retrospectively defined contexts (Leach), listed according to their site location, is found in the archive.

## 2.1: The West Wing - S.W. Range (Lower Bath Suite)

For convenience of discussion the West Wing of the villa is divided into two parts, at the junction between Rooms 1 and 3 (Fig.4). This marked a functional division; with the rooms to the south east comprising a bath house suite set at a lower level than those of the N.W. Range (apart from Room 1). Most of the rooms were cleared by Lysons and again by Clifford, both of whom give summary accounts of their main features (Lysons 1818, 180-2; Clifford 1955, 18-21). Greenfield's final clearance in 1962-3 revealed all the rooms recorded by the earlier excavators; namely, Rooms 3, 4, 5, 6, 7, 7a, 8, 9, 10, 11, 11a, 11b and 12, and further details of drains extending around and away from the baths to the south (Fig. 5).

The core of this suite, and apparently primary elements built as one with most of the N.W.Range, were Rooms 3/4/5 and 6 (of Period 2). The northern room may originally have been one, measuring approximately 7m square, but was subsequently sub-divided into three (in Period 3). Room 5 retains almost intact a fine mosaic pavement of the Corinium school (RCHM 1976, pl. 12), and was heated via hypocaust flue tiles set in the walls, from the furnace in the adjacent Room 12. Reused building material (stone column drums and capitals, Plate 3) was employed as floor supports in the hypocaust below Room 5 (Williams 1972, 113); a further indication of its

Period 3 conversion. There was direct access into the southern Room 6 and, very unusually as recorded in Roman Britain, via a slype into Room 8 to the south west. Around Room 5 to the north and east were, respectively, Room 3 - a latrine through which ran the main northern drain (F6), and Room 4 - a passage leading from Room 6 to the latrine and also to an exit into the South Courtyard. Room 4 represents the only potential location for an access between the N.W. Wing and the Lower Baths, via stairs from an upper storey over Room 1. However, there is no evidence for this or any other direct link, and it has been suggested that the Lower Bath suite could be reached from elsewhere in the villa only via the South Courtyard (Neal 1977, 33). A passageway or verandah providing just such an access was suspected by Clifford in Area 41a (1955, 22), although not apparently corroborated by Greenfield (South Courtyard, below).

The second room ascribed originally to Period 2 - Room 6 - lay immediately to the south, and contained the best part of another mosaic pavement with a design of fishes and sea creatures (RCHM 1976, pl. 11). This was the *frigidarium* in Period 3, and apart from doorways into Room 5 and the passage (Room 4), there was access from Room 6 via steps down into cold plunge baths - Rooms 7 and 7a, and a door westwards into Room 8. Rooms 5 and 6 were covered by a roofed stone building, apparently erected soon after the site was cleared by Lysons and Hicks, and founded upon the original walls of those rooms. Once again, most of the elements now surviving in these rooms should be ascribed to Period 3.

Room 7 of Period 3, butted against the north east wall of Room 6, was an apsidal cold plunge bath, internally lined with plaster and with a floor of brick tiles. Three steps up to the west led via a wide archway into Room 6. Subsidence downhill to the south east had almost detached the foundations of this bath from those of Room 6, and had distorted its remains. Through the foundations of the south east wall a drain (F10) exited to carry water away downhill in the same direction. This was built as two parallel alignments of vertically-set limestone blocks to form a channel which was capped by horizontally-laid stone slabs and infilled by clay silt

A second cold bath, also of Period 3 (Room 7a), was located against the south-east wall of Room 6. Although originally revealed by Lysons, this room was severely affected by land subsidence and had not been re-examined by Clifford (Plate 4). A rectangular structure was defined by mortared wall courses set on ashlar

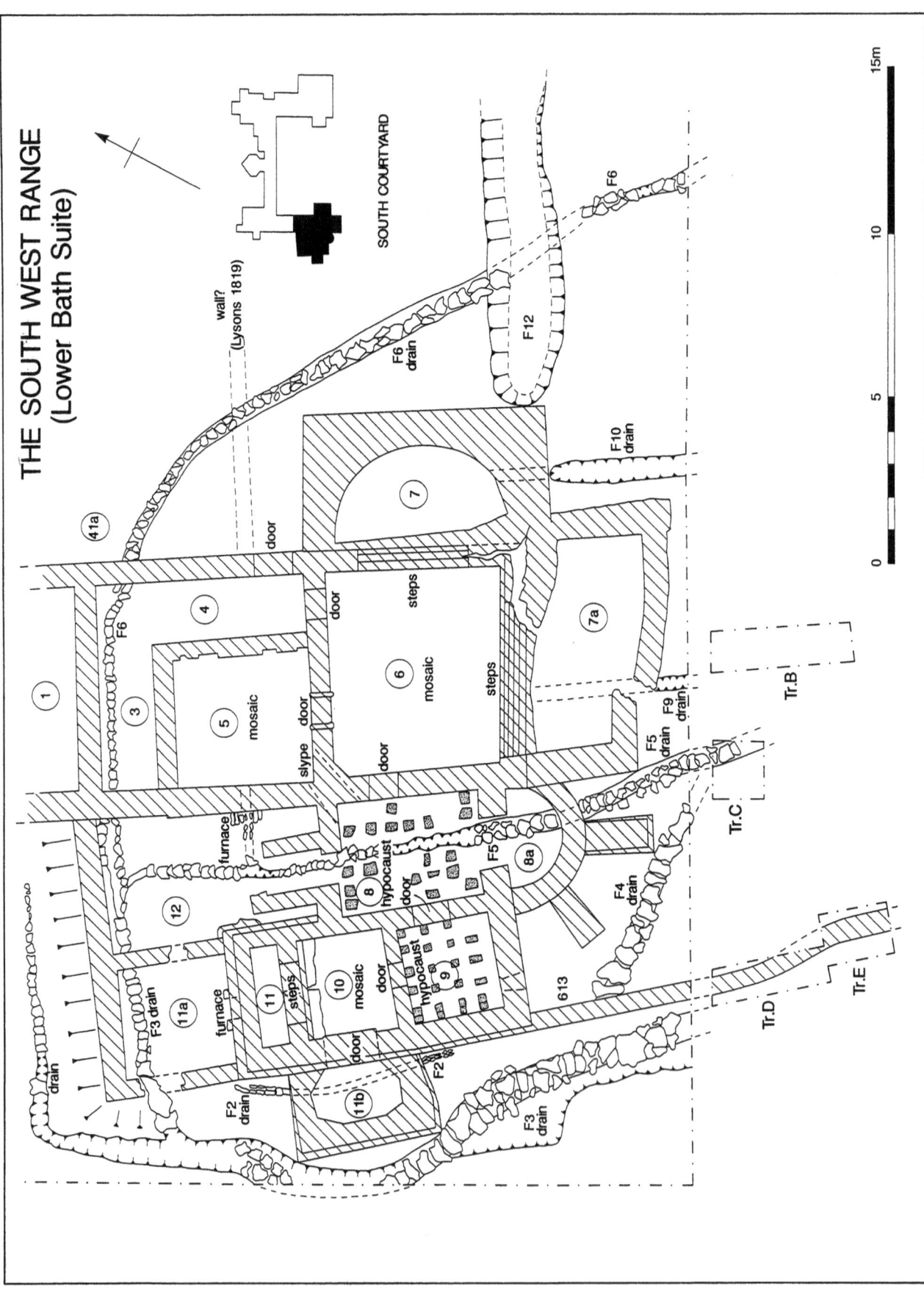

**Figure 5** *South West Range, plan of principal areas and features*

*Plate 4* Room 7a cold bath and foundations distorted by subsidence, Lower Bath Suite; view north.

*Plate 3* Stone column fragments reused in the hypocaust below Room 5, Lower Bath Suite.

foundations. The south-west wall of five surviving courses remained *in situ*, bonded with the south-east wall. The latter, with four surviving courses, was displaced downhill by subsidence, though still bonded with the damaged but still upright 6 courses of the north-east wall. The north-east and south-west walls were also bonded with the north-west-wall, which was butted flat against the south-east wall of Room 6. Up to 8 courses of the north west wall survived, but were partly peeled away from Room 6 behind as a result of the landslip. Upon it were the remains of stone steps which gave access down from Room 6 via a wide and originally arched? opening. A drain (F9) exited south from beneath the broken segments of the south east wall, possibly passing beneath the room.

Within Room 7a survived two phases of concrete and plaster floor, wall and step lining, though badly cracked by subsidence and subsequently weathered following earlier exposure by Lysons. In the south west corner where one area survived unweathered, the primary lining was pink concrete with a powdered brick/tile filler on a sand and stone rubble base. Over its surface was a thin, smoothed plaster skim painted pale green and buff. The second phase of lining was a hard pink concrete with a fragmented tile filler, overlain again with a smooth plaster skim painted pale green/pink. The second phase of lining had been filleted to the earlier wall plaster by plain moulding. This evidence clearly suggests some refurbishment during an extended period of use.

None of the *in situ* floor lining was removed, although in Greenfield's interim report of 1962 (No. 3) it was suggested that the wall foundations of Room 7a were set partly into an earlier rubble-filled wall foundation trench, which thus contributed to their subsidence. This feature was not defined elsewhere in the site records and seems not to have been excavated further. Greenfield's final site plan of 1974 suggests that it linked with the foundation trench (F12) found in 1960 and thought to mark a southern boundary wall of the courtyard, (but see South Courtyard account, below). Later Period 4 deposits within the room included fallen plaster debris from the walls, soil washed into fissures in the floor caused by subsidence, and an area of rubble collapse not removed by Lysons which preserved part of the plaster floors. The remainder of this room was backfilled with rubble from the 19th-century excavations and sealed by turf/topsoil.

To the south west of Room 6 and squeezed somewhat between it and the hot bath suite (Rooms 9/10/11), was Room 8 - the *tepidarium*. Most of this room had been cleared previously by Lysons and then Clifford; the latter also removing a later rubble infill from around the brick hypocaust piers, beneath what might originally have been another decorated mosaic floor pavement. The apsidal south east end (Room 8a) and its exterior, were re-exposed and recorded by Greenfield in 1962 (Plates 5 and 6).

The semi-circular mortared ashlar wall of Room 8a survived as up to-6 courses, butted against the south-east wall of Room 9 and the south-west wall of Room 7a. This was supported to the south by two large buttresses, both of up to 6 mortared ashlar courses bonded with the apse wall, and with fragments of plain cream/white wall plaster still adhering. Their provision was presumably to counter the subsidence which may already have been affecting Rooms 7 and 7a (above). A floor of buff sandy mortar within the apse continued into Room 8, but there was no evidence of the brick hypocaust piers present beneath the main room. Room 8, inserted between Rooms 5/6 and the Period 2 bath house, was of Period 3, with the apse 8a a later addition in that Period (Plate 5).

In the floor of both rooms a stone-lined drain (F5) exited through the base of the apse wall to carry water away downhill to the south east. This comprised a channel of parallel stone blocks containing a base silt and clay fill, capped by stone slabs. At the drain's exit from beneath the apse wall was a water-deposited lime concretion. The drain and floor within Room 8a were sealed by heavy stone rubble; either Lysons' backfill, or more likely, the continuation of infill around the Room 8 hypocaust recorded by Clifford. Coins from this material suggest that it was deposited after AD 378 and should thus be of Period 4.

The hot bath suite comprised Rooms 9, 10, 11and 11a, a single rectangular block with 4 bonded outer walls and bonded partition walls, aligned NW-SE but at an angle diverging away slightly more to the west from that of the main West Wing. This raises the possibility that these rooms are part of some earlier site arrangement, which may even predate the West Wing, but for the purposes of this account they are assigned to Period 2. Rooms 10 and 11 were exposed by Lysons, and subsequently housed within another small roofed building founded upon their original surviving walls. Room 11, the hot bath, was lined with smooth red concrete; its floor resting upon hypocaust tile *pilae* and a double series of roofing tiles to enhance the efficiency of water heating. The bath was approached via steps down from Room 10, also heated by the hypocaust beneath both rooms. This room is floored by another decorated mosaic pavement of geometric design (Clifford 1955, pl. VII), and has the remains of a red plastered seat on the north west wall.

Room 9 was almost square, its upper surviving walls and another decorated mosaic floor pavement having been exposed originally by Lysons. The latter has since been destroyed, but its design was recorded by Lady Cromie, daughter of Sir William Hicks, soon after discovery (*op cit* 19). Further exploration by Greenfield revealed mortared ashlar walls surviving to 6 or 7 courses and resting upon the old ground surface (Plates 6 and 7). A doorway in the north east wall gave access from Room 8, and a very narrow doorway, little more than 0.5m wide, gave access to Room 10. Near the base of the south-east wall an opening permitted drainage out from the hypocaust chambers.

Excavation beneath the floor revealed 19 almost complete tile hypocaust *pilae*. Each complete set comprised 16 horizontally laid tiles separated by lime mortar and set upon a larger *tegula* (Plate 7). A thin layer of clay and charcoal (580) around the base of the *pilae* probably equates with the use of the hypocaust, which was

**Plate 6** *General view east of foundations to Rooms 11b, 9 and 8a, and drains F.3 and F.4, Lower Bath Suite.*

**Plate 5** *Foundations and drain F5 within Room 8a, Lower Bath suite. View north east.*

*Plate 7* Tile pilae, Room 9 hypocaust, Lower Bath Suite. View south west.

*Plate 8* Foundations and hypocaust, Room 11b hot bath, Lower Bath Suite; view north east.

originally linked with that beneath Rooms 10 and 11. Coins within that deposit suggest that the hypocaust may still have been in use up to *c* AD 375, if not later. Beneath this deposit was a building layer or 'floor' of stone, brick and mortar fragments pressed into the old ground surface of green clay. Between the pilae the hypocaust was infilled by two deposits; a claysoil containing much wall plaster and some artefacts, and a layer of stone rubble incorporating fragments of tile, plaster and tesserae. Both deposits suggest deliberate infill with building demolition material, apparently beneath an intact floor, and probably equate to the infilling of Period 4 beneath Rooms 8 and 8a.

Butted against the south corner of Room 9 was an alignment of 3 or 4 mortared wall courses distorted by subsidence and continuing downhill beyond the bounds of the excavation. This continued the alignment of the south-west walls of Rooms 9,10 and 11, but as a boundary wall rather than part of another room. To the east, and cut off by this wall, was a drain (F4) which merged eastwards with the drain F5 exiting from beneath Rooms 8/8a. Built as parallel alignments of stone blocks, the channel contained silt and rubble and was sealed by stone slabs.

Room 11b, opening off Room 10 was butted against the south-west wall footings of Rooms 10 and 11. Its foundations comprised a continuous rectangular mortared ashlar wall surviving to 3 or 4 courses and resting upon a broader unmortared plinth of at least 3 courses (Plate 8). The whole structure rested upon the old ground surface, and its relationship with Roms 9, 10 and 11 suggests that it was added in Period 3. A small drain (F2) comprising a triangular setting of small stone slabs passed through the base of the wall from the north west, to exit again to the south east (Plate 9). This may have been the predecessor to the larger drain (F3) which respects Room 11 (below).

Within the irregular octagonal hypocaust chamber which was linked originally with those beneath Rooms 9-11, were 12 sets of mainly intact tile *piliae*. Each stack stood upon larger *tegula* resting upon the old ground surface, and were bonded with lime mortar. Larger tiles or bricks held with mortar were set upon the *piliae* to form the base for the remains of a pink concrete floor with broken tile filler. The remains of this floor and former lining to the bath had weathered badly since their original exposure by Lysons. Clay silt within the hypocaust, capped by a thin layer of charcoal, had evidently accumulated during its use, before the deposition of further silt following blockage of the flue between Rooms 10 and 11b. A subsequent infill of small compact rubble, mortar and tile fragments in stony soil, up to the underside of the remaining concrete floor, was deliberate, probably matching that introduced beneath other floors in the Lower Baths in Period 4.

Rooms 11a and 12 functioned as service rooms or covered yards (of Period 3) to house the furnaces which heated the baths. Both were cleared previously by Lysons or Clifford, apart from the drains beneath or around them. The rear wall of both rooms to the north west was the most massive, terraced into the hill slope and subsequently affected by subsidence. Two poorly preserved walls, surviving to a maximum of four mortared ashlar courses, extended north west from the ends of Room 11, against which they were butted, to link with the collapsed north-west wall and define the almost square Room 11a. This room contained the furnace which heated Rooms 9-11, whose opening was defined by two short wall stubs bonded into the north-west wall of Room 11. Clifford noted that this opening was narrowed on its west side in the 4th century (Period 4) when the hypocausts beneath Rooms 9 and 11b were infilled and the floors in Rooms 11a and 12 were raised by a deposit containing. 4th-century pottery (1955, 22).

Room 12 housed two furnaces; one to heat Room 5 with an arched opening, and the second to heat Room 8. The latter was blocked at the time of infilling the Room 8/8a hypocaust, when the floor in Rooms 11a and 12 was raised. Greenfield's work in these rooms was confined largely to excavation of the drainage system. The principal drain (F3) continued south west from the latrine drain (F6) in Room 3, comprising parallel settings of stone blocks to form a channel, and paving slabs for its base and lid. The channel was infilled by a series of clay silts and soil, and the drain construction trench infilled with stony clay, tile and mortar debris. The drain was somewhat distorted by subsidence from the north west and may have been reconstructed in part. It was sealed by a layer of stony soil and clay containing charcoal and tile fragments; either the original floor to these rooms or a remnant of the secondary floor recorded by Mrs Clifford (*op cit*). The drain (F5) beneath Room 8 linked up beneath Room 12 with F3, but the latter continued south west to exit beneath the wall of Room 11a and join another drain running around the Lower Baths from the north. The combined drain (F3) then continued south east, to run downhill and beyond the excavation bounds. Rooms 11a & 12 and the exteriors to the south west were all sealed by soil and rubble; Period 5 backfill derived from the excavations of Lysons and/or Clifford.

## 2.2: West Wing - North West Range (Upper Bath Suite) and Exteriors

This comprises the rooms at the north-west end of the West Wing; namely, Rooms 1, 1a, 2, 34a, 45, 46, 48, 49 and 50, and their immediate exteriors (Fig. 6). Apart from Room 1, these rooms lay at a considerably higher level than the South West Range (up to 5m.), and they had been very thoroughly excavated by both Lysons and Hicks and by Clifford, prior to Greenfield's clearance. The following account is mainly therefore a summary of the rooms and their content and suggested function, based upon the earlier published records.

The main structure of the West Wing should be of Period 2 and was continued north west from the primary rooms (3/4/5 and 6) of the Lower Bath Suite, via Room 1 and a stairway (Room 2), to the Upper Baths. Room 1, the first to be opened by Lysons, was paved with sandstone flags (probably from the Forest of Dean), at a level no more than 0.3m above the Lower Bath House floors (Clifford 1955, pl.I). Having been terraced into the slope of the hill, the walls of this room survived in places

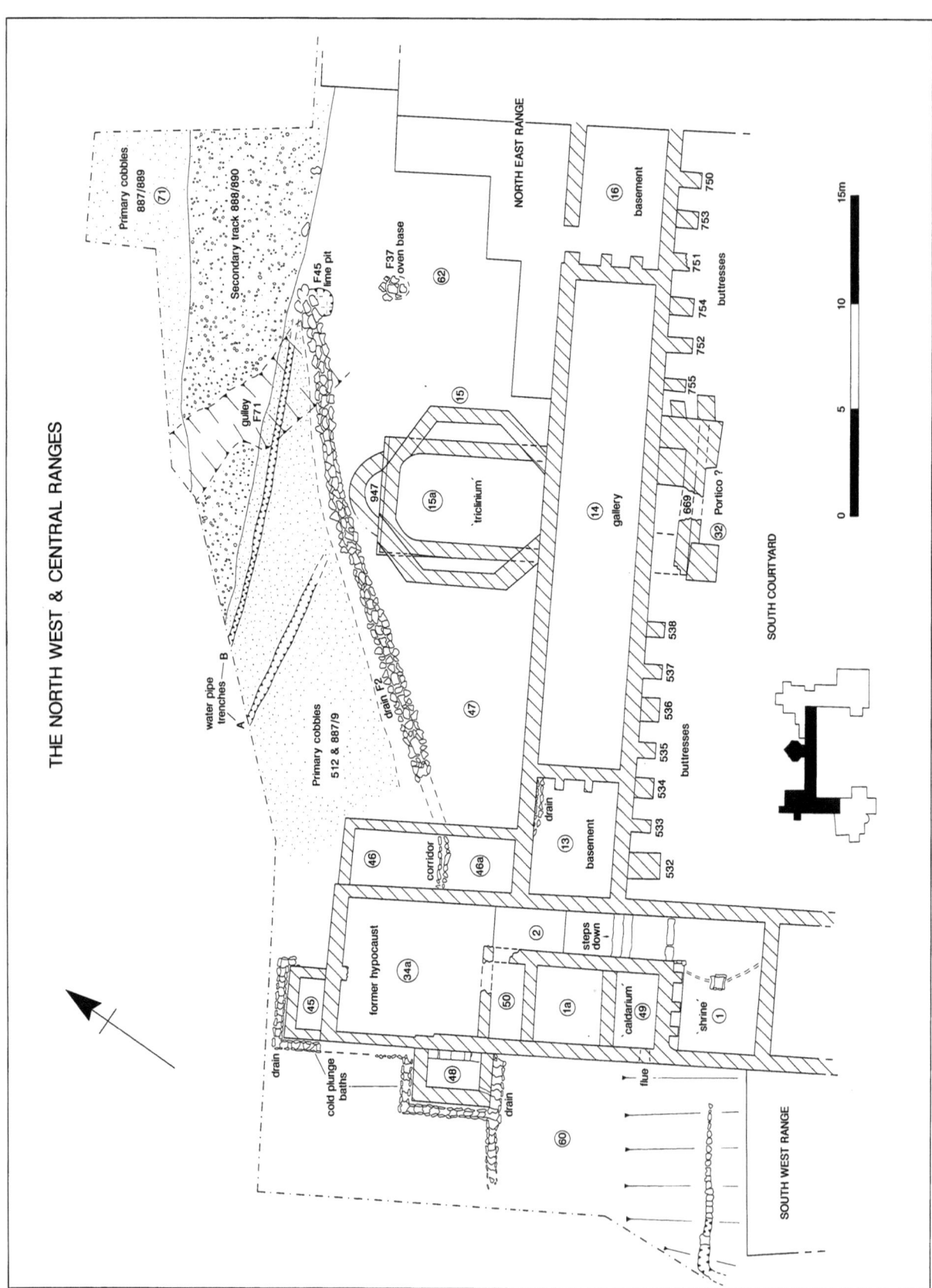

*Figure 6  North West and Central Ranges and exteriors, plan of principal areas and features*

# SITE NARRATIVE

*Plate 10* Rooms 15 and 15a during excavation, Central Range; view south west.

*Plate 9* Drain F.2 exiting from beneath Room 11b, Lower Bath Suite; view north.

almost 2m high. There was no direct link with the lower baths (unless via an upper floor); the only access being from the Upper Baths by the shallow stairway or ramp in Room 2. When originally discovered, both rooms were decorated with panels of painted wall plaster. Three deep niches on a low plinth in the north wall of Room 1 were created by original buttresses, built to support the rooms of the baths above. Between the buttresses and the foot of the stairs was a stone plinth, separated from the floor paving stones by a brick tile border. This has been suggested as the base for an altar (Lysons 1819, 180), and from beneath it ran a tiled water conduit which fed a rectangular cistern defined by flagstones in the centre of the room. The overflow from here was channelled by a drain leading into the latrine of Room 3 to the south. The position, internal arrangements and material found within this room, including the skulls of cattle, sheep/goats, deer antler fragments, and an iron axe, suggest that it functioned primarily as a shrine. It is likely that Room 1 had an upper storey, and that the ceiling of the lower room was at or a little below the floor level of Room 34a (Neal 1977, 34).

The Upper Baths were less well preserved than the Lower Baths, their walls for the most part having been badly robbed, and it is not clear whether both were in contemporary use. The floor of the largest room (34a) survives now as the base level of a hypocaust; an original floor above having been destroyed well before the early 19th-century excavations. This lower level was heavily burnt and disturbed, and lay upon the old ground surface. Greenfield also encountered the base of a furnace channel at this level. Debris above it contained later 4th-century material of Period 4, probably a remnant of the "camping floor" encountered by Clifford at the time of her excavations (1955, pl. V), representing the final occupation phase.

South of Room 34a were three smaller rooms which probably opened off from it. The existing floors of Rooms 1a and 50 are at the same level as 34a and may have shared the same furnace to heat a hypocaust beneath the original floors above. The floor of Room 49 is some 2m lower, but may also have had a hypocaust, heated separately from a flue in the south west wall. This could suggest the site of a hot bath (*caldarium*), in which case this set of rooms would have been a heated bath suite, mirroring the arrangement of Rooms 9, 10 and 11 in the Lower Baths, though perhaps in reverse order.

Opening from Room 34a are the remains of two small rectangular rooms (45 and 48). Of these, the best preserved was Room 48, lined with concrete and retaining three successive floor levels. A lead pipe encased in concrete drained out through the south corner into a drainage channel running around the exterior of both rooms. The walls of both rooms were butted to Room 34a, and a late 3rd-century coin sealed beneath the earliest floor in Room 48 suggests that they were additions of Period 3. Rooms 45 and 48 were possibly cold plunge baths, echoing the more capacious baths in Rooms 7 and 7a of the Lower Baths, although Greenfield suggested that Room 45 may have been heated, which would accord better with the heating of Room 34a.

The operation and use of the Upper Bath Suite can only be adequately understood if upper floors to some rooms are postulated. David Neal's reconstruction of the villa buildings (1977) suggests that access to the Upper Baths from the main building would have been via the corridor of the Central Range. The surviving remains of Room 13 suggest that a corridor lay above a basement and gave access to the suggested room above Room 1 via a passageway above the stairway in Room 2. This route could thus have given entry to the baths, or more directly into Room 1a, but could not have turned north above the stairway where there would have been insufficient headroom. More likely perhaps was a route via Rooms 46 and 46a (probably a single room), indicating a passage from the Central Range corridor (13) which led into Room 34a and to the stairs down into Room 1. Room 46/46a was divided by a drain (the origin of Lysons' division into two?); with the remains of a floor of very small tesserae in a strip to the south, and the remainder of concrete. Greenfield suggests that this room was a secondary addition to the main West Wing and thus perhaps of Period 3. It may also have provided a direct entry to the Upper Baths and the Central Range gallery from the outside, mirroring the access arrangement at the north-east end of the gallery (Rooms 42 and 43).

To the west of the Upper Bath suite some exploration was made of its immediate exterior (Area 60). Much of this area had been previously disturbed by past excavations, and it was not possible to link the surviving walls of the baths with much of the stratigraphy remaining beyond the zone of disturbance. Very little was recorded in this area by the earlier excavators, and Greenfield's records are almost equally sparse. The earliest level was a green clay which should equate with the horizon of natural clay recorded elsewhere beneath the villa. In places this was sealed beneath later hillwash, and an area of metalling was recorded some way to the south west of Room 48 which may also have been laid on the natural clay. Above this metalling was an occupation deposit, presumably surviving beyond the zone of earlier excavation disturbance. Deposits described as rubble or building debris may have been backfill, material deriving from earlier building collapse or robbing, or a combination of both. The open drains around Rooms 45 and 48 were recorded by Clifford, presumably set into the natural ground surface and carrying water away to the south west. Another drain appears to run south west from Room 1, to link up with the drainage system (F3) around the outside of the Lower Baths, but no further details are recorded.

### 2.3: The Central Range

This was the link between the two main wings of the villa, the cross-bar of its essentially H-shaped plan, and conceived as a primary element of the layout in Period 2 (Fig. 6). The Central Range comprises a long room or corridor (Room 14) with two shorter extentions (Rooms 13 and 16) at each end. Opening north from the corridor was a rectangular dining room (Room 15a), subsequently remodelled as an irregular octagon (Room 15), opposite what was probably a portico (Room 32). A small group of rooms to the north east (Rooms 41, 42, 43 and 52) are

*Plate 11* Rooms 15 and 15a excavated, Central Range; view south west.

*Plate 12* Rooms 15 and 15a excavated, Central Range; view east.

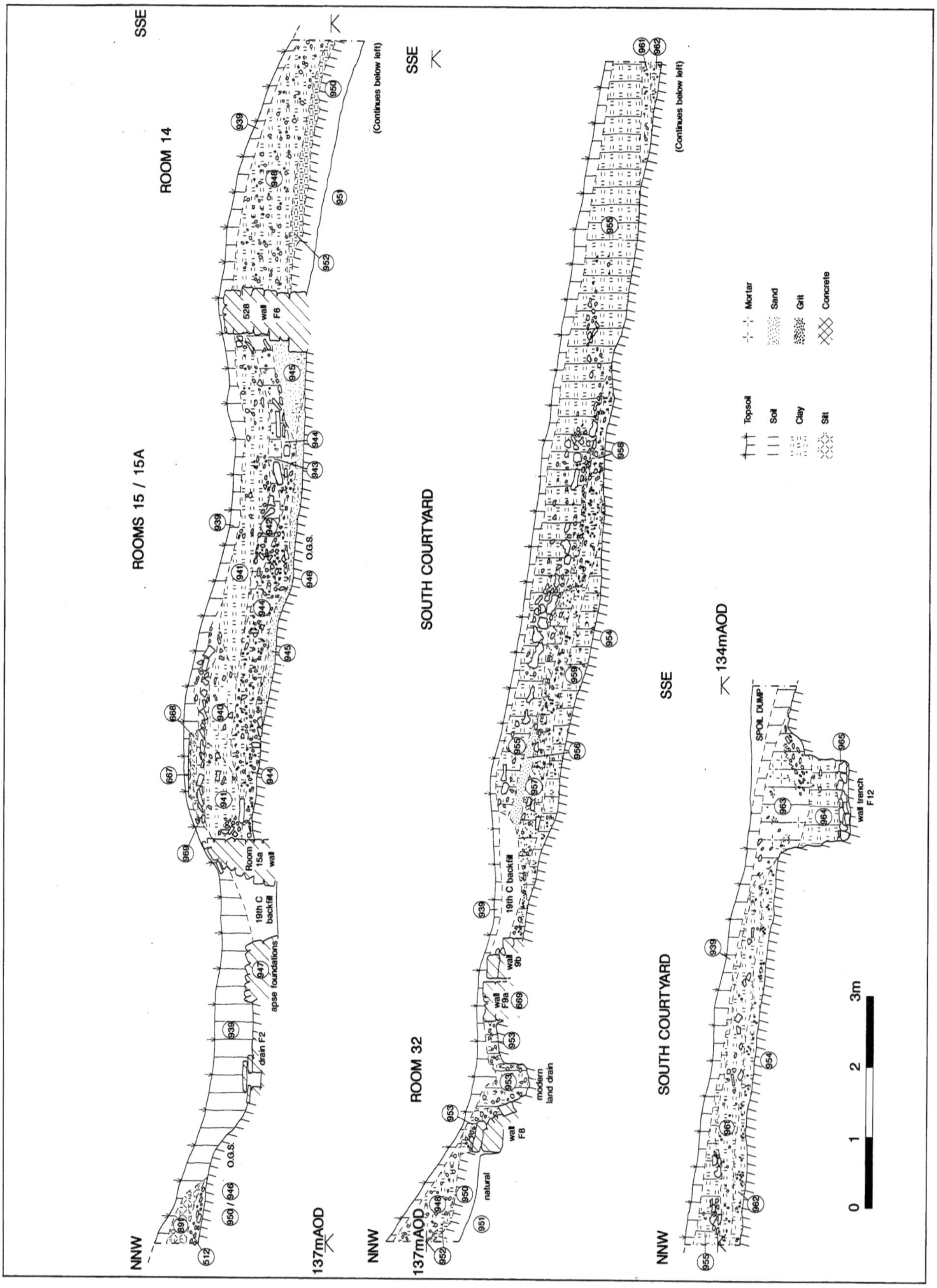

# GREAT WITCOMBE ROMAN VILLA, GLOUCESTERSHIRE

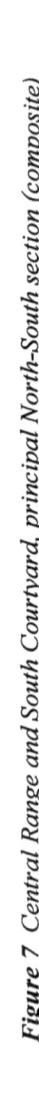

*Figure 7 Central Range and South Courtyard, principal North-South section (composite)*

Plate 14  Drain F2 north of Rooms 15 and 15a, Central Range; view south west.

Plate 13  Portico foundations, Room 32, Central Range; view south west.

more conveniently discussed in the account of the North East Wing (below).

Room 13 occupies the south-west end of the corridor, and had been thoroughly cleared by Lysons and then Clifford. Its north-west and south-east walls continue as one build from the corridor Room 14; its north-east wall abutting these walls with two buttresses bonded into its face within Room 13. The floor of this room lies as much as 2m. below the original floor level of the corridor, and it has been suggested that the corridor originally continued at the same level westwards, above the existing room (Neal 1977, 34). If so, Room 13 should be regarded as a basement, with access from the ramp or stairway in Room 2. No original floor survived in the main corridor section, Room 14, only a thin layer of clay surviving undisturbed above the natural stony clay horizon beneath the Central Range.

Rooms 15/15a open to the north and midway along the corridor and are interpreted as a dining room (triclinium), where Greenfield was able to excavate the most complete sequence of features and deposits surviving in this part of the villa (Plate 10). This had undergone several modifications, but seems to have begun in Period 2 as a rectangular room (15a) whose north-east and south-west walls were butted against the north-west wall (528) of Room 14 (Fig.7). The two exterior base courses were stepped out, while the north east and north west corners were rounded internally. These walls were set into the old ground surface of stony clay (946), equivalent to horizons recorded elsewhere (e.g. 542/950). The earliest level within Room 15a was a foundation of clean crushed limestone (945), possibly for the original floor which had not survived. Above this were deposits of clay soil (944), occupation deposits with burning (943), and fine soil with rubble and tile etc.(942). These may have been levelling up for a second phase of floor in 15a. If so, this could equate with the small apse butted against the exterior of the north wall foundations. Only the pitched foundations (947) of this extension had survived, and it is possible that this was in fact part of the Period 3 remodelling as Room 15, or even secondary to it (Plate 11).

Room 15 was defined as the Period 3 remodelling which converted the rectangular 15a (with or without an apse) into an irregular octagonal room. The walls and their foundations (966) were of more massive construction than their predecessors, and built partly over them, though apparently re-using the earlier walls to the north (Plate 12). Dumps of clay soil with stone rubble and some mortar (940 and 941) had been used to raise the floor level once again within this room and seal the demolished sections of Room 15a walls (965). Above this was a sequence of floor makeup, beginning with a loose rubble of large limestone blocks (969), a layer of crushed stone with clay and mortar fragments and some wall plaster and tesserae (668), which formed the base for a small surviving area of buff/pink cement (667). The latter formed the base for the tiled stone floor recorded originally by Lysons. This was a chequer pattern in dark grey and white limestone squares with some triangles, only a fragment of which survived.

No original floor levels had survived in the raised corridor or gallery, Room 14, although deposits of dumped clay and rubble makeup (948) may relate to a Period 3 floor. This was almost certainly on the same level as that of the octagonal dining room; Room 14 and the gallery as a whole being thus situated at second floor level above the courtyard below. The south-east wall to this and the adjacent extentions, Rooms 13 and 16 (F8), was badly broken down. This may have followed its exposure in Lysons' excavation, but probably resulted also from ground instability. In Period 2 this was countered by a series of buttresses along the two-storey south face of this wall (from west to east 533, 535, 537, and 752, 751 and 750), which were reinforced by a second set in Period 3. The latter survived as only one or two courses of large mortared stone slabs butted against the south wall (from west to east: 532, 534, 536, 538, and 755, 754 and 753).

Between the two sets of buttresses were the poorly recorded remains of Room 32, a structure interpreted primarily as a portico. The mortared rubble foundations (669) had deteriorated further since their original exposure by Lysons, but were evidently butted against the south wall (Plate 14). This structure could have provided further support for the gallery wall, and incorporated at least one of the Period 2 buttresses within it. Given the original height of the corridor above the South Courtyard, and the drains issuing from it, the suggestion has been made that Room 32 was also a nymphaeum or ornamental water cistern, perhaps combined with a staircase from the courtyard which could also have given access to the Lower Bath House in Period 3 (Neal 1977, 36).

There was no clear surviving evidence of final (Period 4) occupation or activity in the Central Range; any such having probably been destroyed by previous excavators. Post-Roman evidence of Period 5 comprised backfill and topsoil deposits (939) over Rooms 15/15a and 14, and their continuation over the west end of Rooms 14 and 13. Two small features are also probably of this Period; a post hole which cut the wall footings of Room 15, and a land drain (953) cut across the 'portico' 32 but apparently sealed beneath Lysons' backfill and topsoil.

**2.4: The North Exteriors**

Areas 47 and 62 to the north of the villa buildings were, for the most part, severely disturbed by Lysons' and Hicks' clearance, which had divorced the structural remains from any associated stratigraphy which may originally have been present. Further north, excavation in Area 71 encountered more intact stratigraphy (Fig. 6).

The one level surviving virtually throughout all three areas was the old ground surface and natural subsoil underlying the villa. This is identified variously as clay layers, sometimes, as beneath the Central Range (950) overlaying a natural 'clayey brash' subsoil (951). Two other deposits surviving in this area; 'a black/red-brown sandy clay' between the drain F2 and the north-west wall of Room 15, and a patch of 'ashy silt' cut by the drain could have been pre-villa contexts, but there is no other record of their position or relationships.

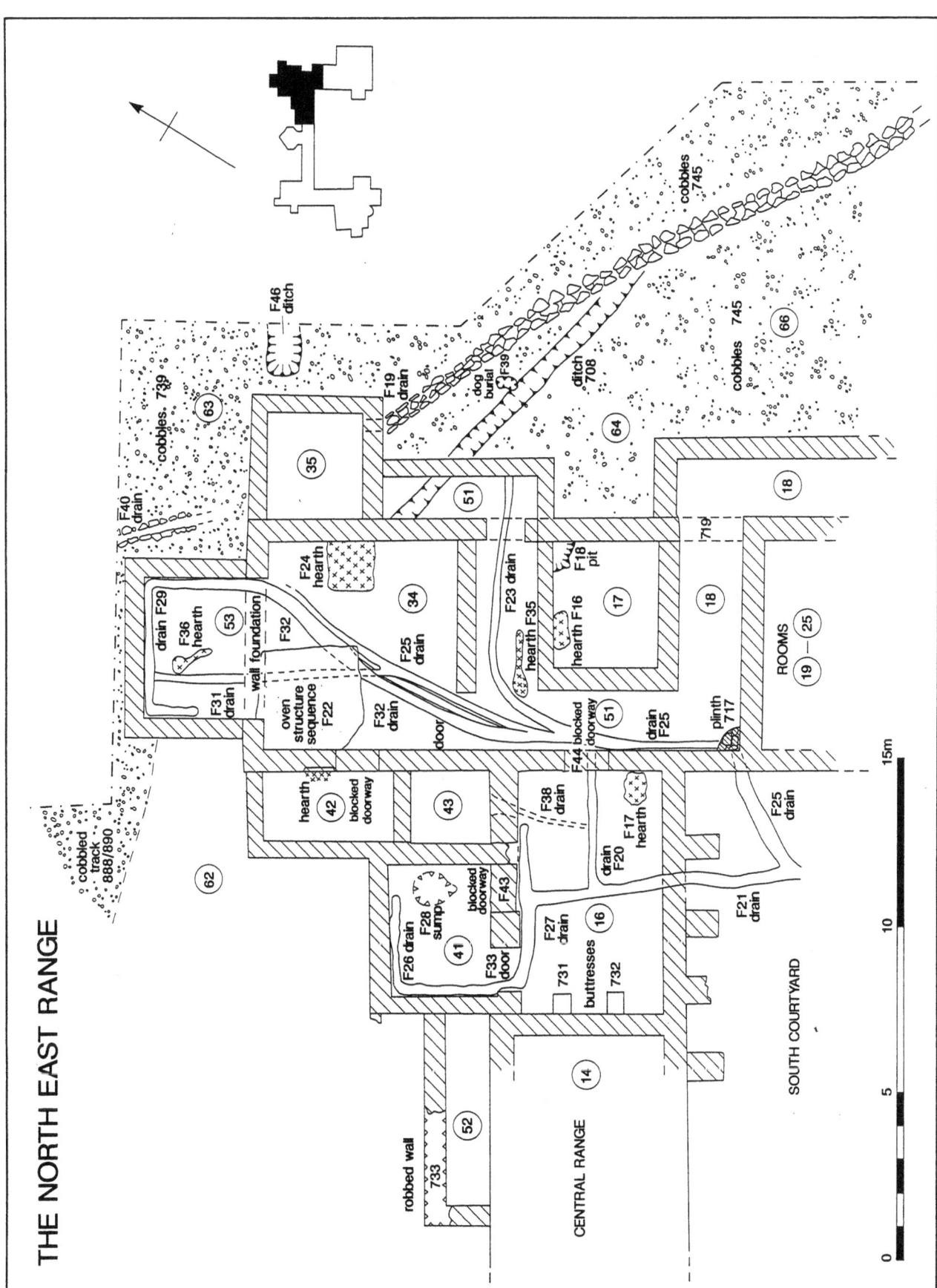

Figure 8 *North East Range and exteriors, plan of principal areas and features*

A cobbled track (887/9) approached the West Wing of the villa from the north east in Period 2, although its relationship with the building was destroyed by 19th-century trenching. This was originally defined in Area 47 and again in Area 71, apparently continuing around the East Wing. A road makeup was also recorded beneath the cobbles in Area 71 which may have led to an exterior entry to the West Wing in its primary phase, and possibly later to Room 46. Deposits of soil and occupation along the north side of the track may have accumulated during its use.

Parallel and south east of the track was a stone-lined and capped drain (F2) at a lower level, although its relationship with the former is uncertain (Pl.14). Originating uphill beyond Area 71, its relationship to Room 46 in the West Wing was destroyed by the 19th-century excavations, but it may have been continued by the drain dividing Room 46 which eventually fed into the tank at the centre of Room 1. A clay-silt fill within the drain was probably of much later date, while the remnants of a rubble backfilled construction trench had also been disturbed by Lysons' excavation.

A second phase of cobbling (888/890) lay along the south-eastern edge of the primary track in Area 71 and probably 47, sealing the drain F2, though much had been destroyed by earlier excavation (Pl.15).. The presence of such a track reinforces the suggestion of a main entrance into the villa via the North East Range rooms (East Wing, below).

In Area 63 (Fig. 8) the primary track was cut by part of another stone-lined drain (F40), and by a gully (F46). A stone oven base (F37), found originally by Lysons or Hicks, and a lime filled pit (F45) were found in Area 62 (Fig. 6). In Area 71 a group of inadequately recorded features included a circular mortar patch (F67) separated by silt from another mortar spread. Two shallow gullies (F69 and F70) were linked at right-angles; the former possibly cut by a shallow pit (F68). These features seem to have been cut into the secondary road, while another gulley (F71) apparently cut the primary road cobbles; but not all are necessarily of Period 3.

Beyond the zone affected by Lysons and Hicks' clearance some intact features and deposits should belong to Period 4. A complex of deposits to the west may represent collapse or robbing of the villa structure since its desertion. Further equivalent deposits were recorded north of Rooms 15/15a, in Area 62 and above the cobbled street north of the East Wing; the latter probably equating with rubble and silt above the cobbles further to the north west in Area 71. Two shallow ditches are also recorded in this area, Trenches A and B; the presence of iron pipe collar joints in one suggesting that they had contained wooden pipes supplying water to the Central and North east Ranges in Periods 3 or 4. All these deposits and features were cut or overlain by the excavations and backfill of Lysons and Hicks (Period 5). In Area 47 this backfill lay against the north wall of the Central Range gallery and partly infilled the drain F2. In Area 71 a dump of wall plaster above the drain Trench B appears to have been redeposited in further backfill, which continued to the north around the East Wing.

**2.5: The East Wing: North East Range**

The East Wing comprises a suite of rooms forming the eastern arm of the basic 'H' villa plan. For convenience of discussion it is sub-divided into a North East and a South East range. All the rooms of the North East Range had been located and cleared previously by Lysons and Hicks, but were not re-investigated by Mrs Clifford. Several floors and some internal features, including hearths and drains, remained for investigation by Greenfield (Fig. 8).

Although physically part of the Central Range, it is more convenient to consider Room 16 in this section of the account. As part of the primary villa structure of Period 2, this room effectively continues the gallery (Room 14) a further 7m or so further east to link it with the East Wing. Its surviving floor lies over 2m below the estimated floor level of the gallery, however, and Room 16 would have required an upper storey for it to have continued the gallery at the same level to the end of the Central Range. In its present form it virtually matches Room 13 to the west, with buttresses (731 and 732) in the lower room supporting the dividing wall with Room 14. An original centrally-placed doorway in the north-west wall may have been one of the main entrances into the villa buildings of Period 2. This was subsequently blocked, probably in Period 3, when Rooms 41-43 were added, by rough walling (F43) which rested upon a base of stone chippings above the old ground level. A second original doorway (F44) in the north-east wall gave access to the East Wing at ground level, but was perhaps also blocked in Period 3 (see Room 51, below).

Within Room 16 was a horizon of stony clay interpreted as the old ground surface. Cut into this was a robbed-out drain (F20) which ran from beneath the original north east entrance before turning south east. A second drain (F38) ran from beneath the north-west wall (and the site of the subsequent Room 43) into F20, but was not fully excavated. These drains and the old ground surface were originally sealed beneath a floor make-up of stony clay mixed with mortar and plaster fragments supporting a mortar floor base, which survived only in the north east quarter of the room. More disturbed but equivalent make-up was identified further west, possibly mixed with material of later phases. These floor bases may have supported a tiled stone or tesselated pavement in Period 2.

The Period 3 use of Room 16 was represented by the hearth F17 which contained ash, charcoal, and burnt clay, and a more widely spread rakeout of ashy soil. A new entrance from the Period 3 Room 41 was made in the north-west wall (F33), where a new drainage channel (F27) had also been provided. This drain extended to the north east and was also linked south east with the earlier drain F20, to run out through the south-east exterior wall as the drain F21 into the South Courtyard.

Rooms 41, 42, 43 and 52 are secondary additions of Period 3. They were terraced into the hillside in the angle

*Plate 15  Period 3 cobbled track 888 and 890 approaching the villa from the north east, Area 71; view south west.*

*Plate 16* Rooms 42 and 43 fully excavated, North East Range; view south east.

*Plate 17* View south west from Room 35 across the North East Range, including Rooms 51, 34, 41-3 and 16 (top).

between Rooms 16 and 34 and abutting them (Plates.18 and 20). They are sparsely recorded, but no original floor surfaces appear to have survived. Within Room 41 a drain (F26) followed the insides of two walls, to pass beneath the entrance (F33) into the adjoining Room 16 as F27. A sump (F28) is also recorded towards the north-east corner, but not its relationship to adjacent drains or stratigraphy. In Room 42, heavily burnt stones in a recess close to the blocked entrance into Room 34, indicate the site of a hearth, possibly of Period 4. A ?later partition wall separated this room from the smaller Room 43 to the south east. The narrow Room 52 lay behind the gallery (Room 14), at a higher level than Rooms 41-3; much of its north west wall having been robbed away.

A scheme for the function and operation of these rooms has been proposed by Neal (1977, 35-6). An upper floor above Rooms 42 and 43 would have provided an entrance and corridor from ground level to the north, directly into the Central Range gallery above Room 16, continuing westwards as Room 14. This means of access seems to parallel an arrangement at the west end of the Central Range via the entrance corridor Room 46/46a (above). The terraced lower rooms were level with the other North East Range rooms and the ground surface to the east of the villa. Access from these to the upper rooms of the Central Range would have been via a staircase in Room 41; while the upper corridor may have continued south west along Room 52, perhaps to another entry. Eastwards, the corridor could also have given access to upper storeys above Rooms 34 and 53 (below). As originally defined in Period 2, Room 34 was a rectangular room terraced into the hillside, occupying the north end of the East Wing (Plate 17). Access from the remaining rooms was via a doorway in the south corner; an arrangement which apparently continued throughout its life. A second door in the south-west wall was an exterior entry, blocked by herringbone-laid mortared masonry with the building of Room 42 in Period 3. No old ground surface was defined in this room, but one of its primary features was a drain (F31), comprising a stone-lined channel with a lid of stone slabs. This ran originally from outside the building to the north west and then beneath the room, probably merging with the drain F25 to the south. The latter was a large, stone-lined and capped channel filled with silt, set diagonally across the room and curving slightly on a N-S axis. This exited beneath the south entrance, to run via Room 18, out into the South Courtyard.

Although originally cleared by Lysons and Hicks, several other structures still survived in this room. Against the north-east wall was a hearth (F24) comprising a horseshoe-shaped bank of lightly baked stony clay containing charcoal and ash. This was founded upon a stony rubble base mixed with some burnt clay and charcoal, which sealed a clay silt. Nearby, a patch of stone rubble pressed into a similar clay-silt layer was possibly a remnant of floor foundation. A second and more substantial oven (F22) was located in the west corner of the room (Plate 18). The primary structure comprised two drystone walls butted at right angles to the north-west and south-west walls of the room, and containing an area of hard-baked, burnt soil, probably a sub-floor surface. A second phase oven structure above, survived as a U-shaped setting of squared limestone blocks around a floor base of broken Pennant sandstone flags or roof tile fragments (Plate 19). A deposit of mixed stony soil and rubble above, formed the base for a third oven of Pennant stone flags set within a square of limestone blocks (Plate 20). Its final phase comprised yet another, roughly circular setting of broken sandstone flags, the base for a hearth whose upper structure had disappeared.

Both ovens (F22 and F24) were secondary features within Room 34. The construction of the larger oven appears to follow a reinforcement of the drain F25 by a parallel structure (F32), which eventually merged with F25 in Room 18. This event probably coincided with the construction of Room 53 in Period 3, and the additional drainage from it. The primary phase of the F22 oven structure overlies this secondary drain, suggesting that the whole sequence of hearths and ovens should be of Period 3, possibly continuing into Period 4. The date of F24 is less certain. It may have been a Period 2 structure replaced by F22 in Period 3. The presence of these ovens and their prolonged use suggests that Room 34 functioned primarily as a kitchen, at least from Period 3.

Room 53, also terraced into the hillside, was added to the north end of the North East Range in Period 3. Its creation involved the removal of most of the north-west wall of Room 34, with which it then appears to have been integral, although the opening between the two was partly obstructed by the oven F22. Around the inside of the three exterior walls ran a drain (F29), stone-lined and infilled with silt. This cut across the earlier drain F31 which ran beneath Room 34, and led into the later drain F32 crossing that room. Burnt traces of a small hearth or oven base (F36) were recorded in the centre of the room, but no floor levels, although photographs suggest a terraced surface of natural clay into which the room was cut. The secondary relationship of this room to Room 34, and its surviving features, suggest that it was an extention of the kitchen premises, perhaps as a cool store or processing room, in Period 3.

Room 35 was another addition to Room 34 in Period 3, butted against the north east wall of the latter and also terraced into the slope (Plate 21). No details of its floors or internal features awere recorded or are evident from photographs, and its early 19th-century clearance was thorough. There was no evidence for an entrance from the kitchens, but Lysons' plan suggests access from the corridor (Room 51), which seems most likely. Despite the absence of internal features, Greenfield suggested that this room might have been a latrine. A substantial stone-lined drain (F19) ran away south east from that corner of the room out into Area 64 (Plate 22). An earlier drain (F40) to the north west was apparently cut off by the construction of Room 35, but could have supplied water to it.

Rooms 17, 18 and 51 were Period 3 sub-divisions of a large rectangular earlier room to the south-east of the kitchen (Room 34). A door gave access into Room 16,

*Plate 18* Oven structure F22 with remains of the latest-phase hearth 686, Room 34, North East Range; view south west.

*Plate 19* Second-phase hearth 690/691 in oven F22, Room 34, North East Range; view west.

*Plate 20* Third-phase hearth 687/688 in oven F22, Room 34, North East Range; view south west.

*Plate 21* View south east across Rooms 53, 34, 35 and 51, North East Range.

*Plate 22* Drain F19 exiting Room 35, with Iron Age ditch 708 upper right, North East Range; view south east.

*Plate 23* Drain F23 with re-used quernstone beneath corridor Room 51, North East Range; view north east.

and another into the kitchen, but there was no obvious access at ground floor level into rooms to the south. The original single large room almost certainly had an upper storey, which would have connected with that postulated above Room 34 and others above Rooms 19-25 to the south. Access to these upper rooms could either have been via the gallery above Room 16, to which they will almost certainly have been connected, or by an internal stairway from the ground floor of one of these rooms. Other ground floor features of this Period 2 room are difficult to identify, owing to its secondary modification and the earlier 19th-century clearance.

In Period 3 a corridor (Rooms 18 and 51) was built around three sides of the original room enclosing a smaller rectangular room (Room 17) to the east. Both corridors extended beyond the walls of the Period 2 room to run along the outside of the primary North East Range rooms. The northern corridor (Room 51) breached the earlier wall to provide access to the contemporary? Room 35. What may have been a pre-building clay soil horizon was cut through by a drain (F23) aligned NE-SW along one axis of the corridor (Plate 23). This comprised a stone-lined channel capped with large stone blocks which included one complete quernstone (Fig. 37.14), and a clay-silt infill. The drain merged westwards into the drain F25 from Room 34, but it was not followed east beneath the outer wall of the corridor. The remains of an oven base or hearth (F35) here should represents a feature of the earlier Period 2 room, but it is uncertain whether the drain (F23) belongs to this phase or the later modification. Beneath the north-west extension of the corridor was the continuation of an Iron Age ditch (708) from Area 64 (see below). To the south west, the original doorway from Room 16 (F44) was blocked by three surviving courses of mortared stone and tile above a sequence of black silt, gritty clay, mortar and clay soil, and a base layer of stony clay soil with mortar and charcoal.

Room 18 continued the corridor around the south side of the original room and beyond it, outside to the south east. Within its western half was a spread of rough paving made of limestone and Pennant sandstone roofing slates; possibly the disturbed remains of a Period 3 floor. This layer overlapped the foundations (719) of the demolished wall of the earlier (Period 2) room, which had been breached to extend the corridor to the south east. In the south west corner was a semi-circular plinth of stone blocks (717) in a matrix of stony soil and rubble, sealing the drain F25 at the point where it exited through the wall into the South Courtyard. The south-east extension of Room 18 descended steeply alongside Rooms 19-25, giving access to the South East Range (see below).

Room 17 was surrounded on three sides by the corridor (Rooms 18/51), its north east wall being a retained section of the original Period 2 wall. A clay soil horizon within the room may have been the old ground surface (pre-villa), equivalent with that in the north corridor (Room 51). The remains of a hearth (F16), comprised an oval depression containing dark brown gritty soil and charcoal. In the north-east corner was a pit (F18) containing much burnt stone, claysoil and charcoal, which was associated with an 'occupation layer', possibly overlying the natural clay. If all these features and deposits relate to creation and use of Room 17 in Period 3, they appear to contradict. Neal's suggestion (1977, 35) that the original Period 2 room was demolished to provide a view out from the gallery (Room 14) over the countryside to the north east. This hypothesis indicates that the Period 3 room should then become a small open courtyard flanked on three sides by a corridor, although this would create a problem in gaining access to first floor rooms to the south east (below).

A block of small rooms, 19-25, immediately south east of Rooms 17/18/51 and cleared originally by Lysons and Hicks, were part of the primary building structure (Fig. 9). No original floor levels survive, although they are presumed to have continued on virtually the same plane as the other floors in the North East Range. With the natural fall of the land here, maintenance of that level required that their floors be raised well above the ground. The upstanding structure so created still survives as a strongly buttressed platform above the South East Range. Its outer walls continue the line of the original (Period 2) East Wing of the villa, but the inner walls may not be a true reflection of rooms at ground floor level. The core of the platform was clay, although this has not been investigated by excavation, and some of the cross walls which define Rooms 19-25 were probably for reinforcement, although the division between 19-22 and 23-25 could well have supported a wall above between two separate rooms. The scale of construction here suggests two storeys built upon the foundations, the upper linking across to rooms postulated above 17/18/51 and 34. If so, a stairwell might also be expected in the block, particularly if the original upper storey to Room 17 was removed in Period 3.

## 2.6: The East Wing: South East Range

The South East Range was built at a much lower level than the North East Range; its floors lying as much as six metres below those to the north (Fig. 9). At its core was Room 27, the southern continuation and termination of the East Wing in Period 2. Whether or not this room stood alone at the lower level in that phase is uncertain; all other rooms of this range appear to be secondary to it, but might replace or extend some earlier structural elements. Despite earlier clearance by Lysons and Hicks, some features and deposits had survived to be excavated and recorded by Greenfield

In Room 27 the early 19th-century excavations apparently exposed secondary floor levels, leaving several other contemporary and earlier features and deposits intact, although a sure attribution of these surviving elements to specific phases is not always possible. A broad gap in the south-east wall should mark an original arched? entrance, almost 3m wide and flanked by plinths of large, 1m square chamfered stone base blocks (Plinths 11 and 12). An internal buttress against the north-east wall (behind Plinth 11), and another opposite against the the south-west wall, may have supported another arched opening. These, and the two massive buttresses built as integral components of the

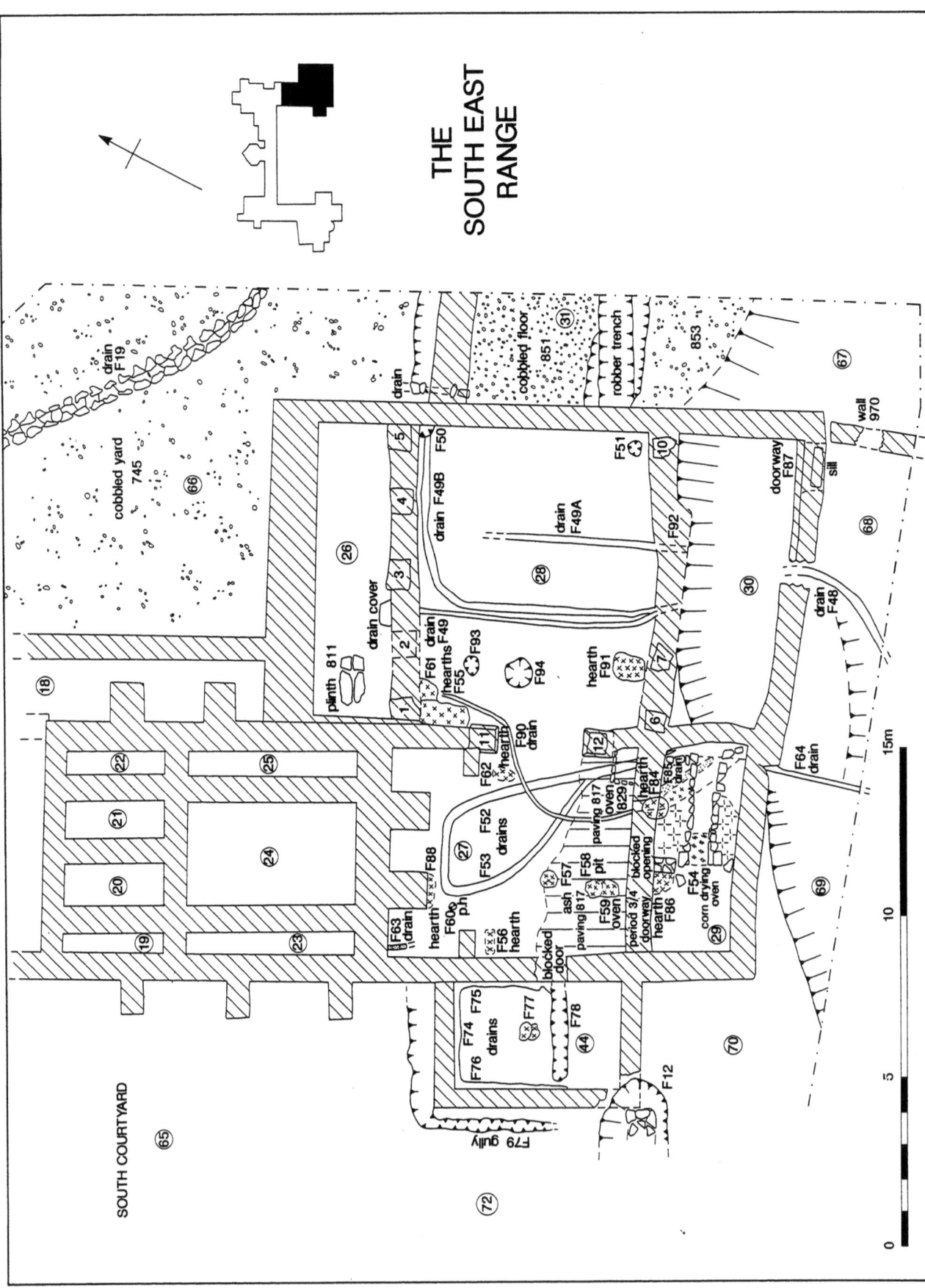

*Figure 9 South East Range and exteriors, plan of principal areas and features*

*Plate 25* Remains of Period 4 floor 817 with re-used paving material in Room 27, South East Range; view east.

*Plate 24* Drains F52 and F53 below Room 27, view south east from Room 23-25 buttresses, South East Range.

north-west wall, supported this end of the East Wing and the postulated upper storey rooms above Room 27 and those to the north west (19-25).

The earliest internal features of Room 27 were probably the drains F52 and F53, which lay beneath later floors and features and should thus be of Period 2 (Plate 24). These comprised a loop around the eastern half of the room, which combined as one (F64) to run out downhill through the later Room 29. Their stone-lined channels were capped by stone slabs and infilled with clay silt, and were presumably cut into the old ground surface below, prior to backfilling with clay and rubble. A later drain (F90) of Period 3? entered Room 27 through the main north-east entrance, curving round to link up with the drain F85 in Room 29. This was not recorded in detail, but photographs show a narrow channel of pitched stones beneath a capping of small horizontal slabs. A third drain (F63) survived as only a short section of re-used clay tile lining beneath limestone slabs and infilled with clay-silt, in the north-west corner of the room. It is unclear whether this drain was a feature of Period 2 or 3.

Most of the evidence for the later use of Room 27 comprised a series of hearths or ovens, and the remains of a rough flagstone floor (817, Plate 25). The latter had survived best along the the south-east wall and comprised Lias and Pennant sandstone flags with some re-used quern and millstones, laid upon rubble which sealed a compacted clay floor. This last was either the old ground surface or possibly a floor of Period 2. Some mixed soil and occupation debris, which contained coin issues up to AD 388-92, above the flagstone floor appear to have been a remnant of Period 4 activity. Also beneath the floor an oval depression (F58) filled with ashy clay lay beneath the remains of an oven (F59) - surviving as an oval of burnt red clay and a patch of charcoal (F57). Further north were the remains of a hearth (F56), close to the blocked doorway into Room 44. This comprised a channel base aligned NE-SW and filled with charcoal and clay. The remains of another hearth (F62) filled with ashy soil and charcoal were located just inside the main north-east entrance. What seems to have been a further oven (F88) was located against the south west buttress to Rooms 19-25, possibly associated with a nearby post-hole (F60). In the east corner of the room an area enclosed by a single-course, rectangular setting of vertical sandstone blocks (829) appears to have been partly overlain by the paving 817. This feature was probably the remains of yet another oven or hearth, and photographs suggest deposits of ash and clay soil beneath or within it.

The series of hearths recorded in Room 27 suggest activity which could identify this room as another kitchen. Less clear is the relationship of these features to each other or to adjacent stratigraphy. It is suspected that several are of Period 2, and it is possible that Room 27 served as a kitchen only in that phase. The latest recorded deposit of rubble and soil sealed the paving 817, probably a remnant of earlier excavation backfill, although the latest event was the excavation of a drainage trench across the room from north east (Room 28) to south west (Room 44). This seems to have been cut by the then Office of Works in the 1920s, with little regard for surviving archaeological remains.

Room 44 was an extension south west from Room 27, from which it was entered by a central doorway. Its north and south walls were butted against Room 27, and it is thus interpreted as part of the Period 3 extension of the South East Range. To the north west the room was terraced into the hill slope, and a 'clay floor' was either the underlying natural or the original floor level. The primary internal feature of the room was a drain (F74, F75 and F76) cut around three sides of the wall foundations. This was built of pitched limestone slabs and infilled with silts, but no connection with other drainage systems or an exit from the room is recorded. Areas of stone rubble makeup above the clay floor represented a foundation for the remains of a paved floor of limestone flags, although the relationship of this floor to other features or its full extent within the room was not recorded. A shallow gully (F78) aligned NE-SW, divided the room and may have been a later cut through the floor. In the centre of the room were the remains of a hearth (F77), whose relationship with the floor is also unknown. The relationship of this room to the kitchen? (F27) and its internal drainage features, are paralleled by Room 53 in the North East Range, and a similar function is thus suggested.

A short segment of herringbone masonary was identified as blocking in the entrance from Room 27, indicating that Room 44 may have been abandoned by Period 4. There is no other record of this feature and at least half was destroyed by the modern drain trench from Room 27 (above). This trench linked with another modern drain cut approximately north-south across Room 44; through the hearth (F77), gully (F78) and floor foundation material, to breach and remove a section of the south-east wall. Around the exterior walls to the north and west a shallow gully (F79) may have been designed to take surface water from the South Courtyard away from them, although there is no record of a lined drain structure. The destruction of the south corner of Room 44 by the robber trench (F12) of the South Courtyard boundary, wall is further evidence that the room was abandoned in Period 4.

Room 29 lies directly south east of Room 27, continuing the line and width of the primary rooms of the East Wing. There is conflicting evidence as to the relationship of this room with Room 27, with which it appears to be one build, although interpretative plans of the villa show it as secondary. An extended sequence of events was revealed by Greenfield; little of the interior having been cleared previously by Lysons and Hicks.

The south-west wall to this room appears to be one build with the equivalent wall of Room 27, and the same relationship may exist between the north-east walls of the two rooms. The dividing wall between Rooms 27 and 29 appears to butt against the south-west wall, but may be bonded with the north-east wall. Located centrally in the dividing wall, a broad entrance over 3m. wide, originally gave access from Room 27. This threshold was marked by worn stones and cream mortar upon the base wall

*Plate 27  Remains of "corn drying oven" F54 in Room 29, South East Range; view east.*

*Plate 26  Part of drain F85 re-using clay imbrex roof tiles, Room 29, South East Range; view north west.*

course. Along the north-east wall a stone-lined and capped drain F64 continued from the linked drains F52 & F53 in Room 27, to exit the room south into Area 69. There were no records of the earliest floor levels or an old ground surface beneath Room 29, but there is a possibility that in its primary form the room was in fact the south-east end of a larger Period 2 Room 27.

Subsequently, two small hearths were located on either side of the north-west entrance. To the right, F84 originated as a base of green clay set with pink mortar, and clay tile fragments. A succession of small hearths (F84A-F84F) followed, comprising deposits of pink mortar, ashy soil, and base structures of tile and burnt stone. Use of these hearths had burnt the stones and mortar of the entrance here. To the south west a second hearth (F86) had partly blocked the original wide entrance, reducing it by half. Only the north-east half remained open, with a step of pebbly mortar to the north at the threshold into Room 27. This hearth comprised a deposit of burnt ashy soil contained by burnt wall stones in the entrance, and a short stub of similarly burnt mortared wall foundation to the north east. In possible association with the F84 hearth sequence, was a short section of drain (F85) lined with re-used *imbrex* tiles, running eastwards into the earlier drain F64 below (Plate 26). These features probably represent activity of Period 3, though further contemporary evidence may have been destroyed by the next phase of use.

A major re-organisation of Room 29 involved blocking the original north-west entrance with mortared courses of stone blocks, and the creation of a new but narrower entry through the west end of the dividing wall from Room 27. This was part of a process which converted Room 29 to house a "corn drying" oven (F54). A dump of clay soil and pitched stone rubble over much of the floor area formed a base for the oven. Above, the T-shaped oven structure survived as two courses of reused stone blocks forming a flue along the axis of the room; two short tapering arms extending to its full width at the east end (Plate 27). The oven was flanked by roughly spread and compacted mortar, founded upon a more extensive stony clay soil packing which also spread out in front to the west. A floor of compacted clay formed the oven base in the arms of the T. A similarly compacted clay occupied the floor of the flue and was baked red-brown from firings at its mouth. Deposits of sooty soil and ash within the flues were residues of its use, sealed beneath dumps of stone rubble and soil originating from the oven's destruction. A final extensive deposit of tumbled stone incorporated a short segment of rough mortared wall on a NW-SE alignment. This feature, the remains of a hearth apparently above the blocked entrance to the room, and a post-hole (F89) nearby within the rubble, may be contemporary or much later intrusions.

It is not clear whether the conversion of Room 29 to accommodate the "corn drying" oven occurred within Period 3 or later, while the fragmentary evidence of an even later episode should be of Period 4 or possibly Period 5. There was no certain record of early 19th-century excavation disturbance or backfill, unless this was represented by the tumbled stone deposit above the oven. The walls to this room were distorted by subsidence down the hill slope, presumably an occurrence following its abandonment.

Rooms 26, 28, 30 and 31 were added to the primary set (19-25, 27 and 29?) as a Period 3 extension of the South East Range (Plate 29). Effectively, they form an aisled hall with some subsidiary rooms. Their construction required a substantial terracing of the hillside, particularly to the north, although their floors were at a slightly higher level than those in the western rooms (27 etc.), and there was some structural instability on the southern down slope. No natural levels were defined by any excavator, and the initial clearance by Lysons and Hicks was relatively thorough.

Room 28 could originally have been built as one unit with Rooms 26 and 30, but the two partition walls dividing off the larger central area (28) from aisles (26 & 30) north and south are more likely to be original elements. The northern partition comprised rubble footings or a single mortared stone course, into which were set large dressed flat blocks of limestone. Four out of an original five were set at regular intervals (Plinths 1-5), although all had weathered following their 19th-century exposure (Plate 28). The southern partition was of similar construction but had suffered subsidence as well as weathering, only three of its original five plinths (Plinths 6-10) surviving. Lysons (1819, 183) records several large stone uprights resting on the plinths between Rooms 28 and 30. Both sets of plinths were evidently bases for stone piers beneath the arched supports for an open, two-storey hall *c* 10m long, with access between into the flanking aisles. A broad arched? opening to the south west would have led into Rooms 27, 29 and 44 (above), and a similar opening opposite would have given access to the exterior via the porchway - Room 31 (below).

Most floor levels in Room 28 appear to have been destroyed, although areas of stony rubble pressed into the underlying natural clay may be remnants of floor foundation. As in many rooms at Great Witcombe, the drainage system was a primary element. Initially, this comprised a stone-lined channel (F49) across the full width of the room (Plate 29). Commencing just inside Room 26, this drain also probably crossed Room 30 (destroyed by subsidence), to link with F48 beyond the building to the south. Another drain (F49B) cut along the inside of the northern partition wall curved south, into or alongside F49. This comprised a channel of pitched stone slabs forming a triangular cross-section with a flat base of re-used clay *tegula* tiles, infilled by clay silts and capped by stone slabs. A third parallel drain (F49A), was also stone-lined, passing separately through the partition wall into Room 30 as F92, and may also have linked with the drain F48 beyond.

In the north-west corner of Room 28 were the sub-rectangular remains of a smelting hearth (F55), with a floor of Pennant sandstone flags containing ash, coal and fragments of lead smelt, and sealed by burnt soil and ash. Beneath, were the remains of another hearth (F61) with a soil and ash-filled flue channel cut into the underlying

*Plate 28* Aisle plinths 3, 4 and 5 between Rooms 26 and 28, drain F49b left, South East Range; view south west.

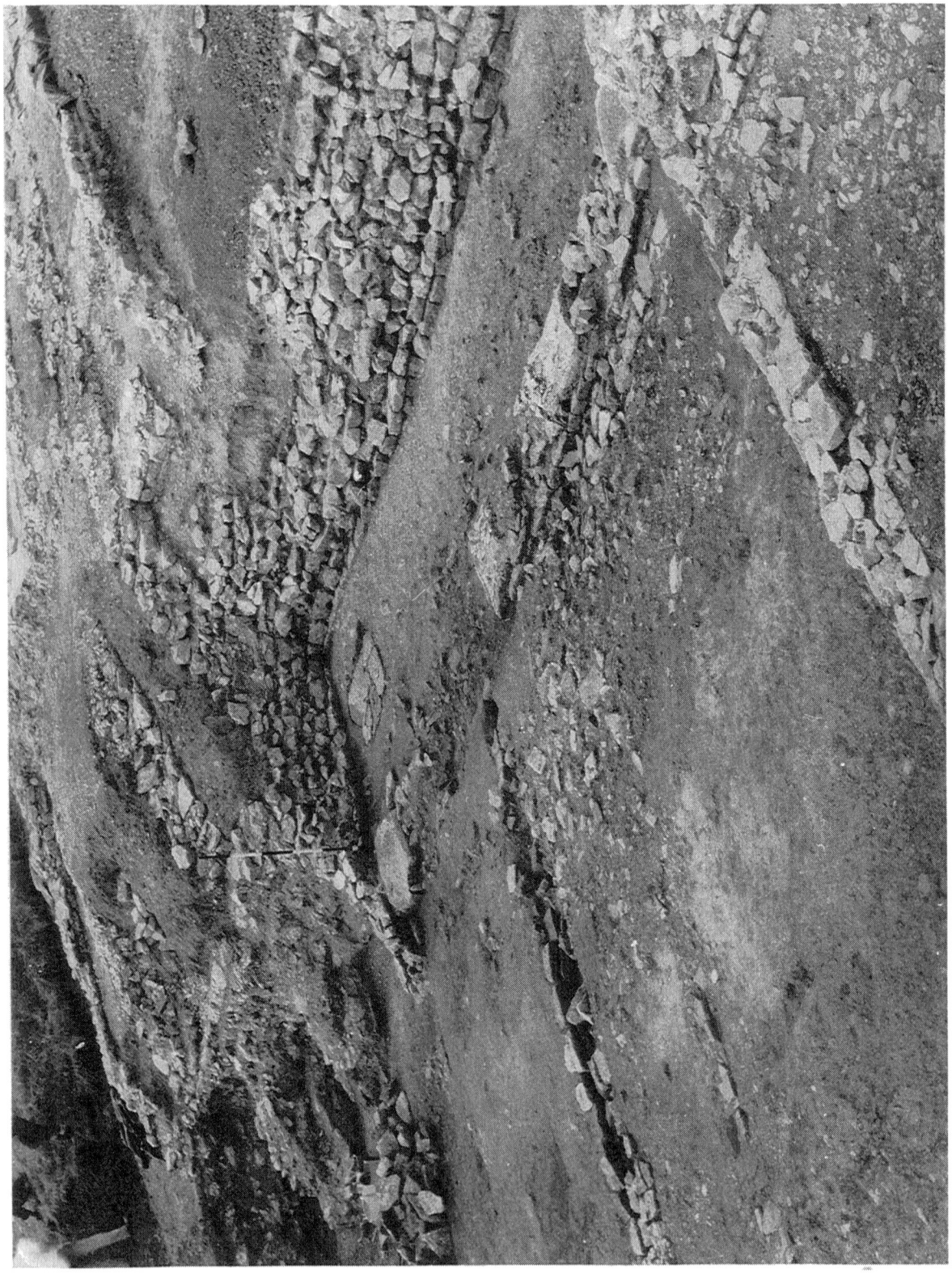

*Plate 29 View west across Rooms 31, 28, 26 and 27 to Rooms 19-25, South East Range.*

*Plate 30* Remains of Room 30 distorted through subsidence, South East Range; view south west.

natural clay. Across the room were the remains of a second oval hearth (F91), partly removed by the 19th-century excavations, which contained soft, purple-brown burnt clay with a considerable quantity of lead melt. Between these hearths was a circular depression (F94) of unknown purpose, containing fills of sandy clay. Also originating in this room and possibly associated with the hearths F55 and F61 was the drain F90, which passed through the south west entry into Room 27 (above). Three small pits or post-holes may all have been much later features of Phases 4 or 5. These comprised F50 in the north corner; F51 in the east corner, and F93 to the west. Two small deposits of stony soil surviving in the east and west corners may have been remnants of Period 4 deposits formerly sealing this room.

Room 26 represents the northern aisle of the hall, separated from the central Room 28 by the open partition wall and Plinths 1-5. This room was deeply terraced into the hill slope, its north-west wall built with very broad rubble foundations to counter the thrust from above, and butted against Rooms 19-25 (Plate 29). Few internal features or deposits survived in this room. At the south-west end a rectangular plinth of four large worn limestone flagstones (811) was set into a stony clay sub-floor level. The plinth exhibited no signs of burning or evidence of associated hearth deposits, and could mark the foot of a stair descending directly to ground floor level from the higher corridor to the north west (Room 18), or from there via an upper room over Room 26 (Neal 1977, 36-8). An adjacent tumble of large stone blocks and occupation deposits may have derived partly from collapse of the north-west wall and should thus be of Period 4. A stone drain cover just inside the room between Plinths 2 and 3 marked the start of the drain F49, but no other details were recorded.

Room 30 was the southern aisle to the hall and equivalent to Room 26. Its remains had suffered severely from subsidence, all four walls having been distorted by movement downhill to the south east (Plate 30). An exterior doorway (F87) was marked by a stone sill in the south-east corner. Further west, the drain F48 exits from Room 30 at a point where the south-east wall is broken into two by the subsidence, though no trace of it survived within the room. The only surviving internal feature was the remnant of disturbed rubble floor foundations above the slumped slope of natural clay. These horizons were sealed by backfill left by the early 19th-century excavators, and a pre-1960 Office of Works spoil dump.

Room 31 was attached to the east end of the aisled hall, its surviving north wall butted against Room 28. The south wall was robbed out, and their east terminations were not reached in Greenfields's excavations. Both walls are of a broader build than most others in the villa, and four surviving courses offset above a wider plinth foundation course are recorded to the north in an even wider foundation trench. A drain passed through the wall here. A cobbled surface of small stone and tile fragments present over the entire exposed floor area probably indicates the former level of floors within the other rooms of the aisled hall. Room 31 has been interpreted as a large covered porch, giving access via a broad arched? entrance into the aisled hall (Rooms 28, 26 and 30) It has been suggested as a single storey structure (Neal 1977, 37), although the size of the wall foundations indicate something on a larger scale. There is no information relating to the outer threshold, which presumably lies just beyond the limit of excavation to the east, but as the main entry into the hall and South East Range, its size suggests that wheeled vehicles could have had access here.

## 2.7: East and South East Exteriors

Exteriors defined as Areas 63 and 64/66, and as 67, 68, 69 and 70, were examined as part of the re-excavation and exposure of the East Wing rooms by Greenfield. As elsewhere around the building, most of the direct relationships between the structure and exterior stratigraphy had been lost through early 19th-century clearance. The following account deals chronologically with features and deposits identified from all areas (Figs. 8 and 9).

Period 1: An 'old ground surface' horizon was identified in several areas, as the earliest pre-villa level. Although no detailed description was given, this is presumed to have been a weathered stony clay, from which some finds were recovered. These horizons were sealed variously by cobbles or occupation deposits, and cut by several features. Of the latter, the earliest was a shallow ditch in Area 64 (708) aligned approximately east-west (Plate 22). Cut away to the east by a later drain (F19), this feature continued west beneath the corridor Room 51 of the North East Range, but was not traced further west. Its position, and Iron Age pottery from its fill indicate that it represents prehistoric occupation on or near the later villa site.

Period 2: Features or deposits which are contemporary with the earliest periods of villa construction and occupation are difficult to identify. Most likely is material from the old ground surface in Area 64/66, and a deposit of occupation soil sealed beneath cobbling in Area 67. The burial of a dog (F39) which cut the Iron Age gully in Area 64 may also be of this Period, but this could equally be of Period 3. In Area 63, the 19th-century clearance stopped above an area of metalling which may continue round to the north into Area 71. as a yard or trackway which probably originated in Period 2, though continuing into Period 3. A short section of ditch (F40) approaching from the north west was either cut through or set into the cobbles. Its stone-lined channel was capped by stone slabs and was either cut off by the addition of Room 35 to the North East Range or supplied water to that room (above), and would thus be of Period 2.

Period 3: The addition of Room 35 to the North East Range also involved the construction of a substantial stone-lined drain (F19) which exited from its south-east corner The channel, packed around with stony rubble, was infilled by two distinct silt deposits and capped by stone blocks. This drain ran south east and beyond the limit of excavation, through an extensive area of cobbles and metalling. Though not recorded, it appears to have cut a Period 2 surface before being sealed by later horizons. The metalling may equate with that in Area 63 but is separated from it by the butt end of a flat-bottomed ditch (F46) which stops just short of Room 35 and continues north east beyond the bounds of excavation. Finds within its fill and the relationship with Room 35 suggest that it belongs to Period 3, possibly as a boundary feature. Above the cobbles in Areas 63 and 64 occupation deposits appear to have survived beyond the zone cleared by Lysons and Hicks, perhaps equating with the latest phase of villa occupation of Period 4.

South of Room 31 in Area 67 may have been another equivalent area of metalling. This was affected by the subsidence downhill, but was limited westwards by a wall (970) extending south east away from the corner of Room 30. No written record of this exists, but photographs show at least three courses of a mortared stone wall, originally butted against the south-east corner of Room 30, surviving as two disturbed segments. This feature appears not to belong to another room and could be the start of a boundary wall to a large walled enclosure, perhaps a garden, laid out on the slopes below the villa. Its western boundary may be the wall (613) extending south east from Room 9 of the Lower Bath Suite (see also the South Courtyard, below).

In Area 68 a drain (F48) exiting south from the subsided Room 30 almost certainly carried water from a drainage system beneath the aisled hall (above). This comprised a stone-lined channel and outlet through the wall, capped by stone slabs and infilled with clay silt. Further west in Area 69 was the continuation downhill of the drain F64, exiting from Room 29. Both these areas (68 and 69) were badly affected by slumping downhill, which may have destroyed or disturbed other deposits or features. An occupation level recorded in Area 70 may equate with similar deposits above the metalling further east (above), all of which may derive from Period 3 and later occupation of the South East Range.

Periods 4-5: Apart from the possibility of occupation deposits above the metalled surfaces around the East Wing continuing to accumulate during Period 4, all other exterior features and deposits relate to desertion and rediscovery of the villa. A hillwash deposit evidently sealed Areas 64/66, and probably most of the villa remains prior to their 19th-century discovery. Lower down, a similar hillwash in Area 67 was mixed with rubble from collapse of the building down the hill. The subsidence of Rooms 29 and 30 resulted in even more confused rubble and hillwash deposits in Areas 68-70. Only in Areas 63, 64 and 66 was backfill from the excavations of Lysons and Hicks specifically identified, although more was doubtless present elsewhere.

## 2.8: South Courtyard

The South Courtyard is defined by the three main wings of the villa to the east, north and west, and by what may have been a wall linking the lower ends of the South East and South West Ranges (Figs.5 and 10). Most of the stratigraphy in a zone adjacent to the exterior walls of all the building ranges had been disturbed or removed by previous excavators. The whole area was eventually excavated by Greenfield over several seasons, and a considerable proportion of undisturbed stratigraphy encountered. The recorded remains are considered where possible in chronological sequence.

Courtyard Layout: The old ground surface or natural subsoil was identified in most areas, but there was no evidence of other Period 1 features or deposits which pre-date the villa. The south-east boundary to the courtyard was marked by a substantial robbed-out wall trench (F12) (Fig.7). This was originally interpreted as a primary element of the villa layout, linking the south-east corner of Room 6 (South West Range) with the south west corner of Room 27 (South East Range). However, butt ends to the trench which respect the later Rooms 7 and 44 suggest that the wall was contemporary with their addition and thus an addition of Period 3. A deliberate robbing and subsequent infill of the wall trench in Period 4 was identified as a series of deposits (including 963 and 964), excavated and recorded in different seasons. The bottom of the trench contained an unrobbed portion of stone rubble wall footings (965) which survived along most of its length. A spread of stone rubble in clay soil downhill, could be debris from the demolition of this wall (Fig. 7).

Surfaces within the courtyard area which should be of Period 2 comprised intermittent horizons of stony clay, within which was a short section of unmortared wall? foundation to the north west, aligned approximately north-south. This does not relate to any other known feature of the courtyard and could even be a remnant of some pre-villa structure. Above the stony clay horizon, though discontinuous and not extending as far as the West Wing and Central Range, was an extensive area of heavy limestone metalling (876). This is likely to have been the main surfacing of the courtyard from Period 2 onwards, though probably repaired subsequently. Evidence of the latter included areas of secondary metalling with mortar patches (880), patches of broken tile (883), rubble and clay soil (869), and similar deposits to the west; all of which may have been laid in Period 3. There is no evidence for any metalling extending beyond the line of the robbed-out southern boundary wall.

One area not strictly part of the South Courtyard is Area 41a to the north west (Fig. 4). Following Lysons' clearance, this area was re-examined by Clifford, who suggested that another room - perhaps an open verandah or corridor - was built here in the corner between the West Wing and the Central Range. In support of this is the wall which Lysons records as extending out into the courtyard from the entrance into Room 4, although the latter would not apparently give direct access to the postulated room. There is no other record of this wall from either Greenfield's or Mrs Clifford's work. At the time of her excavations a large mass of roof tile and building material against the West Wing was interpreted partly as levelling-up, but some as roof collapse upon the remains of a plain? floor of large *tesserae*. There are no further records of this, and nothing was recorded when the area was re-opened by Greenfield which would corroborate the existence of such a room. In view of the suggestion (Neal 1977, 33 and 36) that access to the

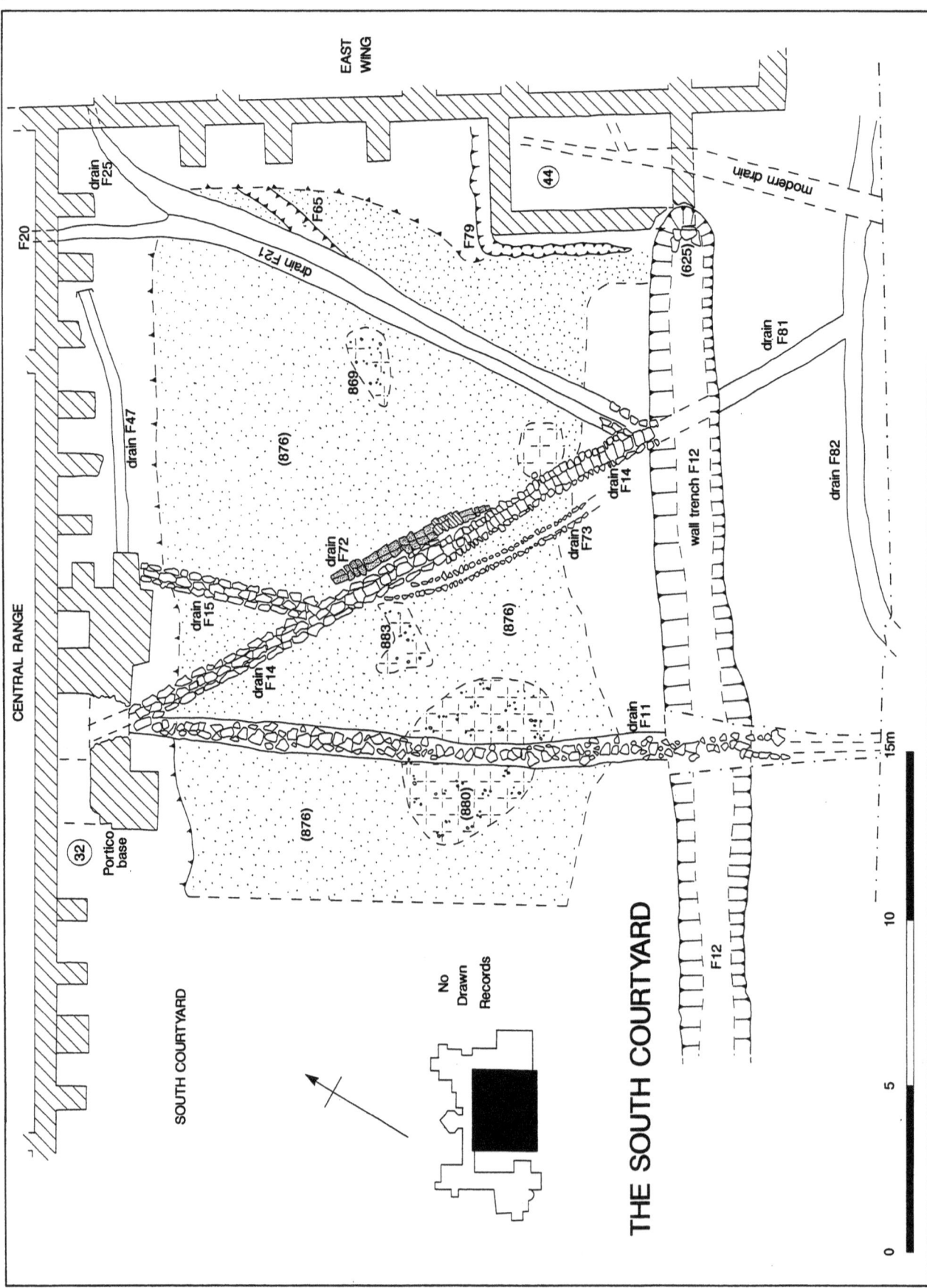

Figure 10 South Courtyard, plan of principal areas and features

*Plate 31* Part of drain F72 re-using clay tegula and decorated flue tiles, South Courtyard; view north west.

Lower Baths from the main living quarters of the villa may have been via the South Courtyard, a verandah or covered passage here in Period 3 would not be out of place (see 2.1, above).

Drainage: While the evidence suggests that the South Courtyard was primarily metalled for much of its existence, several other features were encountered here. The most important were a series of drains, most of which exited from different parts of the villa buildings to cross the courtyard. Most of these were excavated first by Greenfield, but it is not always easy to determine from his records their sequence or relationship with the courtyard surfaces. Exiting south east from the latrine in Room 3 of the South West Range was a drain (F6) which curved downhill to cut across the infilled boundary wall trench F12 (Fig. 5). A double line of vertically-set stone blocks was capped by horizontal slabs and sealed by stony clay soil in a construction trench. The association of this drain with the Lower Bath House almost certainly identifies it as a construction of Period 3, though continuing to function through Period 4.

The main complex of drains occupies the centre of the courtyard, associated with the portico structure (32). A drain (F11) running NW.- SE. from this down the centre, comprised a double row of vertically-set limestone blocks capped by horizontal blocks, set into a construction trench. This appears to cut the upper fills of the robbed courtyard boundary wall and continues south east beyond the excavation site; suggesting that it was a Period 4 drain. From the same point on the portico another, larger drain (F14) ran almost due east. This comprised a channel of vertically-set blocks with a base and lid of limestone slabs, infilled by clay silts. Joining it from the east end of the portico was a second drain (F15) of similar construction; a stone lined channel with limestone slab lid and base, infilled with clay silt. This combined drain (F14/F15), taking all the water from Structure 32, flowed originally through the boundary wall (F12) to the south before being cut away by its robbing trench, although its alignment was then continued by another drain (F81). This stone-lined channel capped with stone slabs ran into another drain (F82), which ran north east-south west across the slope. This was also of stone-lined construction capped with stone slabs, and appears also to have taken some water from the South East Range. What may have been earlier versions of F14 within the main courtyard area were two short drain segments on a similar alignment. To the west and cut by F14 was a drain (F73) with a stone-lined channel, capped with stone slabs and infilled with clay silt. This either terminated or had been destroyed before reaching the southern boundary wall. East of F14 and also cut away by it was a drain (F72) whose channel was formed by clay *tegula* tiles and infilled with silt (Plate 31).

The principal drain in the eastern half of the South Courtyard (F21) ran out through the wall of Room 16 in the Central Range (as F20). A short tributary exited from the south corner of Room 18 (F25), and the combined drain flowed south to link with the drain F14 close to the edge of the boundary wall (F12). A stone-lined channel was capped by stone slabs and infilled with silt within a cutting. This drain probably originated in Period 2 but may have continued in use throughout the life of the villa. A gully (F65) cut by F21 may have been a robbed-out drain, perhaps a forerunner of F25 from the North East Range. Another substantial drain (F47) ran north east from the portico (Structure 32), but terminated before reaching F21. This comprised a channel of vertical limestone blocks, floored and sealed by stone slabs and infilled by silt within the drain trench. The function of this drain is unclear, although it may have linked with F15 and was designed to take surplus water away from the base of the south wall to the Central Range gallery.

Post-villa: Surrounded on three sides and downslope of many of the villa buildings, the South Courtyard had received considerable deposits of debris originating from the decay and collapse of the structure in Period 4. As elsewhere, the substantial remnant of this accumulation was divorced from *in situ* remains of the buildings by the trenches of earlier excavators. The exact disposition and extent of what remained was not always clearly recorded by Greenfield, but a general area location of most deposits is given and their character briefly indicated.

A large proportion of the debris was material derived from collapse and robbing of the Central Range. In Areas 41 and 41a) the succession of deposits began with a silt layer sealed by deposits of stone rubble and mortar, a layer of large stone rubble and clay roof tiles, a spread of shattered clay roof tile, and finally, spreads of finer soil and silt with small stone rubble. An unlocated disturbance within this area (F13) may have been part of this complex or a later intrusion. Towards the centre of the courtyard a similar sequence of deposits began with a layer of soil and small stone rubble beneath a finer sandy silt, both of which were sealed by a thick dump of stony soil with much building stone and tile. In the eastern half of the courtyard (Areas 65 & 72) an initial deposit of silt and rubble was succeeded by a series of stony soils, silt, building rubble and roof tile deposits. Further south the collapse or destruction of the South East Range is represented by more claysoil and rubble deposits, which were then sealed by a clay silt hillwash. An equivalent destruction of the Lower Bath House buildings was marked in Area 61 by deposits of dark soil and rubble and stone rubble with mortar and roof tile. Further downhill to the south east this horizon of dereliction appears to thin out as a spread of smaller rubble and soil above and beyond the infilled robber trench of the southern boundary wall.

The cuts signifying the edges to earlier excavator's trenches were not defined, but a series of deposits can be identified as upcast over earlier levels or backfill within the trenches. These were primarily dumps of mixed stony soil with much stone rubble identified variously from the north-west corner and eastwards around the East Wing. Close to the Lower Bath House a levelled dump of Lysons' spoil sealed a humic soil, sealed in turn by a larger, levelled heaped spoil from the excavations of 1938-9. Sometime after the site was taken over by the Office of Works in 1919, efforts were made to improve drainage from the springs above or beneath the remains. A land drain was cut within Lysons' backfill, parallel with the south wall of the Central Range and also cutting through the portico foundations. This was probably linked to a trench which was cut across the courtyard to carry water away downhill. This drainage is probably contemporary with that cut through several rooms of the South East Range (above) for a similar purpose.

**Appendix**: Index of periodized contexts and features (as redefined from Greenfield)

PERIOD 1: Pre-villa. Relates primarily to old ground surface horizons or natural weathered clay, and occasional evidence of pre-villa activity.

West Wing and Exteriors: 594, 653 (OGS.)

Central Range and North Exteriors: 513, 514, 518, 522, 523, 542, 721, 738, 946, 950 (OGS.); 525, 951 (features)

North East Range and Exteriors: 709, 713, 747, 860 (OGS.); 708, 748 (features)

South East Range: 810, 846

South Courtyard: 542, 627, 757, 872?, 873, 875?, 954

PERIOD 2: Villa I. Most contexts/features are assigned to deposits and structures exclusive of the main building. Walls are rarely described or relationships given, although Greenfield identified the rooms of a primary structural period of the villa which are assigned to this phase. The reliability of attributions is variable, particularly where previous excavators had removed or disturbed much of the original stratigraphy.

West Wing: 657, 659, 660, 661, 662

Central Range: 528, 531, 533, 535, 537, (539-541?), 722, 723, 725, 726?, (730-1?), 750, 751, 752, 780/F20, 787-F38, 942, 943, 944, 945, 947, 952, 965

North Exteriors: 509, 510, 511, 512, 521, 527/F2, 676, 886, 887, 889, 892, 893, 894, 905?

East Range: Room 27 - 821, 822/F56, 823/F57, 824/F58, 825/F59, 827/F62, 828/F88, 906-910/F52 & F53
Room 29 - 839, 841 & 842/F84, 843/F86, 906-908/F64
Room 34 - 699, 700, 763 & 764/F31, 766-768/F25
Room 51 - 707/F35

East Exteriors: 739, 747?, 749/F39?, 856

South Courtyard: 552, 553, 625/F12, 756, 788 - 793/F47, F65, 876, 930 & 931/F72, 959, 962

PERIOD 3: Villa II. Similar problems of recording limitations and uncertain attributions apply to contexts and features of this phase, as in Phase 2. Most of the rooms and structures attributed originally by Greenfield to a secondary structural period of the villa building are assigned to Period 3.

South West Range: Room 7 - 636, 637, 638, 642?, 633-635/F10
Room 7a - 557, 558, 559, 560, 561, 562, 563
Room 8/8a - 564a, 565a, 566a, 567, 568, 569, 570, 571, 572, 573?
Room 9 - 574, 575, 576, 577, 578?, 579?, 580, 581, 582.

Rooms 11a & 12 - 604 - 612/F3, 663, 665
Room 11b - 583, 584, 585, 586, 587, 589, 590, 591, 592, 593

West Exteriors: 596, 598, 599, 600/F4, 601, 602, 603, 604 - 612/F3, 613, 614, 655

Central Range: Rooms 13/14 - 530, 532, 534, 536, 538, (539-541?), 669, 753, 754, 755, 948
Room 15 - 667, 668, 940, 941, 966, 969
Rooms 16, 41, 42, 43 & 52 - 724, 727/F17, 728/F43, 729, (731 & 732?), 781/F26, 782/F27, F28

North Exterior: 516a, 517, 672, 734/F45, 735/F37, 742 & 743/F40, 744/F46, 888, 890, 895, 896/F67, 897, 901/F68?, 902/F69?, 903/F70?, 904/F71, 949

North East Range: Room 17 - 712/F16, 714, 715/F18, 716
Room 18 - 717, 718, 720
Room 34 - 686/F22, 687, 688, 689, 690, 691, 692, 693, 694/F24, 695, 696, 698, 765/F32,
Room 51 - 702, 703, 704, 705, 706, 710, 769-772/F23
Room 53 - 701/F36, 761 & 762/F29

South East Range: Room 26 - 811
Room 27 - 816, 817, 818, 829, 911 & 912/F90, 914 - 916/F63
Room 28 - 794, 795, 797, 799/F50, 801 - 803/F55, 804/F61, 805/F91, 807/F94, 808, 920-924/F49, 925/F92
Room 29 - 830, 831, 833 - 838/F54, 840, 845, 913/F85?
Room 30 - 813, 815/F87
Room 44 - 847, 848, 849/F77, 850/F78, 917-919/F74, F75 & F76

East Exteriors: 740, 742 & 743/F40, 744/F46, 745, 746, 773-777/F19, 853, 854, 862, 926-929/F48, 970

South Courtyard: 619, 639-641/F6, 677-680/F14, 681-684/F15, 783-786/F21, 869, 871, 880, 881, 883/F80, 884/F79, 932-934/F73, 935-936/F81, 937-938/F82, 958, 961

PERIOD 4: Post-villa. Many features and deposits of the latest period of villa use, and its subsequent dereliction, will have been removed by previous excavators. Much of what survives was recorded from around the building perimeters.

West Wing: 564, 565, 566, 652, 656, 658, 666

North Exteriors: 502, 503, 504, 505, 506, 507, 508, 670, 671, 736, 737, 885, 891

East Wing: 711, 719, 796, 798, 809, 819, 832, 835?,

East Exteriors: 852, 855, 857, 858, 859, 861, 1002

South Courtyard: 545, 546, 547, 548, 549, 550, 551, 617, 620, 621-626 & 628/F12, 645, 646-7/F12, 648?,

649, 650/F11, 651, 673-675/F11, 864, 865, 866, 867, 868, 870, 877, 878, 879, 882/F12, 955, 956, 957, 963-964/F12

PERIOD 5: Recent. Previous excavations and backfull, other 19th & 20th-century disturbances, modern turf/topsoil.

All Areas: F13, 501, 519, 520, 524, 526, 529, 543, 544, 554 555, 556, 588, 595, 597, 615, 616, 618, 654, 664,685, 697/F20, 733?, 741, 758, 759, 760, 800/F51, 806/F93, 812, 814, 826/F60, 844/F89, 863, 874, 898, 899, 900, 939, 953, 1000, 1001, 1003, 1004

*NB. An index of all defined Contexts and Features in numerical order, with cross reference to their site location and original Greenfield definition (where given), is available in the site archive.*

Chapter 3

# THE FINDS

Reports on the finds assemblages recovered during Greenfield's excavations are arranged thematically in the following section, according to functional categories. These are defined broadly in line with schemes of categorisation adopted with increasing frequency in recent artifact reports for Romano-British sites (eg Crummy 1983; Woodward and Leach 1993).

Some account of Greenfield's policy for the collection and recording of portable artifacts and other material from the site is given previously. Not all categories were collected or sampled as thoroughly as would now be expected as part of current field practice, notably environmental remains, and this is reflected in the limited scope of certain reports. Furthermore, in one or two instances not all the material originally recovered and recorded by Greenfield could be located and thus fully reported upon. An archive documenting all the recorded finds material was prepared and is available within the larger site archive, in support of the reports published here. The latter provide summaries, in variable detail, of all finds categories, with more detailed discussion and illustration where appropriate of individual groups or pieces. Specified items in the following reports are normally listed in italics with their unique find number (prefixed by 'W'), site context as redefined for this report (prefixed by 'C' or 'F'), locality (Room or Area) and sometimes Period.

## 3.1: PREHISTORIC ARTIFACTS

### Stone
by L. Bevan

Prehistoric artifacts comprise one fragment of a Neolithic polished stone axehead (Fig.11.1), a small assemblage of Iron Age potsherds (below), and seven pieces of humanly-struck flint including a flake knife and a scraper (Fig.11.1-2). The broad flake knife is of probable Neolithic origin and the scraper is a 'thumbnail' type commonly dated to the Early Bronze Age. The remaining flint pieces are struck flakes. All flint finds are residual, relating to low-density prehistoric activities on the site. The segment of a polished axe has not been sectioned to identify its source, but was of a fine grey-green rock, possibly originating in South West England. None of this material is likely to signify anything other than a transient human presence or off-site activity in early prehistoric times.

**Catalogue**

1. Polished stone axe segment: *W1140 C639, A61*
2. Flint scraper: *W994 C664, R15*
3. Flint knife: *W4699 F81/82, A72*

Flint Flakes not illustrated: *W2880, C864/7; W3024, C659; W4510, C877; W4700, F81/82; W4722, C882.*

### Prehistoric pottery
by P. Leach

A small assemblage of prehistoric pottery was recovered from the fills of a small east-west aligned gully (708) cut by the foundations of rooms belonging to the North East Range. Regrettably, this material could not be located among the finds assemblages for analysis. From the excavator's records at least 28 sherds of coarse, handmade, shell-tempered fabric, including three rims, came from this ditch. There is no record of other associated finds, and both ditch and pottery are identified by Greenfield as Iron Age.

A few sherds of similar fabric were identified among the Romano-British pottery assemblages from the South Courtyard (*C759, A65 and C881, A72*), and from *Area 71* (*C886*) to the north. None is illustrated. No other Iron Age contexts appear to have been encountered during the excavations, but the presence of the gulley to the north east may signify the boundary to an earlier settlement which lay in that direction.

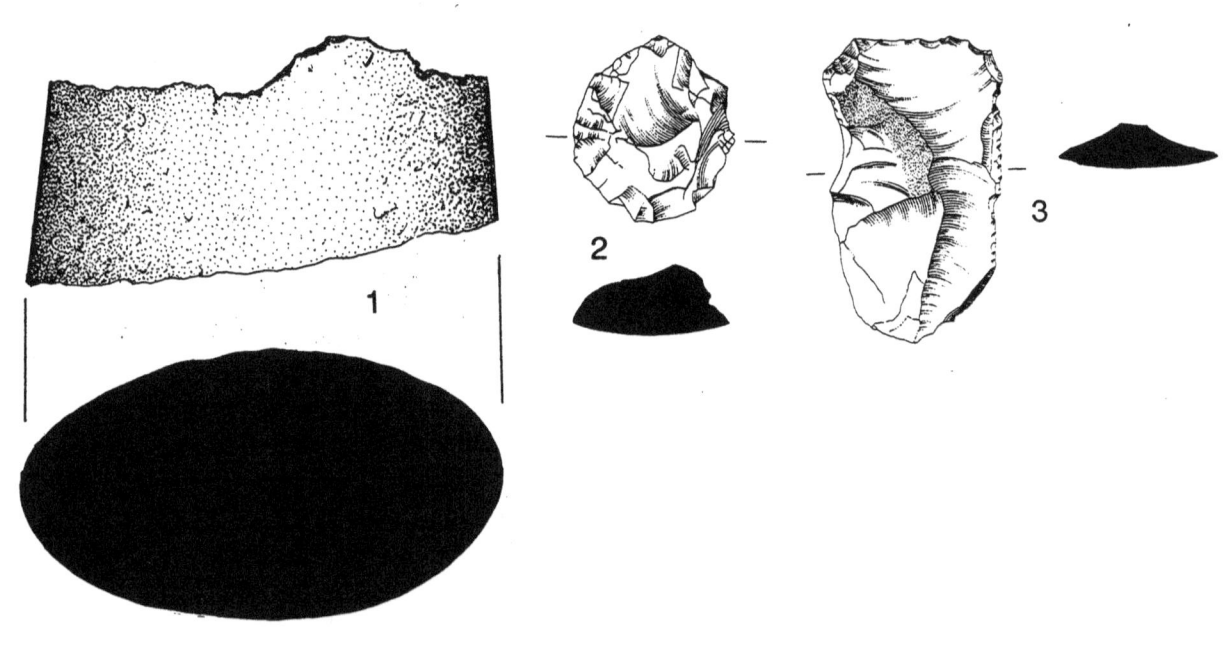

*Figure 11* Prehistoric stone and flint, nos. 1-3 (1:1)

## 3.2: ROMAN

### 3.2.1 VESSELS

### Roman Pottery
*by P. Leach with B. Dickinson, J. Timby and D. Williams*

**Introduction**

No attempt has been made to examine or assess in detail the pottery recovered by previous excavators, although reference is made where appropriate to such material, notably that published by Mrs Clifford (1955). The presentation of ceramics collected in the course of Greenfield's excavations is especially influenced by two factors: the nature of those excavations, and the excavator's collection and site recording policy. In the first instance previous work by Clifford, and particularly by Lysons and Hicks, required much re-excavation by Greenfield of backfilled deposits. This resulted not only in an incomplete ceramic sample from the site as a whole, but also the collection of a substantial proportion of the material from secondary and other post-Roman contexts (approaching 50% of the sample). In the second, account must be taken of Greenfield's discriminatory collecting policy for pottery, and noted on other sites directed by him (e.g. Henley Wood, Watts and Leach 1996). Its retention was apparently based upon the possession of attributes such as 'diagnostic' form, special fabrics or decoration, important sealed groups, and the recognition of mortaria and samian fabrics. Effectively, this has resulted in a surviving assemblage comprising virtually all rims, a small but unknown proportion of the total base and body sherds, and virtually all the mortaria and samian sherds recognised at the time of excavation and initial processing.

As the most numerous class of artifact collected at Great Witcombe, the ceramic assemblage available for study comprised *c* 2,800 sherds weighing almost 90 kg., and representing a minimum of 162 vessels as calculated by estimated vessel equivlents (eves.). All those retained were serially numbered within the excavator's finds recording sequence for Witcombe: W.1-W.4998; samian and mortaria having been additionally identified within sequential catalogues prefixed S1-S149 and M1-M105, respectively. All this material was originally provenanced according to a further numerical sequence of bag numbers, wherein was often included other categories of finds. Wherever possible these bags have subsequently been equated to defined archaeological site contexts.

The basis of this report is the provision of a representative and illustrated pottery fabric and form series for the villa; its quantified and chronological occurrence; support for a site events sequence as determined through the record and interpretation of archaeological stratigraphy; and, if possible, the illustration of any social, economic or cultural patterning within the assemblage. Excepting a handful of prehistoric, medieval or post-medieval sherds, the pottery assemblage was entirely Roman or Romano-British in character. In addition to this material, a few items of pottery with secondary attributes (e.g. counters or spindlewhorls) are considered elsewhere in reports on those finds. Vessels of fired clay are also considered within the pottery report, other classes of this material such as roof, flue or floor tiles are dealt with separately.

**Methodology**

The ceramic vessel assemblage has been classified through the definition of a type fabric and form series. The material was identified and catalogued by a *pro forma*-based record (in archive). The principal Fabric Types were defined by macroscopic examination (with a hand lense) of ceramic matrices and their inclusions; textural attributes; and characteristics such as colour and firing (Peacock 1977). The significance of individual types is emphasised through their association into a smaller number of Groups, whose identity is defined with reference to such criteria as physical character, origin of manufacture or functional attributes. This is an extendable system of classification using an arbitary alphabetical/numerical notation. The index of fabrics defined for this site is summarised in Table 1, with reference to suspected origins, and equations where possible with more widely identified standard types. Full definitions are recorded by *pro-forma* entries and lodged with the archive to this report. Further discussion of the character and significance of the major fabric groups, including specialist contributions on the samian and mortaria fabrics, follows below.

**Table 1: Index of pottery fabric types**

FABRIC GROUP A: reduced coarsewares
Type A1: Severn Valley coarse greyware variant
Type A2: Severn Valley finer greyware variant
Type A3: Alice Holt sandy greyware
Type A4: N.Wiltshire/Cotswold? greyware
Type A5: Midlands shell-tempered ware

FABRIC GROUP B: black burnished reduced coarsewares
Type B1: Dorset Black Burnished ware (BB1)
Type B2: Severn Valley greyware, BB1 imitation
Type B3: Malvernian greyware, BB1 imitation

FABRIC GROUP C: colour coat wares
Type C1: Oxfordshire red colour coat ware (Young 1977, fabric C)
Types C2/6: SW British? wares, variants
Type C3: Nene Valley cream/white ware mortaria
Type C4: Nene Valley colour coat ware
Type C5: N.Wilts/Cotswold? colour coat ware

FABRIC GROUP D: oxidized coarsewares and mortaria
Types D1/4: Severn Valley oxidized ware (Webster 1976)
Type D2: Severn Valley oxidized ware variant
Type D3: Oxfordshire whiteware (Young 1977, Types W and M)
Type D5: Oxfordshire white slipped ware (Young 1977, Type WC)

FABRIC GROUP E: Roman imports
Type E1: Gaulish samian wares (*terra sigillata*)
Type E2: Rhenish/Lezoux colour coat ware
Type E3: Amphora fabrics, various origins
Type E4: Flagon fabric, East Mediterranean source

MISCELLANEOUS GROUP: fired clay
Type FC: Oxidized clay wares, Severn Valley? origin

The definition of a vessel form series is based upon both physical and functional attributes common to a wide spectrum of Roman and Romano-British pottery, which in most instances cuts across the fabric range. Within a simplified range of basic generic forms sub-varieties are distinguished and identified according to an arbitary numerical code. Form definition is linked primarily to function, in the hope of attempting some analysis and interpretation of pottery use on the site. At the crudest level, form distinctions can be made between such categories as storage vessels, cooking, or table wares. A rather more specific breakdown into several principal vessel types (jars, bowls, dishes, etc.) is a starting point for further refinement. In some instances, e.g. amphorae, mortaria or flagons, functional and typological distinctions are clear cut. But in others, vessel forms may occur in such a range of size that functional characteristics may overlap, as for example between some bowl and jar forms; or difficulties arise in distinguishing between some classes of beakers and small jars, or some bowl and dish forms, particularly when the types are normally represented only by fragmentary vessels or a few sherds. In these circumstances a pragmatic approach and a relatively simple system of sub-division is required. The basic vessel form sub-divisions are summarised in Table 2, with reference to the range of pottery fabrics in which they are present.

**Table 2: Roman pottery form series**

FORM 1: Jars
Type 1.1: Short-necked, wide-mouthed, sharp everted rims; Fabrics: A1, A2, A3, B1, B2, B3
Type 1.2/3: Short-necked, wide-mouthed, shallow everted rims; Fabrics: A1, A2, A3, A4, A5, B1, B2, B3, D1, D2, D4?
Type 1.4: Short-necked, shallow or beaded rims; Fabrics: A1, B1, D1
Type 1.5: Short-necked, narrow-mouthed, out-turned rims; Fabrics: A1, A2, A3, B1, C1, C2, D1, D2, D3, D4
Type 1.6: Short-necked, wide-mouthed storage with rolled-over rims; Fabrics: A1

FORM 2: Bowls/Dishes
Type 2.1: Straight/convex-sided, flat or overhanging shallow rims; Fabrics: A1, A2, A5, B1, B2, C1, D1, D2, D4, FC
Type 2.2: Straight/convex sided, plain rim above flange; Fabrics: A1, A5, B1, B2, B3, C1, C4, D1, D2, E1, FC
Type 2.3: Plain rounded rims, shallow, mainly dishes; Fabrics: A1, A2, A3, A5, B1, B2, B3, C1, C4, D1, E1, FC
Type 2.4: Straight/convex-sided, beaded/overturned rims; Fabrics: A1, C1, D1, D4, E1
Type 2.5: Carinated, beaded or plain rounded rims; Fabrics: C1, D1/4
Type 2.6: Shallow, convex-sided, plain or rolled rims, some dishes; Fabrics: C1, D1/4, E1
Type 2.7: Straight/convex-sided, flat or overturned flange rims, includes mortaria; Fabrics: A1, A2, A5, C1, C3, C4, D1, D3, D4, D5, E1

FORM 3: Beakers/Cups
Type 3.1: Globular, narrow out-turned/grooved rims, some handles; Fabrics: A3, B1, C1, C4, C5, D1
Type 3.2: Globular/convex, some indented, long-necked, round/beaded rims; Fabrics: A1, B2, C1, C2/6, C4, E2
Type 3.3: Convex/straight-sided, some indented, everted rims; Fabrics: A1, B2, C1, D1/4
Type 3.4 Straight/concave-sided, plain/beaded rims, some handles; Fabrics: C1, D1/4, D2

FORM 4: Flagons/Bottles
Type 4.1: Globular, narrow or elongated necks, moulded rims, 1/2 handles (flagons); Fabrics: C1, C5, E1
Type 4.2: Globular, long necks, wide mouths, outflaring or moulded rims, 1/2 handles; Fabrics: A1, C2/6, C5, D1
Type 4.3: Globular, long narrow necks, plain or moulded rims; Fabrics: D1/4

FORM 5: Lids
Type 5.1: Shallow, straight or convex-sided, plain or beaded rim, most with central handle boss; Fabrics: B1, B3, C2/6

FORM 6: Amphorae
Type 6.1 Globular or cylindrical bodies, often tapering to base, moulded rolled rims, two handles. No further sub-division by form type or origin; Fabric: E3

Quantification of the assemblage, upon the basis of fabric and form classification, is made, where possible, with reference to chronology. It is unfortunate that due to the degree of previous excavation on the site, as well as the lack of a computerised data base, spatial analysis by these criteria could not be usefully attempted. Most room interiors were severely disturbed, and where contemporary phased contexts survived intact the remaining ceramic sample size was normally too small for useful comparative analysis. In those more extensive areas beyond the confines of the villa buildings, untouched by earlier excavators, the bulk of the assemblage derives from very late or post-villa contexts, many of which relate to clearance from the building and general dumping. Once again, in these circumstances the value of detailed spatial analysis would be questionable.

The fabric quantifications are expressed in terms of sherd count, weight, and estimated vessel equivalents; both in figures and percentages (Table 3 and Fig.19). Given the collection policy adopted by the excavator, sherd count and weight will considerably underrepresent the assemblage size, except perhaps as expressed in percentage terms. The estimating of vessel equivalents is currently regarded as the most reliable technique for quantifying pottery from archaeological contexts, using in this instance the measurement and proportion of rim diameters present (Orton 1975 and 1989). Fortunately, the collecting policy at

Witcombe is well suited to an application of this method. Quantification of form types (Table 4 and Fig. 20) is based solely upon the estimated vessel equivalents.

A complete catalogue of the Great Witcombe pottery, classified by fabric and form types for each individual archaeological site context, is recorded by *pro-forma* and available in the archive. The illustrated material (Figs.12-18) has been selected to show the range of principal forms represented by each fabric type recorded at the site. Significant, well sealed groups and assemblages were rare or absent from areas and deposits excavated by Greenfield, although pottery groups from a general locality or overall phase are reconstructable with reference to the recorded contexts. A relatively full presentation of the material is justified by the local rarity, outside of Gloucester or Cirencester, of significant Roman assemblages which have been analysed in this fashion, and in particular (at the time of writing) any from villas of the Gloucestershire Cotswolds.

**The fabric and form type series**

FABRIC GROUP A
Reduced, coarse greywares; Severn Valley and other British sources (Types A1-A5)

Fabric Type A1
*Fabric:* Variable, medium-light grey sandy fabric, sometimes with abundant mica inclusions; moderately fired, cores often lighter than margins, variable texture.
*Forms:* Principally jars - types 1.1, 1.2/3, 1.5 and 1.6 - and bowls - types 2.1, 2.2, 2.3 and 2.5; occasional beakers - type 3.3 - and flagons - type 4.2. Wheel made, exteriors plain or with some burnished zones; some simple incised linear or combed decoration.

Figs. 12 and 13
1. Jar 1.1, *C775*, *E. exterior, Area 64/66, Period 3*
2. Jar 1.1, *C775*,    "       "       "       "
3. Jar 1.1, *C870*, *S. courtyard, Area 65, Period 4*
4. Jar 1.1, *C777*, *E. exterior, Area 64/66, Period 3*
5. Jar 1.1, *C777*,    "       "       "       "
6. Jar 1.2, *C867*, *S. courtyard, Area 65, Period 4*
7. Jar 1.2, *C777*, *E. exterior, Area 64/66, Period 3*
8. Jar 1.2, *C862*, *E. exterior, Area 70, Period 3*
9. Jar 1.2, *C868*, *S. courtyard, Area 65, Period 4*
10. Jar 1.2/3, *C653*, *W. exterior, Area 60, Period 1*
11. Jar 1.2/3, *C865*, *S. courtyard, Area 65, Period 4*
12. Jar 1.2, *C819*, *E. range, Room 27, Period 4*
13. Jar 1.5, *CF13*, *S. courtyard, Area 41, Period 5*
14. Jar 1.5, *C777*, *E. exterior, Area 64/66, Period 3*
15. Jar 1.5, *CF13*, *S. courtyard, Area 41, Period 5*
16. Jar 1.5, *C650*, *S. courtyard, Area 61, Period 4*
17. Jar 1.5, *C856*, *E. courtyard, Area 67, Period 2*
18. Jar 1.6, *C898*, *S. courtyard, Area 71, Period 5*
19. Bowl 2.1, *C928*, *E. exterior, Area 68, Period 3*
20. Bowl 2.1, *C725*, *Central range, Room 16, Period 2*
21. Bowl 2.1, *C566*, *W. range, Room 7a, Period 4*
22. Bowl 2.2, *C655*, *W. exterior, Area 60, Period 3*
23. Bowl 2.2, *C649*, *S. courtyard, Area 61, Period 4*
24. Bowl 2.2, *C877*, *S. courtyard, Area 72, Period 4*
25. Bowl 2.2, *C725*, *Central range, Room 16, Period 2*
26. Bowl 2.2, *C746*, *E. exterior, Area 64/66, Period 3*
27. Bowl 2.3, *C865*, *S. courtyard, Area 65, Period 4*
28. Bowl 2.3, *C859*, *E. exterior, Area 68/9, Period 4*
29. Bowl 2.3, *C737*, *N. exterior, Area 62, Period 4*
30. Bowl 2.3, *C736*, *N. exterior, Area 62, Period 4*
31. Bowl 2.4, *C675*, *S. courtyard, Area 41a, Period 3*
32. Flagon 4.2, *C774*, *E. exterior, Area 64/66, Period 3*

*Dating and parallels:* A Severn Valley fabric produced as a reduced greyware; probably from the mid-2nd century but continuing into the 3rd and 4th centuries. No local kiln source known, although an abundance of mica temper in some vessels suggests production either in the Forest of Dean or along the upper Severn Estuary where there are outcrops of micaceous Triassic sandstone. Some vessels derive their form from the more familiar oxidized Severn Valley repetoire, but the majority appear to copy Dorset Black Burnished ware forms, probably in response to the latter's importation to the region. As defined at Great Witcombe, this fabric is somewhat variable in character, suggesting several production sources, but further classificatory sub-division was not thought worthwhile for the purposes of this report. It comprised 13.5% of the total assemblage as eves., and is paralleled in the region at rural sites along the upper Severn Estuary (Fulford and Allen 1992, 186), at Gloucester (TF5), Cirencester (TF133), Uley (TF16), and at Frocester and Kingscote (Timby pers. comm.)

Fabric Type A2
*Fabric:* Mid-grey reduced, soapy fabric, lightly gritted; moderately well fired, darker grey surfaces, cores sometimes buff-grey.
*Forms:* Jar types 1.2; Bowl types 2.3, 2.7 including cullenders; Flagon types 4.2. Wheel made, plain exteriors, some with dark grey ?fumed surfaces.

Fig. 13
33. Jar 1.1, *F65, S. courtyard, Period 2*
34. Bowl 2.3, *C650, S. courtyard, Area 61, Period 4*
35. Bowl 2.7, *C878, S. courtyard, Area 72, Period 4*
36. Bowl 2.7, *CF13, S. courtyard, Area 41, Period 5*
37. Flagon 4.2, *C746, E. exterior, Area 64/66, Period 3*

*Dating and parallels*: A reduced Severn Valley fabric, probably a variant of A1. Mainly a 3rd/4th-century product but could begin earlier; no known local kiln source. Comprises 0.8% of the assemblage as eves. No exact parallels documented elsewhere, but possibly included within TF5 at Gloucester.

Fabric Type A3
*Fabric:* Light buff-grey reduced fabric, heavily gritted with coloured quartz and other minerals. Moderately fired, granular texture; exteriors often dark grey or buff-brown.
*Forms:* Jar types 1.1, 1.2, 1.5; Bowl types 2.3; Beaker types 3.3. Wheel made, exteriors normally plain, occasional incised decoration.

Fig. 13
38. Jar 1.2 (Lyne & Jefferies 1979, Class 3B), *C650, S. courtyard, Area 61, Period 4*
39. Jar 1.2 (Lyne & Jefferies 1979, Class 3B), *C859, E. exterior, Area 68/9, Period 4*
40. Jar 1.2 (Lyne & Jefferies 1979, Class 3B), *C774, E. exterior, Area 64/66, Period 3*
41. Jar 1.3 (Lyne & Jefferies 1979, Class 3C), *C865, S. courtyard, Area 65, Period 4*
42. Jar 1.3 (Lyne & Jefferies 1979, Class 3C), *C777, E. exterior, Area 64/66, Period 3*
43. Bowl 2.3/7 (Lyne & Jefferies 1979, Class 6A.8-11), *F13, S. courtyard, Area 41, Period 5*
44. Bowl 2.3/7 (Lyne & Jefferies 1979, Class 6A.8 -11), *unstratified*

*Dating and Parallels*: Alice Holt/Farnham pottery industry fabric, later 3rd and 4th-century types (Lyne and Jefferies 1979). Comprises 1.67% of the assemblage as eves.

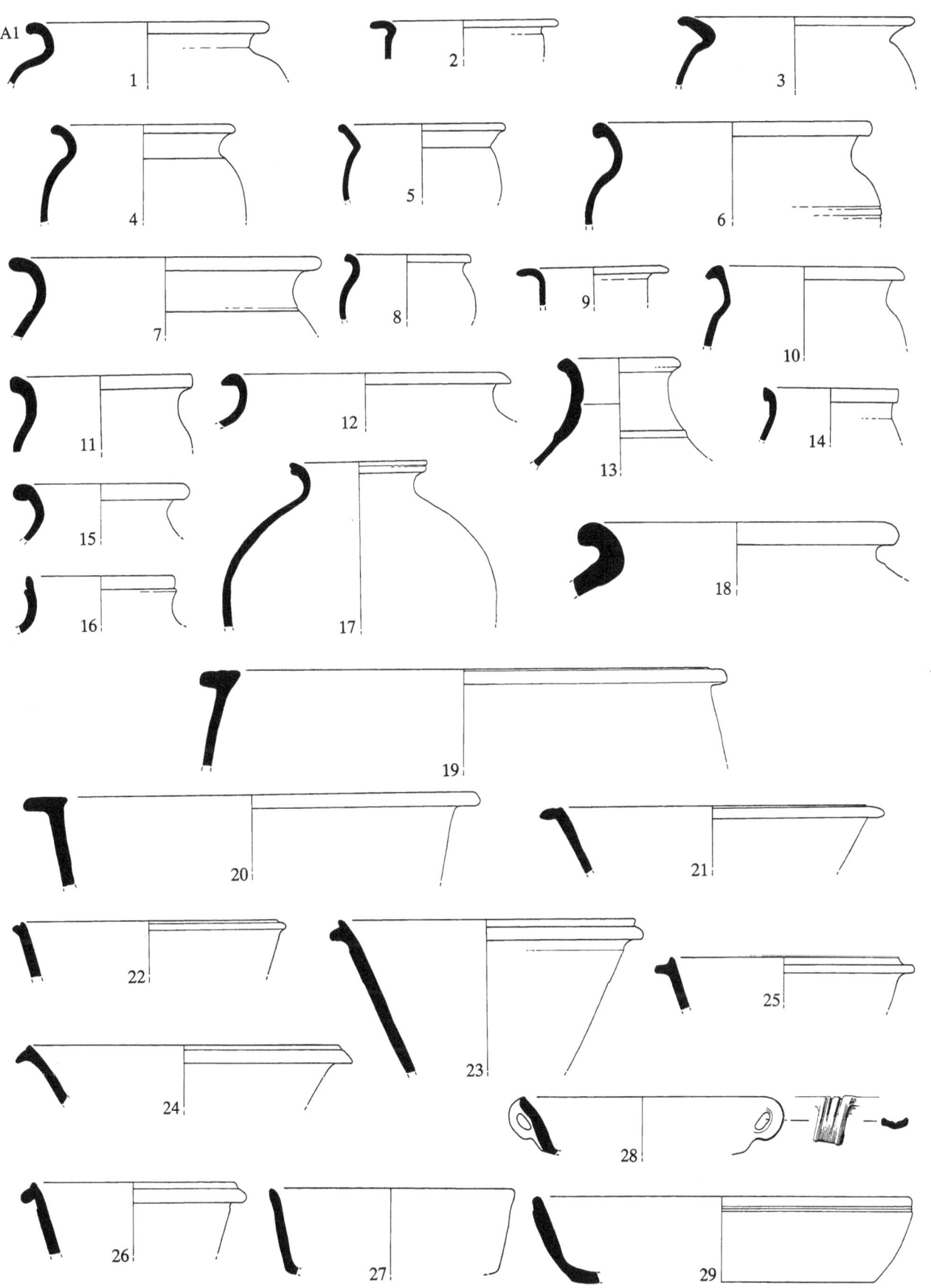

*Figure 12* Roman pottery; Fabric A1, nos. 1-29 (1:4)

Fabric Type A4
*Fabric*: Even, mid-grey, smooth/lightly sanded ware, with occasional large chalk/limestone inclusions; moderately fired.
*Forms*: Jar types 1.2, 1.5. Wheel made, plain exteriors.

Fig. 13
45. Jar 1.3, *F13, S. Courtyard, Area 41, Period 5*
46. Jar 1.5, " " " " "

*Dating and Parallels*: A reduced fabric type of uncertain source, but possibly originating in the 3rd/4th century from the north Wiltshire/Cotswold area. Comprises 0.45% of the assemblage as eves. No parallels known.

Fabric Type A5
*Fabric:* Medium soft, mid/dark grey ware, heavily tempered with coarse grey/white fossil shell; surfaces variable, some buff-brown or light grey.
*Forms:* Jar types 1.2; Bowl types 2.3, 2.7. Hand made, wheel-finished, plain surfaces or with fine exterior corrugations.

Fig. 13
47. Jar 1.3, *C656, W. exterior, Area 60, Period 4*
48. Jar 1.3, *C865, S. courtyard, Area 65, Period 4*
49. Jar 1.3, *C655, W. exterior, Area 60, Period 3*
50. Jar 1.3, *F13, S. courtyard, Area 41, Period 5*
51. Bowl 2.7, *C650, S. courtyard, Area 61, Period 4*
52. Bowl 2.7, *C655, W. exterior, Area 60, Period 3*
53. Bowl 2.3, *F13, S. courtyard, Area 41, Period 5*
54. Bowl 2.3, *F13,* " " " "

*Dating and parallels: South-East Midlands shell*-tempered ware, mainly 4th century and ?later in Gloucestershire. Comprises 8.31% of the assemblage by eves. Locally defined parallels include Gloucester TF22, Cirencester TF155, and Uley TF9 - where it hardly appears before *c* AD 320 and the bulk was deposited post *c* AD 380.

FABRIC GROUP B
Reduced, black burnished coarsewares; Dorset BB1 and local Severn Valley sources (Types B1, B2 and B3).

Fabric Type B1
Fabric: Medium fired, reduced sandy fabric, with abundant quartz sand and other minerals temper. Normally fired black or dark grey, but occasional cream-buff or orange-brown variants, often in patches.
Forms: Most of the common forms in the Dorset BB1 repertoire are represented (Williams 1977), including Jars 1.1, 1.2, 1.4; Bowls & Dishes 2.1, 2.2, 2.3; Beakers 3.1. Exteriors and some interior surfaces characteristically highly burnished; hatched or curvilinear incised designs common, sometimes on unburnished zones.

Figs. 13 and 14
55. Jar 1.1, *C792, S. courtyard, Area 65; Period 2*
56. Jar 1.1, *C647, S. courtyard, Area 61; Period 2*
57. Jar 1.1, *Unstratified*
58. Jar 1.1, *C642, S. courtyard, Area 61; Period 3*
59. Jar 1.1, *C675, S. courtyard, Area 41a; Period 3*
60. Jar 1.1, *C715, E. range, Room 17; Period 3*
61. Jar 1.1, *C725, Central range, Room 16; Period 2*
62. Jar 1.2, *C768, E. range, Room 34; Period 2*
63. Jar 1.4, *C736, N. exterior, Area 62, Period 4*
64. Jar 1.4, *C759, S. courtyard, Area 65, Period 5*
65. Bowl 2.2, *C736, N. exterior, Area 62, Period 4*
66. Bowl 2.2, *C777, E. exterior, Area 64/66, Period 3*
67. Bowl 2.2, *C862, E. exterior, Area 70, Period 3*
68. Bowl 2.2, *C774, E. exterior, Area 64/66, Period 3*
69. Bowl 2.2, *C642, S. courtyard, Area 61, Period 3*
70. Bowl 2.2, *C642, S. courtyard, Area 61, Period 3*
71. Bowl/Dish 2.3, *C649, S. courtyard, Area 61, Period 4*
72. Dish 2.3, *C746, E. exterior, Area 64/66, Period 3*
73. Dish 2.3, *C746, E. exterior, Area 64/66, Period 3*
74. Dish 2.3, *C1001, E. exterior, Area 66, Period 5*
75. Dish 2.3, *C777, E. exterior, Area 64/66, Period 3*
76. Base sherd grafitti 'PV', *C621, S. courtyard, Trench A, Period 2*

*Dating and parallels*: Dorset Black Burnished fabric BB1 (Williams 1977). This product is barely represented in Gloucestershire before the early 2nd century; almost all the datable types at Great Witcombe are 3rd and 4th century. The second largest group within the assemblage, comprising 25.3% by eves. Local parallels include Gloucester TF4, Cirencester TF74, and Uley TF8.

Fabric Type B2
*Fabric:* Medium fired, reduced sandy fabric moderately well tempered with quartz sand and some mica. Dark grey-black surfaces with mica flecks, lightly burnished or sometimes matt.
*Forms:* Jar types 1.2; Bowl types 2.1, 2.2, 2.3; Beaker types 3.2, 3.3; the majority imitate common Dorset BB1 forms (B1). Wheel made or finished vessels, plain, with dark grey-black surface slip, often burnished.

Fig. 14
77. Jar 1.2, *unstratified*
78. Bowl 2.1, *C647, S. courtyard, Area 61, Period 2*
79. Bowl 2.2, *C686, E. range, Room 34, Period 3*
80. Bowl 2.2, *CF65, S. courtyard, Period 2*
81. Bowl 2.2, *C920, S.E. wing, Room 28, Period 3*
82. Bowl 2.2, *C564, W. range, Room 7a, Period 4*
83. Dish 2.3, *C746, E. exterior, Area 64/66, Period 3*
84. Dish 2.3, *C864, S. courtyard, Area 65, Period 65*
85. Bowl/dish 2.3, *C650, S. courtyard, Area 61, Period 4*
86. Beaker 3.2, *C782, Central range, Room 16, Period 3*

*Dating and parallels*: A reduced Severn Valley fabric, probably a finer variant of A1 but produced as a conscious imitation of Dorset BB1. Severn Valley/Forest of Dean, 3rd-4th century, no known kiln source. Comprises 3.3% of the assemblage as eves. Local defined parallels include Gloucester TF5, Cirencester TF133, Uley TF16.

# Roman Pottery

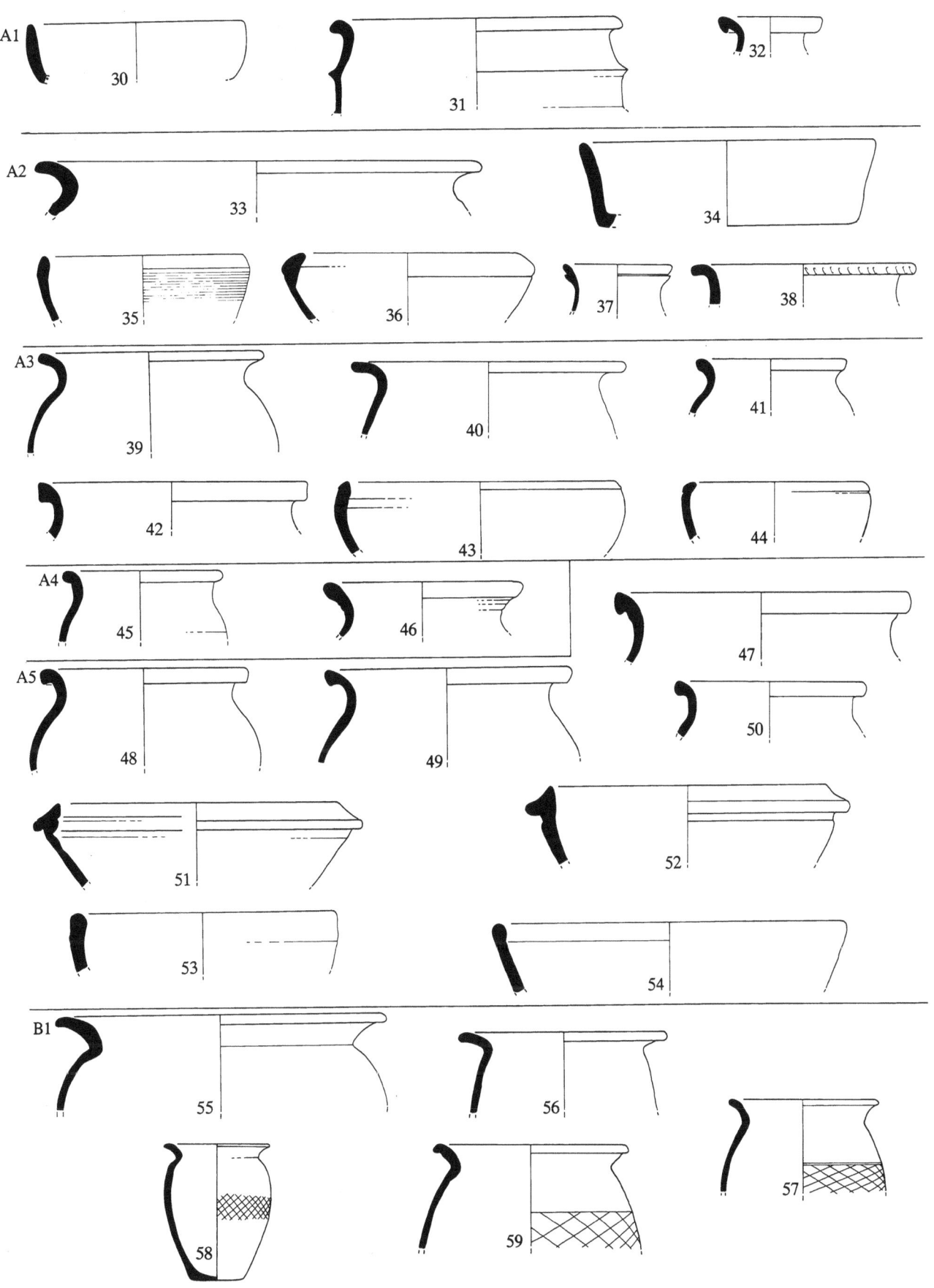

**Figure 13** *Roman pottery; Fabric A1, nos. 30-32; A2, nos. 33-37; A3, nos. 38-44; A4, nos. 45-6; A5, nos. 47-54; B1, nos. 55-59 (1:4)*

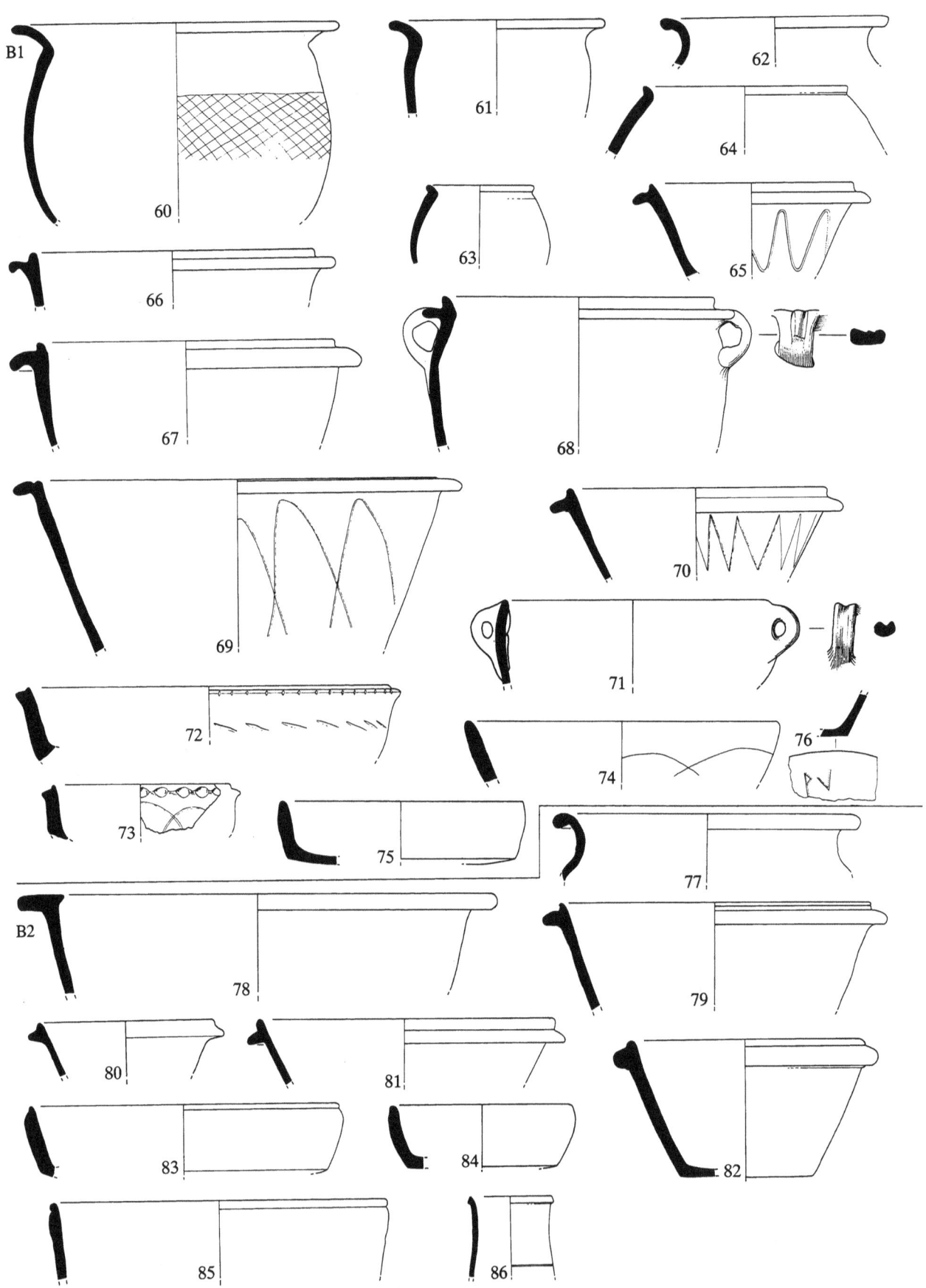

*Figure 14* Roman pottery; Fabric B1, nos. 60-76; B2, nos. 77-86 (1:4)

**Fabric Type B3**
*Fabric:* Moderately fired, reduced buff-grey-black, coarse gritty texture, some coarse palaeozoic rock inclusions of Malvernian origin.
*Forms:* Jar types 1.2; Bowl types 2.2, 2.3; Lids 5.1; some imitating Dorset BB1 forms. Hand made and wheel finished, grey-black surface finish, plain, sometimes burnished.

Fig. 15
87. Jar 1.2, *C816, S.E. wing, Room 27, Period 3*
88. Bowl 2.2, *CF65, S. courtyard, Period 2*
89. Dish 2.3, *C866, S. courtyard, Area 65, Period 4*
90. Lid 5.1, *C819, E. range, Room 27, Period 4*

*Dating and parallels:* A Severn Valley 'Malvernian' type, apparently imitating Dorset BBI wares; probably a 3rd-4th century product. Comprises 0.3% of the assemblage by eves. A possible locally identified parallel is TF206 from Gloucester.

**FABRIC GROUP C**
Oxidized and reduced British colour coat wares (Types C1, C2/6, C3, C4, C5).

**Fabric Type C1**
*Fabric:* Soft, medium fired, oxidized red-orange-buff ware, fine grained and often micaceous, with lustrous or burnished red-orange colour coat.
*Forms:* Principally bowls - including mortaria, and some enclosed types, many imitating samian forms; Bowl types 2.1, 2.2, 2.3, 2.4, 2.6, 2.7; Cup types 3.4; Flagon types 4.1. Wheel made with burnished surfaces; often decorated with bands of rouletting, stamps and sometimes white-painted designs.

Fig. 15
91. Bowl 2.1, *C604, W. range exterior, Period 3*
92. Bowl 2.2, *C858, E. exterior, Area 68/9, Period 4*
93. Dish 2.3, *CF13, S. courtyard, Area 41, Period 5*
94. Bowl 2.4, *C777, E. exterior, Area 64/66, Period 3*
95. Bowl 2.4, *C746, E. exterior, Area 64/66, Period 3*
96. Bowl 2.4, *unstratified*
97. Bowl 2.4, *C715, E. range, Room 17, Period 3*
98. Bowl 2.4, *C958, S. courtyard, Area 41a, Period 3*
99. Bowl 2.4, *F13, S. courtyard, Area 41, Period 5*
100. Bowl 2.4, *C910, E. range, Room 27, Period 2*
101. Bowl 2.4, *C725, Central range, Room 16, Period 2*
102. Bowl 2.4, *C777, E. exterior, Area 64/66, Period 3*
103. Bowl 2.4, *C859, E. exterior, Area 68/9, Period 4*
104. Bowl base, illegible stamp, *C854, E. exterior, Area 67, Period 3*
105. Cup 3.1, *F13, S. courtyard, Area 41, Period 5*
106. Cup 3.1, *F13, S. courtyard, Area 41, Period 5*
107. Beaker 3.2, *C854, E. exterior, Area 67, Period 3*
108. Flagon 4.1, *CF65, S. courtyard, Period 2*
109. Flagon 4.3, *unstratified*

*Dating and parallels:* A later 3rd and 4th-century product of the Oxfordshire pottery industry, corresponding to Young's fabric C (1977, 123-184). Comprises 6.9% of the assemblage by eves, and includes 19% by weight of the total mortaria types recovered (Timby, archive report). Widely distributed throughout southern Britain; local identified equivalents include Gloucester TF12a, Cirencester TF83, Uley TF23.

**Type Fabric C2/C6**
*Fabric:* Fine, well-fired oxidized or partly reduced, somewhat variable (two separate types originally classified may be essentially the same); variable red or grey colour coat on one or both surfaces.
*Forms:* Thin-walled, wheel made enclosed vessels; Beaker types 3.2, Flagon types 4.2, and Lids 5.1. Variable range of colour coats, exterior bodies frequently decorated with barbotine or rouletted bands.

Fig. 15
110. Flagon 4.2, *C649, S. Courtyard, Area 61, Period 4*
111. Lid 5.1, *C854, E. exterior, Area 67, Period 3*

*Dating and parallels:* Varieties of south-west British colour coat products, possibly of several unknown local sources. Mainly 3rd and 4th-century manufacture, some earlier? Comprises 0.7% of the assemblage as eves. Local identified equivalents include Gloucester TF12D, Cirencester TFs105 and 86?, Uley TF17.

**Type Fabrics C3 and C4**
*Fabric:* Fine, well fired, cream iron-free; dark grey angular trituration grits on mortaria; many with red-brown colour coated surfaces.
*Forms:* Wheel made Bowl types 2.2, 2.3 and 2.7 mortaria (separately classified as Fabric C3); Beaker types 3.1, 3.2. Plain or decorated red-brown or grey-black colour coat exterior surfaces; barbotine, rouletted or painted decoration.

Fig. 15
112. Bowl/Jar? 2.4/1.2, *CF65, S. courtyard, Period 2*
113. Dish 2.3, *F13, S. courtyard, Area 41, Period 5*
114. Bowl 2.5?, *C867, S. courtyard, Area 65, Period 4*
115. Beaker 3.1, *C868, S. courtyard, Area 65, Period 4*

*Dating and parallels:* Nene Valley colour coat wares, 3rd and 4th-century types (Howe, Perrin and Mackreth 1980); C3 is distinguished from C4 only as a form group - mortaria. Comprising 0.9% of the assemblage as eves. Locally identified equivalents include Gloucester TF12B, Cirencester TF81 and Uley TF20.

**Type Fabric C5**
*Fabric:* Well-fired, reduced, sandy texture with much small rounded quartz filler; cream or buff-orange exterior colour coat.
*Forms:* Wheel made, enclosed vessels; Beaker types 3.3, Flagon types 4.1. Plain colour coated exterior surfaces, sometimes burnished.

Fig. 15
116. Cup/Beaker 3.1, *C858/9, E. exterior Area 68/9, Period 4*
117. Cup/Beaker 3.3, *C792, S. courtyard, Area 65, Period 2*
118. Flagon 4.3, *C870, S. courtyard, Area 65, Period 4*

*Dating and parallels*: Colour coat wares of unspecified but probably south west British origin; later 2nd and 3rd-century manufacture but no known kiln sources. Comprises 0.7% of the assemblage as eves. Local equivalent fabrics include Gloucester TFs15A and 15B, Cirencester TFs88/95, 96 and 97, Uley TFs13 and 18.

FABRIC GROUP D
Oxidized coarsewares; Severn Valley and other British sources (Types D1 - D5).

Fabric Type D1/D4
*Fabric:* Medium-soft oxidized coarseware, somewhat variable but predominantly buff-red or orange, sometimes with a reduced core (D4 variant), lightly tempered with small grog, iron, mica, and limestone.
*Forms:* Good range of cooking and storage vessels, some table wares; Jar types 1.2, 1.3, 1.5; Bowl types 2.1, 2.2, 2.4, 2.6; Cup/Beaker types 3.3, 3.4; Flagon types 4.3. Wheel made, occasional incised linear decoration and smoothed or burnished zones on exterior surfaces.

Figs. 15-17
(D 1)
119. Jar 1.2, *C854, E. exterior, Area 67, Period 3*
120. Jar 1.2, *C809, E. range, Room 26, Period 4*
121. Jar 1.2, *C774, E. exterior, Area 64/66, Period 3*
122. Jar 1.2, *C744, E. exterior, Area 63, Period 3*
123. Jar 1.2, *CF28, Central range, Room 41, Period 3*
124. Jar 1.2, *C579, S.W. range, Room 9, Period 3*
125. Jar 1.2, *C620, S. courtyard, Trench A, Period 3*
126. Jar 1.2, *C781, Central range, Room 41, Period 3*
127. Jar 1.2, *C781, Central range, Room 41, Period 3*
128. Jar 1.5, *C775, E. exterior, A64/66, Period 3*
129. Jar 1.5, *C648, S. courtyard, Area 61, Period 2*
130. Jar 1.5, *C548, S. courtyard, Area 41, Period 4*
131. Jar 1.5, *F13, S. courtyard, Area 41, Period 5*
132. Jar 1.5, *CF33, Central range, Room 41, Period 3*
133. Jar 1.5, *C786, S. courtyard, Area 65, Period 3*
134. Jar 1.5, *C692, W. range, Room 34, Period 3*
135. Jar 1.5, *C739, E. exterior, Area 63, Period 3*
136. Jar 1.5, *C864, S. courtyard, Area 65, Period 4*
137. Bowl 2.1, *C799, S.E. range, Room 28, Period 3*
138. Bowl 2.1, *C870, S. courtyard, Area 65, Period 4*
139. Bowl 2.1, *C736, N. exterior, Area 62, Period 4*
140. Bowl 2.1, *C650, S. courtyard, Area 61, Period 4*
141. Bowl 2.1, *unstratified*
142. Bowl 2.1, *C859, E. exterior, Area 68/9, Period 4*
143. Bowl 2.1, *C774, E. exterior, Area 64/66, Period 3*
144. Bowl 2.1, *C792, S. courtyard, Area 65, Period 2*
145. Bowl 2.2, *C774, E. exterior, Area 64/66, Period 3*
146. Bowl 2.2, *C774, E. exterior, Area 64/66, Period 3*
147. Dish 2.3, *F13, S. courtyard, Area 41, Period 5*
148. Bowl 2.3, *C619, S. courtyard, Trench A, Period 4*
149. Colander 2.4, *C622, S. courtyard, Trench A, Period 2*
150. Bowl 2.4, *C700, E. range, Room 34, Period 2*
151. Bowl 2.4, *C768, E. range, Room 34/51, Period 2*
152. Bowl 2.4, *C859, E. exterior, Area 68/9, Period 4*
153. Bowl 2.4, *F13, S. courtyard, Area 41, Period 5*
154. Bowl 2.4, *C579, S.W. range, Room 9, Period 3*
155. Bowl 2.4, *C700, E. range, Room 34, Period 2*
156. Bowl 2.4, *C725, Central range, Room 16, Period 2*
157. Bowl 2.4, *C650, S. courtyard, Area 61, Period 4*
158. Bowl 2.4, *C578, S.W. range, Room 9, Period 3*
159. Bowl 2.7, *C746, E. exterior, Area 64/66, Period 3*
160. Beaker 3.2, *C736, N. exterior, Area 62, Period 4*
161. Mug 3.4, *C736, N. exterior, Area 62, Period 4*
162. Mug 3.4, *C736, N. exterior, Area 62, Period 4*
163. Flagon 4.3, *C746, E. exterior, Area 64/66, Period 3*
(D 4)
164. Bowl 2.1, *C725, Central range, Room 16, Period 2*
165. Bowl 2.7, *C700, E. range, Room 34, Period 2*

*Dating and parallels*: Oxidized Severn Valley coarseware, mainly of the 2nd century but originating in the later 1st; may continue into early 3rd (Webster 1976). Common, widely distributed type in the wider Severn Valley region, probably several kiln sources; this type may originate from potteries at or near Gloucester. The largest fabric group comprising 30% of the assemblage as eves. Comparable, locally identified fabrics include Gloucester TF11B, Cirencester TFs.106-110, Uley TF10.

Fabric Type D2
*Fabric:* Moderately hard and well fired, coarse texture, with characteristic reduced grey core and oxidized buff-orange exteriors, speckled with medium sized multicoloured inclusions, including grog, iron and calcite/limestone. Not always readily distinguished from D1.
*Forms:* Plain, hand made, wheel-finished, coarse and often thick-walled storage vessels; Jar types 1.2, 1.3, 1.5; some table wares; Bowl types 2.2.

Fig. 17
166. Jar 1.2, *C699, E. range, Room 34, Period 2*
167. Jar 1.3, *C854, E. exterior, Area 67, Period 3*
168. Jar 1.5, *C920, S.E. range, Room 28, Period 3*
169. Bowl 2.2, *C777, E. exterior, Area 64/66, Period 3*

*Dating and parallels*: Oxidized Severn Valley ware variant of D1, commonly as a coarser, storage jar type. 2nd/3rd?-century Severn Valley manufacture (Webster 1976). Comprised 2.3% of the assemblage as eves. Local equivalent fabrics include Gloucester TF23, Cirencester TF10, Uley TF11.

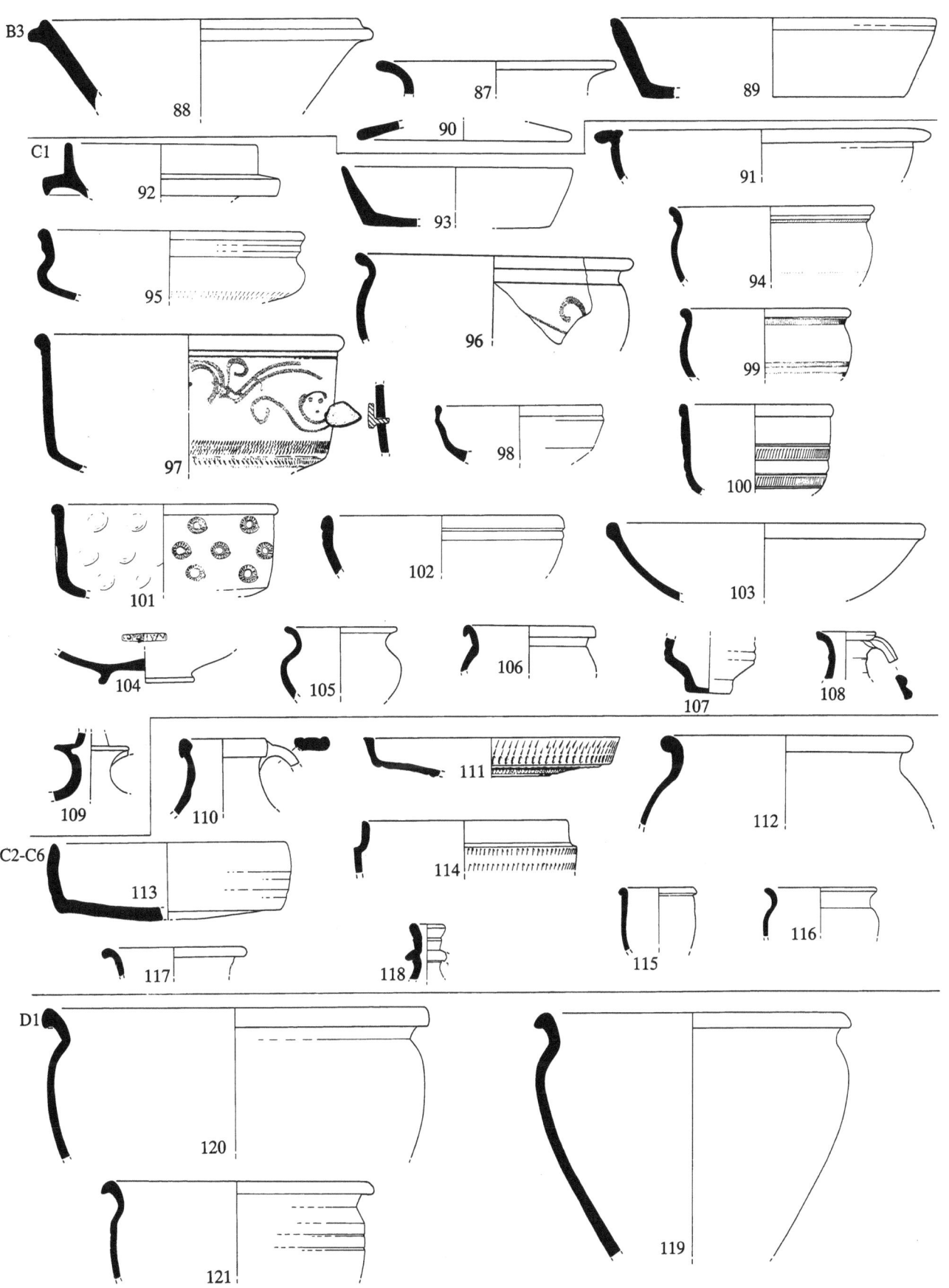

*Figure 15* Roman pottery; Fabric B3, nos. 87-90; C1, nos. 91-109; C2-C6, nos. 110-118; D1, nos. 119-121 (1:4)

Fabric Type D3
*Fabric:* Well-fired, even, cream/white oxidized sandy texture, small quartz sand temper.
*Forms:* Bowl and mortaria types 2.6, 2.7, and some enclosed forms. Wheel made, plain or colour-washed surfaces; pink and red rounded quartz trituration grits on mortaria. None illustrated.
*Dating and parallels:* Oxfordshire whiteware fabric of 3rd and 4th century manufacture. Defined by Young (1977) as sub-types M (mortaria) and W (other whiteware forms). Comprised 4.6% of the assemblege as eves., and over 70% by weight of all the mortaria recovered by Greenfield (Timby, archive report). Equivalent locally defined fabrics include Gloucester TFs.9A and 13, Cirencester TFs.84 and 90, Uley TFs.24 and 26.

Fabric Type D5
*Fabric:* Moderately fired, soft micaceous, buff-orange or pink body, sometimes with a reduced grey core; pink and red rounded quartz trituration grits.
*Forms:* Mortaria type 2.7; plain, wheel made, cream-buff or white surface slip.
None illustrated.
*Dating and parallels:* Oxfordshire white slipped ware mortaria (Young 1977, Type WC); 3rd and 4th-century product. Comprised 0.8% of the assemblage as eves., and some 7% by weight of all the mortaria (Timby, archive report).

FABRIC GROUP E
Imported wares, including samian and amphorae (Types E1 - E4).

Fabric Type E 1: samian wares *by B. Dickinson*

Apart from one Flavian sherd from La Graufesenque and one Trajanic piece from Les Martres-de-Veyre, all the samian in this collection comes either from Lezoux or East Gaul. A rather limited range of forms is represented, the commonest being 31, 31R, 33, 38 and the gritted mortarium, form 45. Some of the bowls of form 38 are heavily worn inside, as if they had been used as mortaria. Earlier forms made at Lezoux, such as 18/31R and 27, are entirely absent, which suggests that Central Gaulish samian was not reaching the site before *c* AD160-65, at the earliest. The proportion of decorated ware is very low, which could reflect a lack of prosperity.

The quantities of Lezoux and East Gaulish ware are almost exactly the same and, unusually, Trier ware accounts for just over 25% of the latter. The rest of the East Gaulish ware is from Rheinzabern, though there may be one Argonne piece. The high proportion of East Gaulish ware is consistent with occupation in the 3rd century, though it is not possible to say how late samian continued to be used on the site. Earlier clearances of the site at Witcombe may also have distorted the pattern of samian representation in Greenfield's collection. Samian comprised 3.1% of the total pottery assemblage by eves.

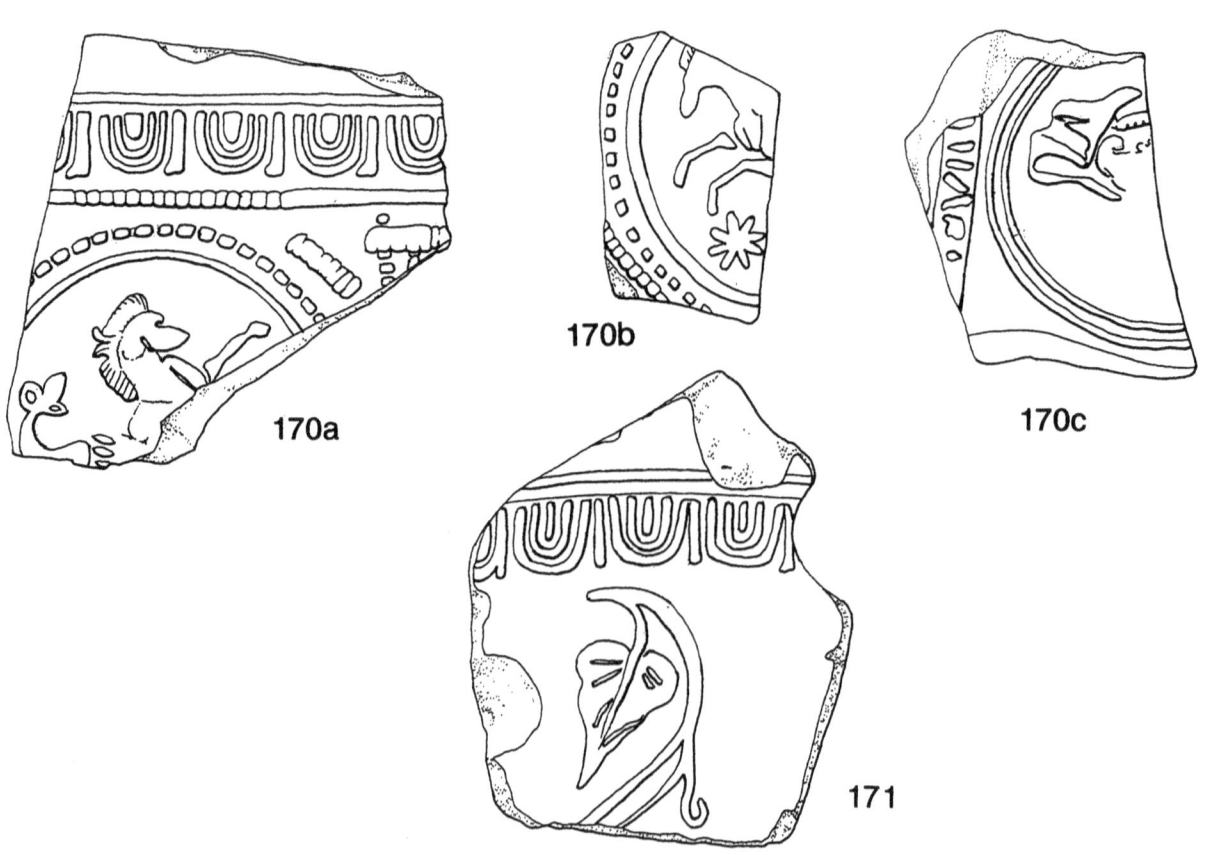

*Figure 18* Decorated samian (Fabric E), nos. 170a, b, c and 171 (1:1)

Fig. 18
170a, b, c. Form 30, Central Gaulish. A bowl in the style of Do(v)eccus i of Lezoux. The ovolo is Rogers B161. Two of the panels (a and b) contain medallions with beaded outer borders (Rogers E8), each containing a sea horse (D.35 and 33, the latter over the eight-petalled rosette, Rogers C167). Both panels have astragali across the corners. Another panel (c) probably contains a festoon. *c* AD165-200; (a) *unstratified*; (b and c) *C884, Area 72, S.courtyard, Period 3.*
171. Form 37, East Gaulish. A bowl in the style of Verecundus of Rheinzabern, with ovolo (Ricken-Fischer 1963, E10) and wreath (*op cit.*,p52), impressed vertically, cf. Ricken 1948, Taf 172, 16, 18 and 19; 173, 4. The inside of the bowl is very worn. Late 2nd or early 3rd century; *C878, Area 72, S. courtyard, Period 4.*

Fig. 17
172. Flagon, Oswald & Price 1920, pl.LXXXIII, 2. Central Gaulish, Antonine. *C744, Area 63, E. exterior, Period 3*

Fabric Type E.2: Rhenish/Lezoux wares

*Fabric:* Well-fired, fine oxidized red-orange body; dark red-brown or black lustrous colour coat.
*Form:* Beaker/cup 3.2; fine, thin-walled, wheel made or moulded tablewares. Plain, or exteriors decorated with rouletting, barbotine, white paint or moulded designs.

Fig. 17
173. Beaker 3.2, C782, Room 16,Central range, Period 3

*Dating and parallels*: Rhenish Ware colour coat import, later 2nd - 3rd century, Central Gaul or Germany (Symonds 1992). Comprised 0.2% of the assemblage as eves. Local equivalent fabrics include Gloucester TF12J, Cirencester TF80, Uley TF19.

Fabric Type E3: Amphorae

Only a small collection of diagnostic amphorae sherds were retained by Greenfield, all apparently from Dressel 20 globular amphorae of southern Spanish origin (Peacock and Williams 1986). These comprise 0.4% of the assemblage as eves. The two rims illustrated are probably from later 2nd-century vessels.

Fig. 17
174. Amphora 5.2, *C621, S. courtyard,Trench A, Period 2*
175. Amphora 5.2, *C689, E. range,Room 34, Period 3*

Fabric Type E4: Late Roman imported pottery
*by D. Williams (A.M.L. Report 82/88)*

Fig. 17
176. Four sherds comprising the footring and ribbed body sherds of a flagon in a hard rough fabric, slightly micaceous and with frequent light and dark coloured inclusions protruding through the surfaces. Pinkish-red inner surfaces and core, cream/buff outer surface colour coat. Thin sectioning and study under a petrological microscope shows a groundmass of small quartz grains and mica flecks (mainly muscovite but with some biotite); a scatter of lava pieces, some with a trachytic texture; plagioclase and potash felspar; larger quartz and a little limestone. The vessel evidently originates in an area of recent volcanic rocks, most probably from a source around the Aegean or Anatolia, since this is the region of origin of many ribbed amphorae found in late Roman and post-Roman Britain (Tomber and Williams 1986). Flat-bottomed jars/flagons with ribbed bodies were made in similar fabrics in this region (Robinson 1959). *C768, E. range Rooms 34/51, Period 2-3.*

FABRIC GROUP F
Miscellaneous types, fired clay (Fabric Type FC).

Fabric Type FC
*Fabric:* Medium soft, micaceous fired clay, oxidized buff-orange with some grog temper; similar to roof and flue tile.
*Forms:* Bowl types 2.1, 2.2, 2.3, and other miscellaneous forms; surfaces sometimes smoothed or with incised decoration.

Fig. 17
177. Bowl 2.1, *C854, E. exterior, Area 67, Period 3*
178. Bowl 2.1, *C867, S. courtyard, Area 65, Period 4*
179. Bowl 2.2, *C737, N. exterior, Area 62, Period 4*
180. Bowl 2.2, *unstratified*
181. Bowl 2.2, *C715, E. range, Room 17, Period 3*
182. Bowl/dish 2.3, *C854, E. exterior,Area 67, Period 3*
183. Bowl/dish 2.3, *C746, E. exterior, Area 64/66, Period 3*
184. Pedestal/candleholder?, *C768, E. range, Room 34/51, Period 2*

*Dating and parallels*: The fabric of these vessels is virtually indistinguishable from the clay fired to make tile, brick, roof finials, etc.; suggesting a relatively local product, possibly a manufacturing source in or near Gloucester. Its occurrence at Witcombe suggests a 3rd or 4th-century product, where it comprised 1.1% of the total assemblage as eves. Similar vessels and other non- structural objects are recorded at Uley and Kingscote.

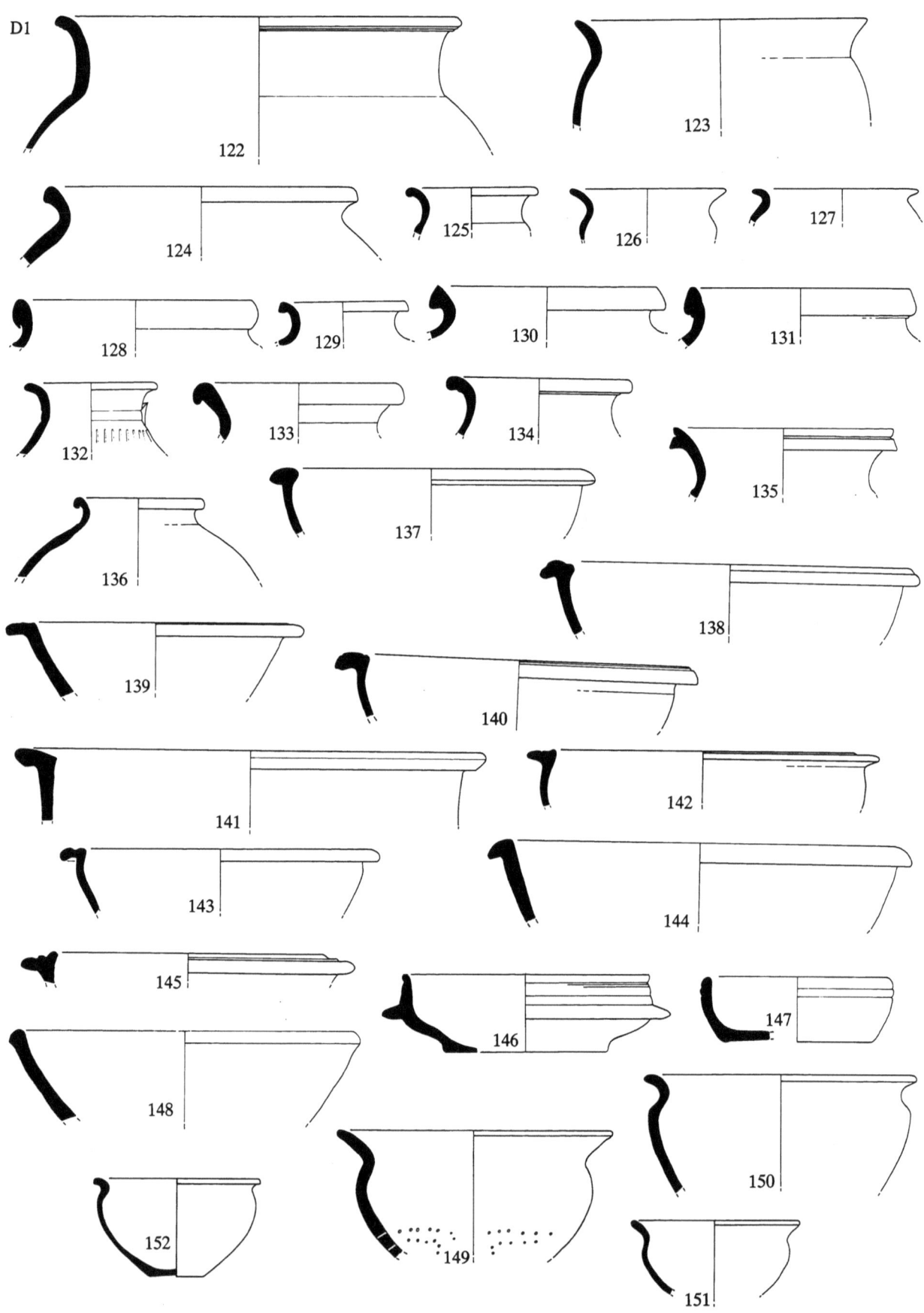

*Figure 16* Roman pottery; Fabric D1, nos. 122-152 (1:4)

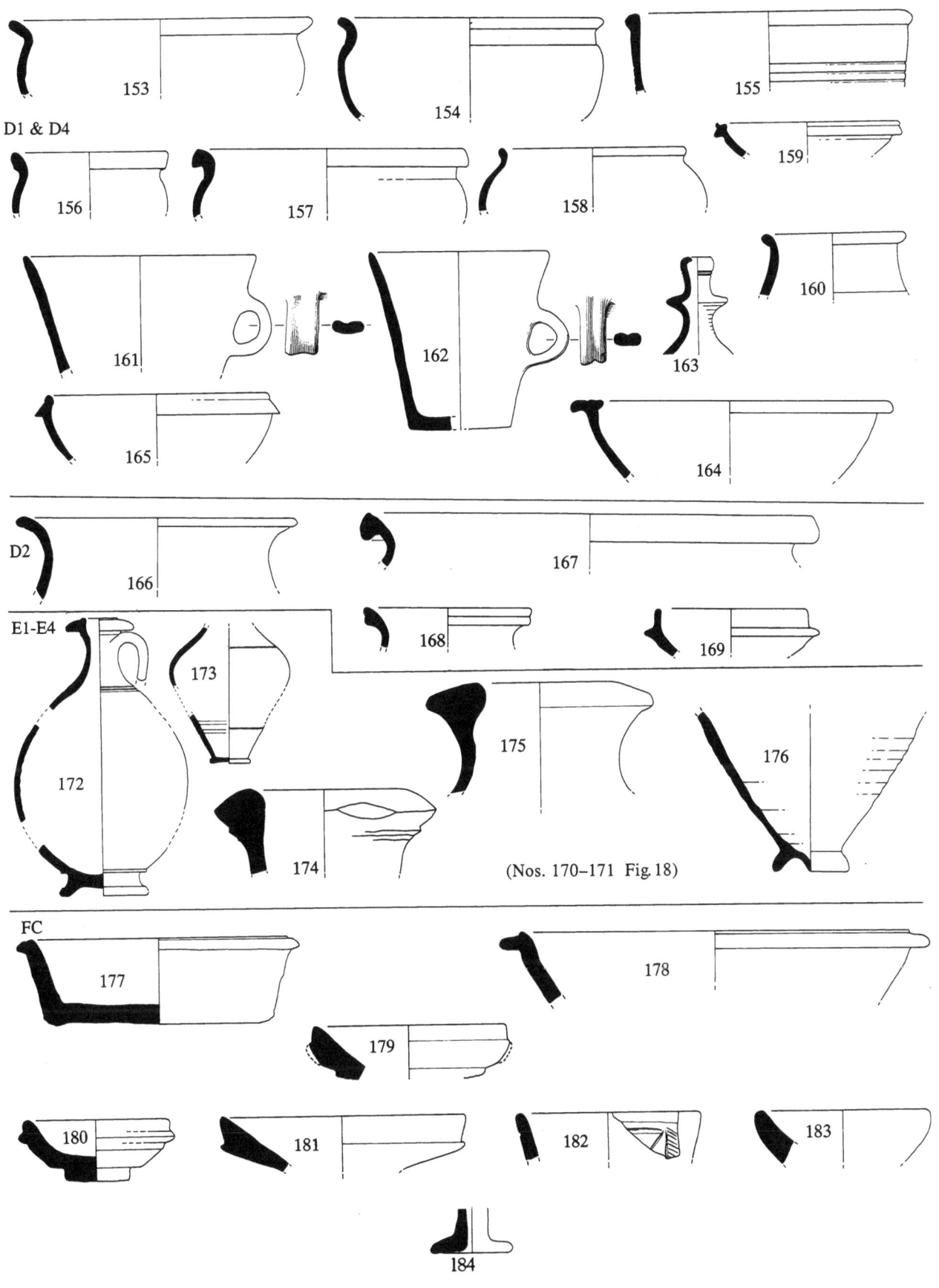

*Figure 17* Roman pottery; Fabrics D1 & D4, nos. 153-165; D2, nos. 166-169; E1-E4, nos. 172-4; FC, nos. 177-184 (1:4)

**Discussion**

Since this report deals essentially with material excavated by Ernest Greenfield, any wider interpretation of the Great Witcombe pottery assemblage is inevitably constrained by the nature and location of the deposits available to him for excavation, and by his own methods of recording and recovery. This discussion focusses upon the themes of chronology and supply, and forms and function, although the data is not always adequate for their full consideration, nor for other aspects such as intra-site patterning.

**Chronology and supply**

A chronological representation of the assemblage according to the main fabric types is shown in Figure 19 and Table 3. From these it is immediately apparent that almost half was obtained from contexts representing either the final phase of occupation on the site or its abandonment and decay up to the present time. The problem of residuality is widely recognised in Romano-British pottery studies, though less easily quantified and assessed. Equally, it is recognised that the patterning perceived in a chronological analysis will be more a reflection of deposition and loss than contemporaneity of product. In this instance, virtually everything from Periods 4 and 5 must be regarded as residual, deriving from earlier Periods of site occupation and in some cases subject to more than one episode of deposition. At the other end of the range Period 1 is represented by such a small sample that it is unlikely to be statistically valid. Furthermore, unless errors of attribution relating to specific contexts or the Period as a whole have crept in, the presence of types which should post-date Period 1 (e.g. Oxford red colour coat or East Midlands shell tempered wares) suggest a degree of later contamination and thus additional distortion of the ceramic spectrum. Only Periods 2 and 3, spanning the greater part of the 3rd and 4th centuries, have ceramic assemblage samples of sufficient size for the purposes of characterisation and comparison, reflecting the main span of occupation and development of the villa.

Two ceramic groups dominate the assemblages throughout; Severn Valley wares of both oxidized and reduced fabrics (A1, A2, D1, D2, D4 and possibly B2), and Dorset Black Burnished Ware (B1). The oxidized wares are the largest single group throughout, representing over 30% of the assemblage overall and in each Period except 4/5. The reduced fabrics make up between $c$ 12% and 17% of the total, apparently increasing in proportion over time. Dorset Black Burnished Ware representation varies between $c$ 34% and 20%, exhibiting an equivalent decline over time, particularly if material assigned to Period 1 and to Periods 4 and 5 is included.

Among the smaller groups certain trends are discernable, reflecting chronologies of production and/or deposition. The third largest group from the Oxford potteries (C1, D3 and D5) represented between $c$ 7% and 16% of the assemblage, deposition increasing markedly over time. Two other late Roman types originating from Alice Holt (A3) and the East Midlands (A5), also appear to be deposited in increasing proportions with time. The opposite trend is apparent among imports of generally earlier origin. Samian (E1), Rhenish Wares (E2) and Amphorae (E3) all decline in the later Periods (Samian from 5% in Period 2 to 2.4% in Periods 4/5), although the quantity of material in the other groups is very small. The recognition that such trends within the Witcombe assemblage correspond with what might be expected as more general and widespread patterns of ceramic occurrence in Roman Britain, increases confidence in the validity of this analysis.

Given the predominantly later Roman (3rd and 4th-century) character of the assemblage its relatively limited range of sources is to be expected (Fig. 21); many higher status sites of earlier periods (urban and rural) exhibit much greater diversity.. That these should be dominated by products of the Severn Valley industries is equally unsurprising, in view of the location of Great Witcombe close to known or suspected manufacturing sites around Gloucester. More unusual, however, is the prominence of the most typical oxidized wares (D1/4 and D2). For many years these were regarded as primarily later 1st and earlier 2nd-century products, and indeed, their abundance at this site was interpreted by Clifford (1955) as evidence for its relatively early foundation. More recently it has been demonstrated that these wares were in production for much longer (Webster 1977), and in this region were still in use during the 4th century (e.g. in Gloucester, Heighway 1983). The scarcity (still) of other comparatively published local ceramic assemblages from rural sites limits a more informed assessment of the significance of this phenomenon at Witcombe, although at Uley by contrast, there is a very marked decline in oxidized Severn Valley wares after the 2nd century (Woodward and Leach 1993). Their predominance at Witcombe may reflect no more than proximity to production sources, although a greater preference for oxidized over reduced wares may also be some reflection of the status of the site.

Products of the Dorset Black Burnished industry (B1) were already in plentiful local supply by the time the villa was built. As the second largest group, these always dominated the local reduced coarsewares (A1 and A2), with which they were presumably in some competition, but their popularity appears to decline over time. To some extent this decline is balanced by an increase in East Midlands shell tempered ware (A5), and a small influx from the Alice Holt industry in Hampshire (A3). The local reduced wares also show a modest increase, although their sources may be more diverse. Similar patterns emerge among the latest assemblages at Uley (*op cit*) and in Gloucester, and perhaps also in Cirencester (McWhirr 1986).

The fine wares are dominated by products of the Oxfordshire industry, notably the red slipped wares (C1), which came to replace Samian in this region after the early 3rd century. Samian itself (E1) declines progressively within the assemblage from Period 2, though likely to have continued longer in use before being finally discarded. The predominance of Antonine and later types doubtless reflects

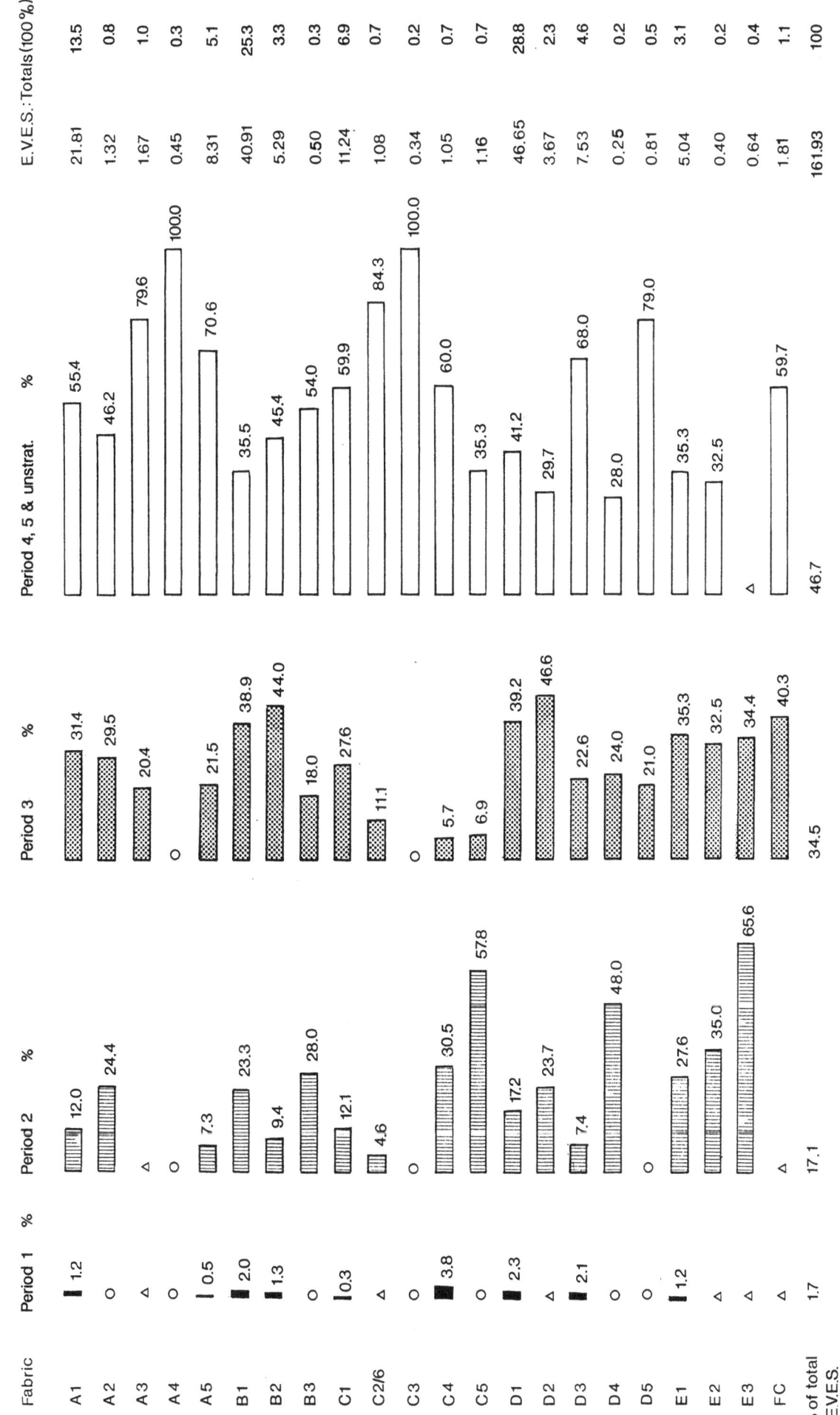

Figure 19 Roman pottery; chronological representation of fabric types by eves. (%)

| Fabric | Weight (gms) | | Sherds | | Eve Pd.1 | | Eve Pd.2 | | Eve Pd.3 | | Eve Pd.4, 5 and u/s | | Eve Total | |
|---|---|---|---|---|---|---|---|---|---|---|---|---|---|---|
| A.1 | 9274 | (10.4) | 293 | (10.5) | .25 | (9.3) | 2.61 | (9.4) | 6.86 | (12.8) | 12.09 | (16.0) | 21.81 | (13.5) |
| A.2 | 540 | (0.6) | 14 | (0.5) | - | | .32 | (1.2) | .39 | (0.7) | .61 | (0.7) | 1.32 | (0.8) |
| A.3 | 753 | (0.8) | 25 | (0.9) | * | | * | | .34 | (0.6) | 1.33 | (1.8) | 1.67 | (1.0) |
| A.4 | 106 | (0.1) | 4 | (0.1) | - | | - | | - | | .45 | (0.6) | .45 | (0.3) |
| A.5 | 2277 | (2.5) | 88 | (3.1) | .04 | (1.5) | .61 | (2.2) | 1.79 | (3.2) | 5.87 | (7.8) | 8.31 | (5.1) |
| B.1 | 18425 | (20.6) | 651 | (23.3) | .91 | (33.8) | 9.55 | (34.5) | 15.93 | (28.5) | 14.52 | (19.2) | 40.91 | (25.3) |
| B.2 | 2058 | (2.3) | 70 | (2.5) | .06 | (2.2) | .50 | (1.8) | 2.33 | (4.2) | 2.40 | (3.2) | 5.29 | (3.3) |
| B.3 | 537 | (0.6) | 17 | (0.6) | - | | .14 | (0.5) | .09 | (0.2) | .27 | (0.4) | .50 | (0.3) |
| C.1 | 5813 | (6.5) | 303 | (10.8) | .05 | (1.9) | 1.36 | (4.9) | 3.10 | (5.5) | 6.73 | (8.9) | 11.24 | (6.9) |
| C.2/6 | 669 | (0.7) | 57 | (2.0) | * | | .05 | (0.2) | .12 | (0.2) | .91 | (1.2) | 1.08 | (0.7) |
| C.3 | 184 | (0.2) | 4 | (0.1) | - | | - | | - | | .34 | (0.4) | .34 | (0.2) |
| C.4 | 826 | (0.9) | 49 | (1.8) | .04 | (1.5) | .32 | (1.2) | .06 | (0.1) | .63 | (0.8) | 1.05 | (0.7) |
| C.5 | 173 | (0.2) | 18 | (0.6) | - | | .67 | (2.4) | .08 | (0.1) | .41 | (0.5) | 1.16 | (0.7) |
| D.1 | 22911 | (25.6) | 678 | (24.2) | 1.10 | (40.9) | 8.04 | (29.1) | 18.31 | (32.8) | 19.20 | (25.4) | 46.65 | (28.8) |
| D.2 | 3992 | (4.5) | 101 | (3.6) | * | | .87 | (3.1) | 1.71 | (3.1) | 1.09 | (1.4) | 3.67 | (2.3) |
| D.3 | 6327 | (7.1) | 100 | (3.6) | .15 | (5.6) | .56 | (2.0) | 1.70 | (3.1) | 5.12 | (6.8) | 7.53 | (4.6) |
| D.4 | 471 | (0.5) | 12 | (0.4) | - | | .12 | (0.4) | .06 | (0.1) | .07 | (0.1) | .25 | (0.2) |
| D.5 | 490 | (0.5) | 9 | (0.3) | - | | - | | .17 | (0.3) | .64 | (0.8) | .81 | (0.5) |
| E.1 | 2859 | (3.2) | 163 | (5.8) | .09 | (3.3) | 1.39 | (5.0) | 1.78 | (3.2) | 1.78 | (2.4) | 5.04 | (3.1) |
| E.2 | 245 | (0.3) | 70 | (2.5) | * | | .14 | (0.5) | .13 | (0.2) | .13 | (0.2) | .40 | (0.2) |
| E.3 | 3578 | (4.0) | 34 | (1.2) | * | | .42 | (1.5) | .22 | (0.4) | * | | .64 | (0.4) |
| F.C. | 7125 | (8.0) | 44 | (1.6) | * | | * | | .73 | (1.3) | 1.08 | (1.4) | 1.81 | (1.1) |
| Totals | 89633 (100%) | | 2804 (100%) | | 2.69 (1.7%) | | 27.67 (17.1%) | | 55.90 (34.5%) | | 75.67 (46.7%) | | 161.93 (100%) | |

excluded from totals: prehistoric 165 gms, 24 sherds
medieval/post-medieval 27 gms, 2 sherds

\*: present but not quantifiable
( ) = %

*Table 3 Roman pottery quantification by e.v.e. per fabric type and period*

the later foundation date of the villa, at a time when Samian supplies to Britain were probably in decline. Other imports are even scarcer; Rhenish Wares (E2) are barely represented, and amphorae (E3) are not common. A few other British sources for colour coat tablewares include the Nene Valley industry and one or two other miscellaneous types of relatively ?local origin, but no products of the New Forest potteries appear to have reached the site. Some finer wares were produced in the oxidized Severn Valley fabrics, notably handled mugs (form 3.4). The pattern at Uley seems broadly similar in the latest phases, although New Forest wares are present there in small quantities.

**Forms and function**

Figure 20 and Table 4 show the proportions of principal form types present according to their occurrence as fabrics and through time. In crude terms, jars, used either for cooking or for storage, were the most numerous vessels (over 50%). Bowls represent the second major group (38%), once again multifunctional, dividing largely between storage and table ware, although mortaria (Type 2.7) were used primarily to prepare food, while others could well have been used in an oven. Unequivocally identifiable tablewares (cups, beakers and flagons) make up the balance, representing just over 13% of the total assemblage. The proportions of storage, cooking and tablewares seem in fact to be roughly equivalent in this assemblage, although the latter may be somewhat under-represented. In reality, quite a high proportion of Roman pottery types were probably multifunctional to some extent throughout the course of their use, whatever their original purpose may have been. Can we, nevertheless, perceive any significant patterning in their site occurrence at Witcombe?

At present one of the main impediments to assessing the significance of such patterning is the extreme scarcity of published rural site assemblages which have been analysed in a comparable way. In the Cotswold region West Hill, Uley (Woodward and Leach 1993) is probably the closest, though from a site of rather different status. There also, the proportions of storage, cooking and tablewares were roughly equivalent; while at Gatcombe (Branigan 1977a), from what may have been the service or ancilliary buildings of a large villa, tableware representation was markedly lower. With the availability of more modern analyses of assemblages from the region and neighbouring areas (e.g. Frocester and Kingscote, settlements in the Upper Thames Valley, or urban groups from Cirencester and Gloucester) it should be possible to make far more detailed studies of the role of different vessel types and their sources, both within and between individual sites of comparable or contrasting status.

The value of any intra-site analyses will clearly also be constrained by the degree of previous excavation at Witcombe; a factor which also limits the potential for perceiving internal site patterning. Much of the in-context material was recovered from the building exteriors; internal room assemblages representing only a residue which had survived earlier clearances. For example, the functional significance of any assemblage patterning within the more complete deposits excavated around the building is difficult to assess without reference to comparable assemblages from rooms, while the surviving residue from such rooms is hardly adequate to provide any reliable reflection of their former use. In these circumstances no detailed analysis of the fabrics and vessel forms located to each room or area of excavation was considered justifiable, although the relevant data is available in the archive.

**Lids**
*by L. Bevan*

At least 14 objects adapted for use as lids with pottery vessels or possibly other containers were recovered, which (except two made from ceramic vessel bases and three from clay tiles) were made from Pennant or Old Red sandstone floor and roofing tiles. The majority were roughly circular in shape while others were sub-rectangular. Diameters were in the general range of 30-55mm, with some larger examples between 70-90mm. Whilst the presence of these lids suggests an association with food storage, these easily portable artefacts did not occur in significant groups or in any great quantity. None are illustrated but they are summarised as follows:

*Room 9*: 1 pottery vessel base, 1 stone tile: *Area 61*: 1 stone tile; *Area 64/66*: 2 stone; *Area 65*: 2 stone tiles, 1 clay *imbrex* tile; *Area 68*: 1 clay tile; *Area 70*: 1 stone; *Area 71*: 1stone, 1 pottery vessel base; *Area 72*: 2 stone; *Unstratified:* 1 stone; 1 clay box tile.

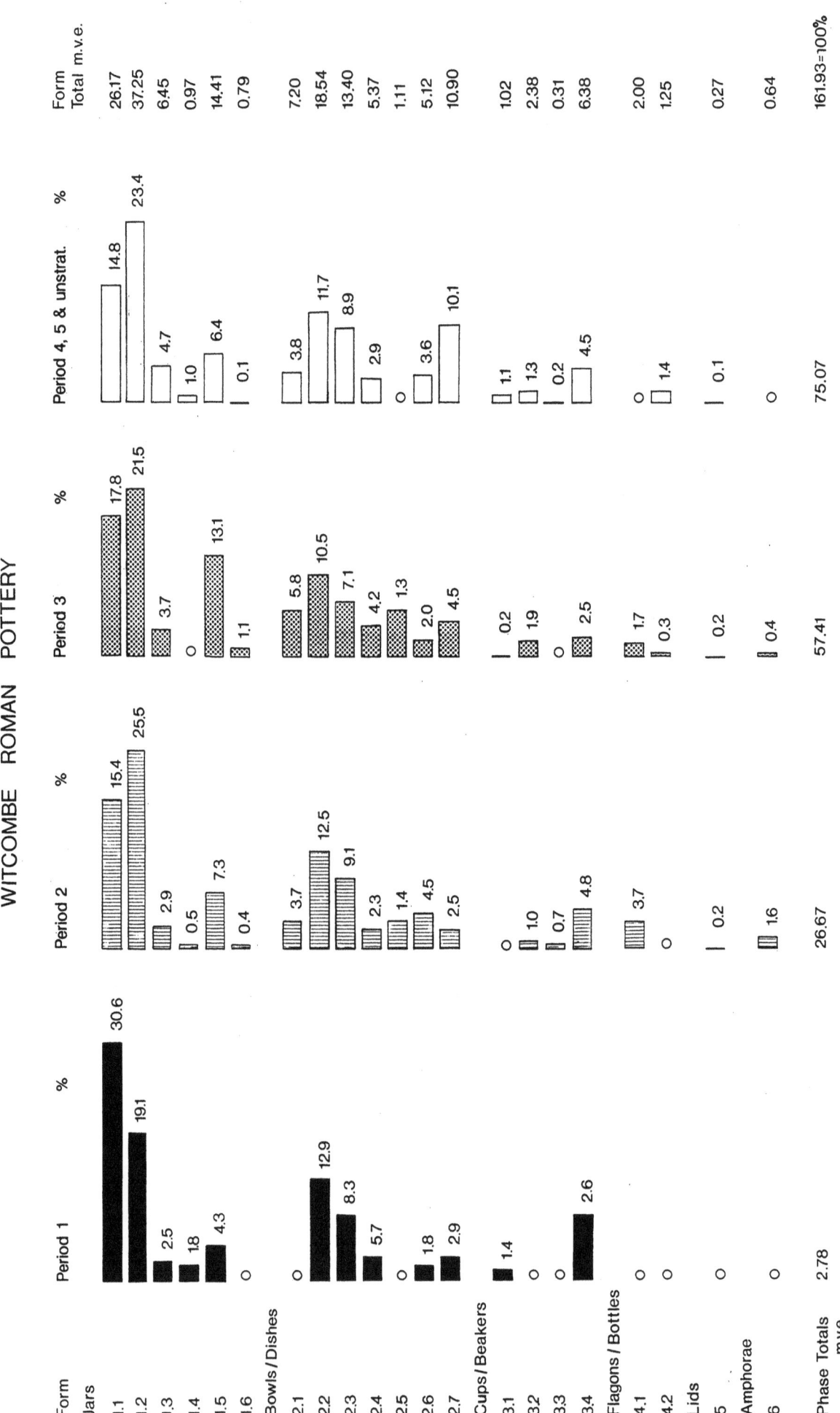

*Figure 20 Roman pottery; chronological representation of form types by eves: (%)*

## FABRICS

| Form Types | A.1 | A.2 | A.3 | A.4 | A.5 | B.1 | B.2 | B.3 | C.1 | C.2/6 | C.3 | C.4 | C.5 | D.1 | D.2 | D.3 | D.4 | D.5 | E.1 | E.2 | E.3 | FC | % | e.v.e.s | |
|---|---|---|---|---|---|---|---|---|---|---|---|---|---|---|---|---|---|---|---|---|---|---|---|---|---|
| 1.1 | 3.75 | .26 | .19 | | | 21.25 | .63 | .09 | | | | | | | | | | | | | | | 16.2 | 26.17 } | |
| 1.2 | 8.44 | .38 | .93 | .45 | 6.72 | .61 | .40 | .07 | | | | | | 18.15 | 1.10 | | | | | | | | 23.0 | 37.25 } | JARS |
| 1.3 | .53 | .07 | .10 | | .54 | .25 | .13 | | .06 | | | | | 3.87 | .83 | .07 | | | | | | | 4.0 | .96 } | 86.04 eve |
| 1.4 | .56 | | | | | .07 | | | | | | | | .34 | | | | | | | | | 8.9 | 14.41 } | (53.2%) |
| 1.5 | 2.59 | .25 | .10 | | | .13 | | | .10 | .09 | | | .17 | 9.62 | 1.24 | .05 | .07 | | | | | | 0.6 | .97 } | |
| 1.6 | .79 | | | | | | | | | | | | | | | | | | | | | | 0.5 | .79 } | |
| 2.1 | .81 | .04 | | | .06 | 2.21 | .23 | | .23 | | | | | 2.95 | .31 | | .06 | | | | | .30 | 4.4 | 7.20 } | |
| 2.2 | 1.47 | | | | .10 | 9.87 | 1.48 | .08 | 2.52 | | | | | .51 | .11 | | | | 1.32 | | | 1.08 | 11.41 } | 18.54 | |
| 2.3 | 2.26 | .19 | .12 | | .57 | 6.39 | 1.80 | .16 | .06 | | | .38 | | .42 | | | | | .62 | | | .43 | 8.3 | 13.40 } | BOWLS |
| 2.4 | .05 | | | | | | | | 3.69 | | | | | 1.30 | | .06 | | | .27 | | | | 3.3 | 5.37 } | 61.64 eve |
| 2.5 | | | | | | | | | .06 | | | | | 1.05 | | | | | | | | | 0.7 | 1.11 } | (38.0%) |
| 2.6 | | | | | | | | | 1.78 | | | | | 1.60 | | | | | 1.74 | | | | 3.2 | 5.12 } | |
| 2.7 | .14 | .13 | | | .32 | | | | 1.34 | | .34 | .21 | | .05 | | 7.41 | .06 | .81 | .09 | | | | 6.7 | 10.90 } | |
| 3.1 | | | .23 | | | .08 | | | .11 | | | .22 | .24 | .14 | | | | | | | | | 0.6 | 1.02 } | BEAKERS/ |
| 3.2 | .25 | | | | | | .50 | | .67 | .32 | | .24 | | | | | | | | .40 | | | 1.5 | 2.38 } | CUPS |
| 3.3 | .03 | | | | | | .12 | | .07 | | | | | .09 | | | | | | | | | 0.2 | .31 } | 10.09 eve |
| 3.4 | | | | | | | | | .05 | | | | | 6.25 | .08 | | | | | | | | 3.9 | 6.38 } | (6.2%) |
| 4.1 | | | | | | | | | .50 | | | | .50 | | | | | | 1.00 | | | | 1.2 | 2.00 } | FLAGONS |
| 4.2 | .14 | | | | | | | | | .55 | | | .25 | .31 | | | | | | | | | 0.8 | 1.25 } | 3.25 eve |
| 4.3 | | | | | | | | | | | | | | | | | | | | | | | - | - } | (2.0%) |
| 5 | | | | | | .05 | | .10 | | .12 | | | | | | | | | | | .64 | | 0.2 | .27 | |
| 6 | | | | | | | | | | | | | | | | | | | | | | | 0.4 | .64 | |
| Totals | 21.81 | 1.32 | 1.67 | .45 | 8.31 | 40.91 | 5.29 | .50 | 11.24 | 1.08 | .34 | 1.05 | 1.16 | 46.65 | 3.67 | 7.53 | .25 | .81 | 5.04 | .40 | .64 | 1.81 | 100% | 161.93 | |

*Table 4 Roman Pottery, quantification of forms by e.v.e. per fabric type*

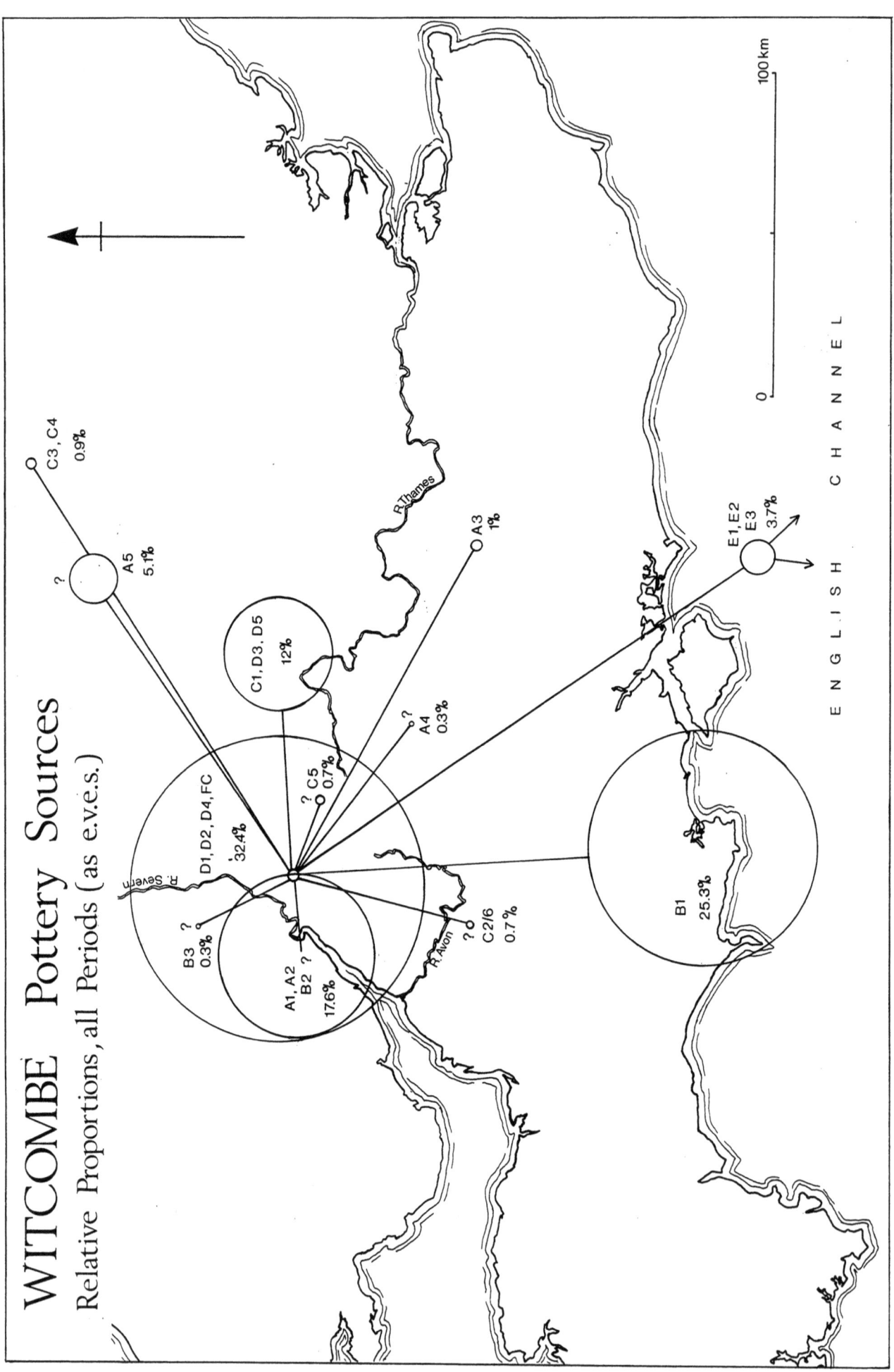

*Figure 21 Sources of Roman pottery at Witcombe*

## Vessel Glass

*By J. Price and S. Cottam*

A total of 188 fragments of vessel glass were found at Witcombe. The glass was generally well preserved, with little weathering. The assemblage ranges in date from the 1st to the 4th century, but there are very few early pieces and the majority of the vessels are of 2nd to 3rd-century type. the glass is notable for the quality and variety of the tablewares, and includes some forms rarely found in Roman Britain (Figure 22).

Very few fragments can be dated to the 1st century. These include two cast fragments, one from a dark blue pillar moulded bowl (no. 1) and the other from a colourless handled bowl (no. 2), although the latter could possibly be from a 3rdcentury vessel. Pillar moulded bowls (Isings 1957, form 3) are commonly found on 1st-century sites in Britain and throughout the Roman Empire. Strongly coloured bowls are rarely found after the Neronian period and are very much less common than the blue/green bowls which continue in use until the end of the 1st century. It is therefore interesting that the only fragment of this form from Witcombe should come from a strongly coloured bowl. Dark blue bowls have been found in pre-Flavian contexts at Camulodunum (Harden 1947, 302 no. 65; Charlesworth 1985, M3:F7 no. 44, fig. 81), Chichester (Charlesworth 1978, 267 no. 3), Brandon Camp (Price 1987a, 74 no. 2), and Kingsholm, Gloucester (Price and Cool 1985, 45 no. 2, fig.17). Other examples from dated contexts include fragments from a Neronian-early Flavian context at the Lunt, Bagindon (Charlesworth 1975, 38 no. 2), and from a Flavian early 2nd-century context at Godmanchester (Green 1960, fig.6.1). The Witcombe fragment comes from a high quality vessel from the early period of production; the thin wall has been carefully ground above the surviving rib.

The cast colourless body and handle fragment (no. 2) probably comes from a two-handled bowl, or scyphos (Isings 1957, form 39). The complete vessel, ground from a cast blank, had a vertical rim, a slightly convex body, and probably two narrow handles, bordered by carved supports at the rim edge. No decoration is visible on the Witcombe fragment, and scyphoi were usually undecorated, although a piece from Fishbourne has wavy wheel-cut grooves on the body (Harden and Price 1971, 336 no. 32, fig. 138).

Colourless cast and blown vessels are very uncommon in the Roman world before the Flavian period, so a Flavian or later date is likely for this piece. A substantially complete colourless *scyphos* with a cylindrical body was found in a pit dated to the mid-Flavian period at St Swithin's House in the Walbrook Valley, London (Price 1991, 159 no. 610, flg. l 13). At Vindonissa a fragment from a colourless *scyphos* was found in the Schutthugel, a largely Flavian assemblage (Berger 1960, 83, pl.14. 215). Other fragments of handles and bodies have been found in Britain, for example at Richborough and Wroxeter (both unpublished), and York (Harden 1962, 136, fig.88 H.G. 223), although few of these are closely dated.

Five strongly coloured fragments probably come from lst-century blown vessels (nos. 6-8 + listed fragments). The dark blue fragment (no. 6) comes from a carinated bowl which may have had a tubular rim. Carinated tubular rimmed bowls (Isings 1957, form 45) were made in both strongly coloured and blue/green glass and are common in many parts of the Roman Empire in the 1st and early 2nd centuries. The complete vessel has a tubular rim, a shallow or deep straight-sided upper body, sometimes decorated with ribs, a strong carination and an applied base ring. Like most other strong coloured vessels, deep blue bowls are uncommon after the Neronian period. Similar vessels have been found in Claudian and Neronian contexts at Camulodunum (Harden 1947, 304 no. 81, pl. LXXXVIII), a deep blue rim came from the Neronian assemblage at Kingsholm, Gloucester (Price and Cool 1985, 46 no. 24, fig. 1 8), and a largely complete deep blue bowl was found in a Neronian context at Long Melford, Sussex (Avent and Howlett 1980, 246, fig. 41).

The dark yellow/green fragment (no. 8) is most unusual. It comes from the angular handle of a long-necked jug of 1st - mid 2nd century date (Isings 1957, forms 52 and 55). Conical, ovoid or globular jugs with either concave bases or pushed-in base rings were made in both strongly coloured and blue/green glass and are found in the north-western provinces. Strong colours usually indicate a 1st-century date, and conical jugs in strong colours have been found in Flavian burials at Winchester (Harden 1967) and Radnage, Bucks. (Skilbeck 1923, fig. 2c). The strong green colour of this fragment has only rarely been noted on jugs of these forms in Roman Britain. Two conical jugs in olive-green glass were found at Towcester in a pit dated to A.D.155-65 (Price 1980, 66 nos. 7-8, fig. 15). This pit group, along with strongly coloured jugs from similarly dated groups at Harlow (Price 1987b, 193 no. 20, fig.3) and Alcester (Price and Cottam forthcoming, no. 9), indicates that this form in certain strong colours continued in use until the mid 2nd century. The handles of the jug from Radnage and of no. 7 from the body of the vessels, and it is possible that the body of the jug from Witcombe may have been a different colour from the surviving handle fragment.

The yellow/brown ribbed body fragment (no. 7) comes from a convex-walled vessel, possibly a jug of the type discussed above, or a jar (Isings 1957, form 67c). Ribbed or plain ovoid and globular jars were made in a strongly coloured and blue/green glass and also common in 1st and early 2nd-century contexts in the north-western provinces. Several strongly coloured and blue/green examples were found at Verularnium in contexts ranging from the later 1st century to the mid 2nd century (Charlesworth 1972, 204-5 ix nos. 1-7, fig.76.25-6; Charlesworth 1984, 166 nos. 246252, fig.67.105-6), and yellow/brown ribbed jars have been found at Silchester

(Boon 1974a, 232 fig.36.5), Brading, Isle of Wight (Tomalin 1987, 43 B3) and Boxfield Farm, Stevenage (Price and Cottam forthcoming, no. 3).

The excavations at Witcombe produced a very small quantity of blue/green glass. The small number of fragments and the narrow range of vessels is noteworthy, as this colour is usually the commonest on 1st to 3rd-century sites in Britain. Apart from the blue/green bottles discussed further below, the recognisable fragments represent a minimum of one cup, two jars, three jugs and a flask or unguent bottle.

Number 48 is a fragment of a tubular base ring found on cups, small bowls, jars and jugs. The two rim fragments (nos. 39-40) are also too small to be easily identifiable, but they may come from jars. Similar rolled rims have been found on blue/green jars from 1st-2nd-century contexts at Verulamium (Charlesworth 1972, 205, fig.76.29-30), and on a blue/green indented jar from the Antonine pit at Harlow, Essex (Price 1978b, 195 no. 24, fig.3).

The two handle fragments (nos. 43-4) come from jugs, though their forms are not certain. Variants of blue.green jugs are found from the 1st to 3rd centuries. Number 44 is particularly large and poorly made and perhaps belongs to a bottle rather than to a jug. The rim and neck fragments (nos. 41-2) may also come from jugs or flasks.

The very limited range and plainness of the blue/green tableware from Witcombe forms a remarkable contrast with the colourless tableware (nos. 9-38), which shows a rich variety of decoration. These vessels, dating to the 2nd and 3rd centuries, form a particularly interesting group, and illustrate the wide range of decorated tableware available during this period.

Number 3 is the only fragment of mould-blown tableware to have been found at Witcombe. The fragment is too small to be positively identified but may come from a convex-sided vessel, perhaps a cup or bowl, or a flask. Flasks blown in the form of heads or bunches of grapes and other fruit shapes were made in the Rhineland in the later 2nd and 3rd centuries (Isings 1957, 78 and 91a). Many examples are known from Cologne, in green, blue/green and colourless glass (Fremersdorf 1961, 71 taf. 143-7, 166-176). These vessels are unusual in Roman Britain, and the only parallel for this piece appears to be a yellowish fragment from Wall, with raised mould-blown dots (Harden 1963/4, 41 no. 5).

One of the most interesting features of the Witcombe assemblage is the range and quality of the 2nd to 3rd-century colourless vessels. The complete absence of fire-rounded rims is notable as fire rounded rims are the commonest type of rims found on colourless cups and bowls of the later 2nd and early 3rd century in Roman Britain. In particular a site of this period would be expected to produce numerous examples of colourless cylindrical cups with fire-rounded rims and double base rings (Isings 1957, form 85b). However, only rims which have been cracked-off and ground are present, with at least five cups and two flasks represented.

Numbers 4 and 5 very probably came from the same vessel. The first is a base fragment with two opaque white trails, one marvered around the edge of the base, and the other an unmarvered trail on the upper surface. Number 5 is impressed with a scallop shell design, and this ornament connects the Witcombe vessel with a small group of highly decorated flasks and stemmed beakers found in the north-western provinces and probably made in the Rhineland.

This group has been discussed in detail in connection with fragments found at the Roman villa at Rapsley, Surrey (Harden 1968a). The colourless scallop shell trails from Rapsley are very similar in form to the Witcombe trail, probably standing proud of the vessel in a vertical strip, with pinched folds pressed in between the shells to join the vessel wall.

Harden compared the Rapsley vessel with a tall narrow beaker on a stemmed foot found in an early 4th-century inhumation burial in Kartauserhof, Cologne (Doppelfeld 1959), and the Witcombe fragments can also be compared with this and with another very similar beaker found in a cremation burial in the Luxemburger Strasse cemetery in Cologne in 1969 (Harden et al .1987, 252 no. 142). The Kartauserhof vessel was found in association with a coin of Constantine dating to AD 313-7, and on the basis of this, shell-decorated beakers were dated to the early 4th century (Doppelfeld 1975, 17-23). However, a recent review of the Luxemberger Strasse cremation burial has dated the associated finds, including the pottery and other glass vessels to the early 3rd century (Von Boeselager 1989). Von Boeselager has therefore argued that the Kartauserhof beaker was old when buried, and has redated these vessels to the first quarter of the 3rd-century. The early 3rd-century context in which the fragments from Rapsley villa were found confirms this new dating.

Other fragmentary shell beakers have been found in a cremation dated by associated finds to the later 2nd century at Stein, Limburg (Isings 1971, 18 no. 47, Fig. 4), in a cremation burial at Bouille-Courdault (Vendee), and two fragments were found in a pit at Heldenburg, probably filled before AD 233 (Von Boeselager 1989, 34). The fragment from Witcombe appears to be the only shell from this group to be made in opaque white glass, although opaque white trails occur in the decoration of several of the vessels.

Four rim fragments (nos. 9-11) come from three cups with horizontal wheel-cut or abraded bands of 2nd-century type. The exact shape of these vessels cannot be reconstructed from such small fragments, but they may be similar in form to vessels found in the Antonine pit at Park Street, Towcester (Price 1980, 63-4 nos. 3-5, fig. 14) and other 2nd-century sites in Roman Britain.

Numbers 11 and 12 are made in rather bubbly glass with carelessly executed abraded bands, and they may alternatively come from 4th-century vessels.

The greenish-colourless tubular pushed-in base ring no. 14 comes from a narrow, thin-walled straight-sided vessel made in bubbly glass. It is difficult to find substantially complete vessels with similar bases from Roman Britain, although nearly identical colourless base-rings have been found at Exeter (Allan 1991, 228 no. 62, fig. 96) and Water Newton (unpublished). It may perhaps come from a tall conical beaker with a narrow lower body. Examples are known in late 3rd and 4th century contexts in the Rhineland (Isings 1957, form 109; Fremersdorf and Polonyi-Fremersdorf 1984, 13-41 nos. 35-41).

Two colourless rim fragments (nos. 12-13) are probably from 3rd-century drinking cups. A vessel with this form of cracked-off and ground rim with a horizontal abraded band below was found in the mid-3rd century cemetery at Brougham, Cumbria (Cool 1990, 171, fig. 2.8). A cup with a slightly outurned cracked-off rim but with a similar convex body to the fragments from Witcombe was found in a drain at East Grimstead villa, Wiltshire (Sumner 1924, 43, pl.VIII.3). This vessel also had an applied pad base, similar to no. 22. Number 22 has a pointil scar on the underside of the base suggesting that it may have come from a cup or bowl with a fire-rounded rim or applied or pulled-out decoration. A very similar pad base, also with a pointil mark, was found at the King Harry Lane site at Verulamium (Price 1989, 44 no. 284, fig. 26).

Number 15 comes from a colourless funnel-mouthed globular flask with a cracked-off and ground rim, a wide funnel mouth and short neck, tapering in. Flasks of this type with a globular body and either a pushed-in base ring or a concave base (Isings 1957, form 104a and b), have frequently been found in 3rd and 4th-century burials in the north western provinces. Several are known from burials at Cologne (Fremersdorf and Fremersdorf-Polonyi 1984, 40- 1 nos. 100- 103), Strasbourg (Arvellier and Arvellier-Dulong 1985, 129-133, 258-263, nos. 279-283) and elsewhere. In Britain complete flasks of this type have been found in burials at Chilgrove near Chichester, associated with 3rd or 4th-century vessels (Harcourt 1846, pl. 9) and Aldgate, London (Harden and Green 1978, 163-175). The flask from London, which has a concave base, has similar wheel-cutting below the rim and halfway down the funnel neck of the vessel. Harden dated this vessel to the 3rd rather than the 4th century, and the good quality colourless glass of the Witcombe example also suggests a 3rd-century date. Another flask of this type, with a wider neck, may be represented by four rim and neck fragments (no. 16).

The convex body fragments (nos. 17-18) are decorated with an unusually complex wheel-cut design. The complete vessel probably had six groups of six concentric wheel-cut circles, intersecting at regular intervals around the circumference, crossed by three pairs of horizontal wheel-cut lines. These fragments probably came from at least one globular flask which is likely to have had a vertical cracked-off rim, a narrow cylindrical neck, a globular body and a concave base (cf. Isings 1957, form 103). These flasks are found in 3rd century contexts in the Rhineland (Fremersdorf 1967, taf. 11, 110-13, 115-7; Fremersdorf and Polonyi-Fremersdorf 1984, 36-40, taf. 89-100) and elsewhere in the Roman Empire. They are usually colourless and frequently decorated with combinations of wheel-cut lines. Highly decorated examples such as this vessel are very much less common, and include the series of flasks decorated with waterfront scenes of Baiae and Puteoli, Italy (Harden et. al. 1987, 208-9, no. 116), as well as facet-cut and painted flasks (Fremersdorf 1967, 112 taf. 117, 196 taf. 279).

No exact parallel for the fragments at Witcombe has been found, though two colourless flasks of this form, decorated with more simple combinations of wheel-cut circles and horizontal lines were found in burials in Cologne (Fremersdorf 1967, 110 taf. 112). Examples of this form are rare in Roman Britain, although a complete flask, decorated with horizontal wheel-cut lines, was found in a grave at York (Harden 1962, 141 pl. 67, H.G.33). Other possible fragmentary examples have been found at Poundbury (Charlesworth and Price 1987, MF2 E12 and F3) and Shakenoak (Harden 1968b, 78 no. 21, fig. 26.8). However, the complexity of the wheel-cutting on the vessel from Witcombe appears to be unique in Roman Britain. A further flask, or possibly a jug is represented by a wide cylindrical neck fragment (no. 20).

Number 20 comes from a separately blown foot with a cracked-off and ground edge. This form of foot is found on some late 1st to early 2nd-century cups or beakers, with facet-cut decoration (Isings 1957, form 21). However, some late 2nd to 3rd-century vessels also have bases of this type, for example the colourless flask from the burial at Hauxton, Cambridgeshire (Harden 1958, 12 no. 1, fig. 5 pl. IIIa), and this later date may be preferable for the fragment from Witcombe.

The undecorated curved fragment (no. 21), may perhaps come from the shoulder of a small colourless cylindrical bottle or flask, similar to the examples found at York (Harden 1962, 140, Fig. 90 H.G.146.3-4) or from the lower body of a narrow beaker, but the fragment is too small to identify with any certainty. The two concave base fragments (nos. 23-4) could come from bowls, or possibly flasks, such as the globular flasks discussed above (nos. 16- 19).

The pale greenish/colourless straight sided fragment (no. 25) is difficult to identify. It appears to come from the corner angle of a thin-walled square-sectioned vessel, perhaps a Mercury flask of 2nd to 3rd-century date. These vessels have mould-blown bodies and often have a raised inscription or design on the base, and occasionally also on the sides of the vessel (Isings 1957, form 84). The form is not common in Britain, though a complete example is known from a 2nd-century burial at Chester (Newstead 1914, no. 3 pl.XXXI fig. 2), and a rim and neck fragment came from Fishbourne (Harden and Price 1971, 358, fig.142.87).

The five facet-cut fragments (nos. 26-29) come from hemispherical or shallow cups or small bowls. Vessels decorated in this way were produced in the 2nd, 3rd and 4th centuries. They have been found on several sites in Roman Britain, and are also common in the lower Rhineland (Fremersdorf 1967, taf. 55, 57, 60-2, 66-7). These vessels were made in colourless glass and are decorated with combinations of linear and facet cutting. One of the earliest dated examples of this type in Roman Britain comes from the Antonine pit at Towcester. This hemispherical bowl was made in good quality glass and decorated with a combination of wheel-cut lines and oval facets (Price 1980, 63 no.1, fig. 14).

Vessels with more complex decorative schemes are probably slightly later in date. Highly decorated examples have been found at Silchester (Boon 1974a, 232, fig. 36.4), York (Harden 1962, 137, fig.88, H.G.162 and 210), and Verulamium (Charlesworth 1972, 206 fig. 78.48-53). Rice grain and circular facets are very commonly found, either separately, as on bowls from Colchester (Hull 1958, 79, fig. 35 no.1), Verulamium (Charlesworth 1984, 154 no. 84, fig. 632.36) and Shakenoak (Harden 1968b, 76 no.7, fig.26.5), or together as on nos. 27-8 and 30 from Witcombe.

Number 26 comes from the lower body of a hemispherical bowl, and shows two rows of circular facets alternating with an I-shaped design made up of three rice grain facets and divided horizontally by a single row of rice grain facets. A similar arrangement can be seen on a complete bowl from a burial at Leuna Merseburg (Fremersdorf 1967, taf.77), on fragments from Piercebridge (Charlesworth 1959, 44, fig. 3.9), and more closely set on a bowl from Verulamium (Charlesworth 1972, fig.78.52), although the circular facets on these pieces have raised central points.

Number 28 is a straight-sided fragment and may come from the upper body of a deeper convex bowl. The narrow and wide horizontal rice grain facets on no.28 are identical to those below the rim on the deeper bag-shaped vessels from Verulamium (Charlesworth 1972, 206, fig. 78.48-51). Number 29 has vertical rice grain facets and circular facets divided by a wheel-cut line, similar to examples from York (Harden 1962, 137, fig. 88 H.G.205.1), Strasbourg (Arveiller-Dulong and Arveiller 1985, 107 no. 205), Cologne and elsewhere (Fremersdorf 1967, taf. 80- 1).

The body fragment no. 31 is difficult to identify, although the decoration is interesting. The colourless trails have been nipped together to form a vertical Y shape. This form of decoration was used on several vessel types of the late 2nd to 4th-centuries. Cups, bowls and beakers decorated in this manner have been found in the Luxemburger-Strasse cemetery and elsewhere in Cologne (Fremersdorf 1959, 714, taf. 108-150). A jug from Limburg, Holland has similar decoration (Fremersdorf and Polonyi-Fremersdorf 1984, 84 no. 190) as does a complete colourless flask from the burial at Hauxton, Cambridge (Harden 1958, 12 no. 1 fig. 5, pl. IIIa).

Two colourless body fragments (nos. 32-3), may possibly come from the same vessel. Numerous cups, bowls, flasks and other forms with irregular trailed 'snake thread' decoration, usually scored across, have been found in burials in the Rhineland, particularly around Cologne in the late 2nd and 3rd centuries (Fremersdorf 1959 passim), and were probably manufactured in this area. Fragments with coloured and colourless scored trails of this type, have been found on several 2nd to 3rd-century sites in Britain, including fragments with colourless trails at York (Blossom Street site, unpublished), Caerwent (Boon 1974b, 116 no. 17, flg. 2) and Cirencester (Charlesworth 1971, 88 no.16, fig. 11). The irregular colourless unscored trails on the Witcombe fragments may come from the thick terminals of snake thread motifs, though a completely different form of applied decoration cannot be ruled out.

Number 36 is a body fragment which was decorated with pulled-out points. Decoration similar to this occurs on hemispherical cups, beakers and flasks of 3rd-century date, in combination with lugs or ribs, as on vessels from Chichester (Down 1979, 163 no. 9), Braintree (Drury 1976, 37, fig. 19.6), from the mid-3rd century cemetery at Brougham, Cumbria (Cool 1990, 170, fig. 1.2), Malton (Price and Cool forthcoming, no. 11) and elsewhere. Vessels decorated with pulled-out points only are less common, although these can be seen on a colourless bowl from Stonham Aspal, Suffolk (Charlesworth 1967, 240a, fig. 38), Brougham (Cool 1990, 170, flg. 1.2) and on a bowl and a flask found in Cologne (Fremersdorf and Polnyi-Fremersdorf 1984, 27 no. 69). Number 38, which has the trace of a change of angle, may come from the lower body of a similar vessel.

Thirty three fragments (just under 18% of the vessel glass) probably come from late-Roman vessels. These include one polychrome, seven yellow/green and five pale blue/green fragments, with the remainder pale green or greenish/colourless. Although several of the vessel forms discussed above continued in use beyond the 3rd century, the form, colour and quality of the following group of fragments suggest that they date exclusively to the 4th century.

The second fragment of polychrome glass from Witcombe is a colourless convex body fragment decorated with blobs of peacock blue and pale blue (no. 50). It comes from a hemispherical bowl of 4th-century date; the complete vessel very probably had a cracked-off rim and a simple concave base (Isings 1957, form 96). The coloured blobs may have been arranged in a regular pattern around the vessel, a feature frequently noticed on vessels with large blobs. Fourth-century colourless hemispherical bowls and conical beakers with this type of decoration are quite commonly found in the Rhineland (Fremersdorf 1962, taf. 1-23). Other forms such as segmental bowls and flasks are also occasionally decorated in this manner (Harden et. al. 1987, 114-5 nos. 47-8). They have been recognised at several sites in Roman Britain. At Barnsley Park villa at least three vessels, probably conical beakers, with applied purple and emerald green blobs were found (Price 1982a, 175 no. 2, fig.59). A colourless fragment with a dark blue blob was found at Frocester Court villa (Price 1979, fig. 16.3), and a fragment with a dark green blob at Ilchester (Price 1982b, fig.112.23). At Porchester Castle four fragments from convex-sided vessels with blue and bluish-green blobs were found (Harden 1975, 371 no. 10c, fig. 198). Other similarly decorated fragments from conical beakers have been found at Caister-by-Yarmouth (dark blue-green and blue blobs; Price and Cool forthcoming, nos. 99-102) and Wroxeter (blue blobs; Harden 1975/6, no. 1). The combination of peacock blue and pale blue blobs on the Witcombe example appears to be unique in Roman Britain. Very similar peacock blue blobs in combination with yellow/brown blobs can be seen on a segmental bowl from Luxemburger Strasse, Cologne (Harden et. al. 1987, 115 no. 48).

The greenish colourless claw no.51, is an uncommon find on a Roman site. Claws are better known on beakers of the 5th and 6th centuries from Britain and the northwest Continent, than on vessels of the Roman period. There is no doubt that this almost colourless claw is of Roman date, although the form of vessel which it decorated is almost impossible to determine. The claw was formed by applying a small inflated blob of glass to the body of the vessel and then pulling this out and down. Two complete colourless vessels with claw decoration, dated to the 3rd and 4th centuries, are known from burials in Cologne. The first is a beaker with two rows of claws, the top row being decorated with applied dark blue jaws and fins to resemble dolphins (Fremersdorf 1961, 24-5 taf. 16-7; Harden et al. 1987, 256 no. 145). The second is a two-handled stemmed cup with irregular claws which are very similar to the claw from Witcombe (Fremersdorf 1961, 23 taf. 15).

The most common forms of 4th-century drinking vessels in Britain were the conical beaker and the hemispherical cup. Both forms have cracked-off rims and are often decorated with horizontal abraded bands. Number 53 is a rim fragment from a conical beaker, similar to vessels found at the Lankhills cemetery, Winchester (Harden 1979, fig.27.382, 391, 530 and 634) and at Porchester (Harden 1975, 371 nos. 11-12, Silchester (Boon 1974a, fig. 36.8), Frocester Court villa (Price 1979, 41 nos. 9 and 11, fig. 16) and many other occupation and burial sites. The base fragment (no. 56) probably comes from a similar vessel.

Further rim fragments (nos. 54-5) may also come from conical beakers, or possibly hemispherical cups, similar to vessels from Lankhills cemetery (Harden 1979, fig. 27.62 and 385), Alchester Road, Towcester (Price and Cool 1983, fig. 46. 19-21) and many other sites.

Five fragments of good quality, greenish colourless glass (no. 52) also come from a hemispherical or truncated conical cup or bowl. The colour is somewhat unusual at this period, but the unfinished cracked-off rim and the poorly executed abraded bands suggest a 4th-century date.

The small body fragments come from a convex-sided vessel with shallow diagonal ribbing (no. 57 + listed fragment). Although these fragments are too small for the vessel form to be identified, the decoration is known in Britain on several convex and straight-sided yellow/green or colourless 4th-century vessel types. These include ovoid jugs (e.g. Thorpe 1935, pl. IVc), cylindrical bowls (e.g. Price 1986, no 4, fig. 117) and hexagonal bottles (e.g. Price 1982a, 183-4 nos. 46-7, fig. 60). Three blue/green base fragments, nos. 45-48, are too small to be identified. Blue/green vessels are generally produced in the 1st and 2nd centuries, but the poor quality, very bubbly glass of these examples may indicate a late Roman date.

## Bottle Glass

About 15% of the vessel glass came from blue/green bottles (27 fragments). This very low proportion of the total assemblage suggests that the main accumulation of the vessel glass at Witcombe took place after the late 2nd century, when blue/green bottles went out of use. Nevertheless, the rim of no. 58 has a triangular section, frequently noted on bottles of the Neronian and early Flavian periods in Britain. Rim neck and handle fragments are formed in a similar manner on both cylindrical and prismatic blue/green bottles, so it is not possible to determine the form of those represented by nos. 58-60. However, all the listed body fragments are from prismatic bottles, and it is unlikely that any cylindrical bottles, which went out of use at the end of the 1st or early 2nd century are represented here.

Prismatic bottles are very common during the 1st and 2nd centuries, and are usually the most numerous single vessel type on sites of this period. They were used as general household containers for liquids or semi-liquids. The complete vessel, almost invariably blown in a body mould with a separate base piece, had a folded rim, cylindrical neck, straight-sided body, flat base and an angular handle applied to the shoulder and neck and usually with reeded decoration on the lower part. The most common form of prismatic bottle was square, although rectangular, hexagonal and other polygonal forms are known. The base was almost always decorated with a raised design, of which the most common was one or more concentric circles, sometimes with corner supports such as no. 61. Number 62 has an unusual design at the edge of the base, probably caused by an irregular mould.

## Catalogue of the vessel glass (Fig. 22)

*Abbreviations*
PH present height
RD rim diameter
BD base diameter
WT wall thickness
Dim Dimensions
T Thickness
A Area
R Room
C Context
u/s unstratified
W find number
(all measurements in millimetres)

Pillar moulded bowl
1. Upper body fragment. Deep blue. Straight side below rim edge; wheel polished on interior and exterior; small part of one rib. Dim 15x10, T 2; *W2911, C863, A65*

Cast
2. Rim fragment of cast bowl with handle. Colourless; small bubbles. Vertical rim, small external rib on rim edge widening towards broken handle, two carved projections; slightly convex-curved side. Surfaces ground and wheel polished. PH 24, RD c.120, WT 3-2; *W2417-20, C854, A67*

Mould blown
3. Body fragment. Colourless; some small bubbles; strain cracks. Slightly convexcurved. Parts of two circular mouldings in shallow relief with edges of 4 other mouldings. Surfaces slightly heat distorted. Dim 20x16, WT 2; *W4489/90, C877, A72*

Blown
Polychrome
4. Base fragment of beaker or flask. Slightly green-tinged/colourless with many small bubbles, and opaque white. Part of separately blown foot with fire-rounded edge and slightly concave upper surface. Opaque white thick marvered trail applied to edge of foot; opaque white thin unmarvered trail applied close to central stem (now missing). PH 10, BD 70, T 2.5; *W3733, C856, A67*

5. Fragment from opaque white ribbon trail applied to body of vessel at intervals with slightly angular-profiled, free-standing loops between. Fragment broken top and bottom and forms majority of one free-standing loop. Impressed with pincers to produce a scallop shell pattern on front and back. Length 16, section 14x3; *W2860, u/s*

Deep Blue
6. Body fragment. Occasional small bubbles. Carinated side. Dim 34x20, WT 0.5
2.5; *W1065, C942, R15/15a*
Also 1 deep blue undecorated body fragment. *W995, C671, R15/15a*

Yellow/Brown
7. Body fragment. Light yellow/brown; occasional small bubbles; strain crack.
Convex-curved. 1 narrow rib. Dim 22x11, WT 1.5; *W576, u/s*
Also 1 undecorated light yellow/brown body fragment. *W4921, C877, A72*

Yellow/Green
8. Handle fragment of jug. dark yellow/green appearing almost emerald; many elongated bubbles; dulled surfaces; strain cracks. part of an angular ribbon handle with central rib. Length 21, section 26x4; *W1864, C512, A47*

Colourless
9. Rim fragment of beaker. Occasional small bubbles. Curved rim, edge cracked off and ground. One wheel cut line on upper body with abrasions either side. PH 10, RD 70, WT 1; *W4228, u/s*

10. Rim fragment of conical beaker. Green-tinged colourless; occasional bubbles, some large. Curved rim, edge cracked off and smoothed; straight side sloping in slightly. Faint band of abraded lines below rim edge; lightly abraded band on upper body. PH 30, RD 60, WT 0.5; *W4489/90, C877, A72*

11. Two rim fragments of beaker. Slightly greenish-tinged colourless. Some small bubbles. Curved rim, edge cracked off but not ground; straight side sloping in. Abraded band on upper body. PH 12, RD c. 80, WT 0.5; *W2913, C863, A65*
Also one similar upper body fragment of beaker with abraded band. *W1589, C738, A62*
Also 8 body fragments with abraded bands
*W997, u/s*
*W1824, C768, R34/51*
*W2006, C784, A65*
*W2109, C746, A64/66*
*W2292, C775, A64/66* (3 fr.)
*W3707, C868, A65*

12. Rim and upper body fragment of ovoid beaker. Some small bubbles, dulled surfaces. Vertical rim, edge cracked off and ground and now much chipped; convex curved side Abraded horizontal band below rim. PH 41, RD 80, WT 1; *W816, C620, Tr.A*

13. Rim fragment of beaker or cup. Some small bubbles. Vertical rim7 edge cracked off and ground; straight side. Narrow horizontal abraded line. PH 22, RD 85, WT 1; *W1345, C954, A41a*

14. Lower body and complete base fragment of beaker. Green-tinged colourless; many small bubbles. Narrow straight side sloping in steeply to outsplayed tubular pushed-in base ring; concave base with small central kick. PH 4, BD 39, WT 1; *W4224, u/s*

15. Rim and neck fragment of funnel-mouthed flask. Occasional bubbles; dulled surfaces. Funnel mouth, rim edge cracked off and ground, body curving out almost horizontally. One wheel-cut line below rim edge and two on neck. PH 42, RD 50, WT 2; *W1493, C780, R16*

16. Two rim and two body fragments of funnel-mouthed flask joining in two pairs. Some small bubbles, streakily weathered surfaces. Funnel mouth, rim edge cracked off and ground, beginning to curve out to body. Two abraded bands on upper neck and at junction with body. PH 45, RD 65, WT 1.5; *W1507 & W1510, C782, R16*

17. Seven body fragments of globular flask, six joining. Occasional small bubbles; dulled surfaces. Convex curved side. Intersecting sets of three pairs of concentric circular wheel-cut lines, parts of three sets extant,

GLASS

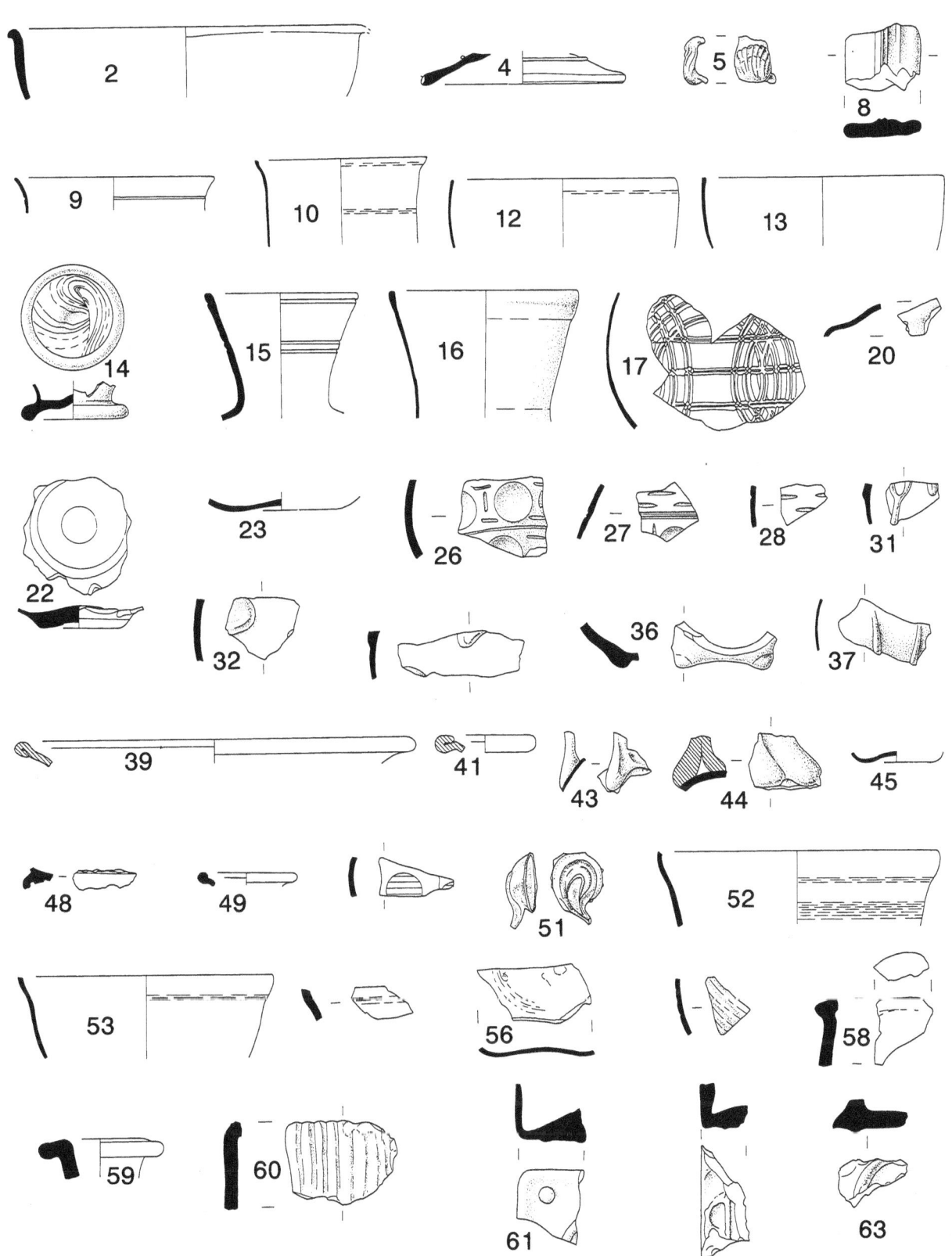

*Figure 22* Roman vessel glass, numbered from catalogue (1:2)

arranged around body; three sets of horizontal wheel-cut lines around widest part of body. Dim (joined frags.) 58x40, WT 1-2; *W1509, C782, R16*

18. Body fragment, dulled surfaces. Convex-curved body. Parts of two curved wheel-cut lines. Dim 16x14, Wt 2; *W2962, C867, A65*

19. Neck fragment of flask or jug. Slightly green-tinged; many cylindrical bubbles. Wide cylindrical neck. PH 33, ND c. 32, WT 2; *W836, C620, Tr.A*

20. Base fragment of beaker? Small bubbles; dulled surfaces. Part of separately blown foot, rim cracked off and ground with concave upper surface. Dim 24x14, T 2; *W1618, C736, A62*

21. Body fragment; some small bubbles, inside surface crazed. Part of side curving into a ?shoulder/?lower bod above base. Dim 35x23, WT 1-2.5; *W4225, u/s.*

22. Complete base of cup. Green-tinged colourless; small bubbles. Side sloping in to concave base with applied circular pad. Circular pontil scar with small amounts of additional glass. Base worn. BD 28, WT 1.5, scar, dim 11. *W2887, u/s.*

23. Base fragment of cup or flask. Slightly green-tinged, colourless; small bubbles. Convex-curved side sloping into shallow concave base. Base worn. PH *c*.5, BD *c*. 30, WT 1; *W2051, C1000, A66*

24. Base fragment; ?flask. Slightly green-tinged, colourless. small bubbles. Convex-curved side sloping into convex base, mostly missing. PH 13, WT 2; *W1769, u/s.*

25. Body fragment. ?unguent bottle. Slightly green-tinged, colourless; some small bubbles. Part of square-sectioned side. PH 19, WT 1.5; *W2934, C864, A65*

26. Two joining? lower body fragments of facet-cut bowl. Small bubbles; clouded, pitted surfaces; strain cracks. Convex-curved side. Row of circular facets alternating with three rice grain facets arranged in an 'I' shape above a lightly abraded band; parts of one circular and one horizontal rice grain facet below. Dim 31x26, WT 2-3; *W4216, C918, R44.*

27. Body fragment of facet-cut bowl. Clouded surfaces; strain cracks. Convex-curved side. Three horizontal rice grain facets arranged in two rows above two horizontal wheel-cut lines; tip of one vertical rice grain facet and part of one circular facet below. Dim 21x20, WT 1.5; *W4244, C918, R44.*

28. Body fragment; some small bubbles. Straight side. Parts of two horizontal rice grain facets above horizontal oval facet cut. Dim 16x13, WT l; *W4227, u/s.*

29. Body fragment; green-tinged, colourless; occasional bubbles. Convex-curved side. Lower part of one vertical rice grain facet above lightly abraded horizontal band; part of one circular facet below. Dim 29x20; *W1640, u/s.*

30. Body fragment; many bubbles. Straight side. One wheel-cut band. Dim 19x10, WT 2; *W2934, C864, A65.*

31. Body fragment; some small bubbles. Convex-curved side. Terminal of one trail and two others pinched together to form a "Y" shape. Dim 18x14, WT l; *W3329, C886, A71.*

32. Body fragment; small bubbles. Convex-curved side. Part of applied oval selfcoloured blob, also tip of a second blob. Dim 26x21, WT 2; *W1O99, u/s.*

33. Body fragment, small bubbles. Convex-curved side. Parts of two applied selfcoloured blobs. Dim 43x16, WT 2; *W1105,C676, R15/15a.*

(Nos.32 and 33 probably from the same vessel)

34. Body fragment; occasional small bubbles. Straight side. One chipped trail. Dim 10x7, WT 0.5; *W4240, C918, R44.*

35. Body fragment; green-tinged, colourless; small bubbles. Convex-curved side. One trail. Dim 15x13, WT 1; *W1526, C716, R17.*

36. Lower body and base fragment?; some small bubbles. Side sloping in steeply to edge of concave base. Two pinched-up knobs at edge of base. PH 16, WT 4; *W2788, C916, R27.*

37. Body fragment; dulled surfaces; occasional small bubbles. Thin convex-curved side. Terminals of two pinched-up ribs. Dim 31x15, WT 1.5; *W54 ,u/s*

38. Body fragment; clouded surfaces. Convex-curved side. Trace of change of angle. terminal of one pinched-up rib or lug. Dim 36x30, WT 3; *W4942, u/s.* Also 19 undecorated colourless body fragments.

*W1126, u/s.* (2 frags.)
*W1186, C948, R14/15*
*W1527, C716, R17*
*W1702, u/s*
*W2002, u/s*
*W2109, C746, A64/66* (2f.)
*W2709, u/s* (2 fr., very bubbly)
*W2913, C863, A65* (2f.)
*W3710, C892, A71*
*W3712, C892, A71*
*W4107/8, C793, A65*
*W4187, C870, A65*
*W4241and W4242, C918, R44*
*W4826, C856, A67*

Blue/Green

39. Rim fragment of jar. Some bubbles; streaky green impurities. Out-turned rim, edge rolled down and in. RD c. 130-140, WT 2; *W2900, C863, A65.*

40. Rim fragment of jar. Some small bubbles. Out-turned rim, edge rolled up and in. RD *c*. 40, WT 1.5; *W4216, C918, R44*

41. Rim fragment of jug, flask or bottle. Some small bubbles. Rim bent out, up, in and flattened. RD *c*. 35; *W4991, C806, R28*

42. Neck fragment of jug or flask. Occasional small bubbles. Cylindrical neck with tooling marks at junction with body. Dim 20x13, WT 4; *W3701, C868, C65*

43. Handle and body fragment of jug. Small bubbles; elongated in handle. Edge of lower handle attachment of handle with side rib retaining small part of side. Dim (of side) 15x12, WT 1; *WSS, u/s.*

44. Handle and shoulder fragment of jug or bottle. Elongated bubbles and streaky green impurity in handle. Handle with at least two thick rounded ribs retaining part of side. Dim (of side) 20x17, WT 1; *W193, F13, A41a*

45. Bade fragment of beaker? Occasional small bubbles. Side sloping in steeply to shallow concave base. BD *c*. 20, WT 1; *W1658, C726, R16*

46. Base fragment. Some small bubbles. Concave base.

Dim 28x21; *W280, F13, A41a*

47. Base fragment. Many bubbles. Fragment from centre of concave base. Dim l9x13; *W4193, C872, A65*

48. Base fragment of bowl, flask or jug. Fragment from edge of base with tubular pushed-in base ring (now broken); side grozed. Dim 21xl1; *W1976, C874/759, A65*

49. Rim fragment of flask or unguent bottle. Out-bent rim, edge rolled up and in. RD *c.* 30; *W3699, C868, A65*

Also 27 undecorated blue/green body fragments.
*W196, F13, A41a*
*W991, C526, A47*
*W1192 and W1277, C950, R14/15*
*W1310, C953, R14* (2f.)
*W1386, C956, A41a*
*W1508, C782, R16*
*W1583, C737, A62*
*W1747, u/s*
*W1865, C512, A47*
*W2039, u/s*
*W2042, C1001, A66*
*W2109, C746, A64/66*
*W2209, C775, A64/66*
*W2721, C822, R27*
*W2913, C863, A65 (4f.)*
*W2934, C864, A65*
*W2946, C866, A65*
*W2957, C865, A65*
*W3334, C885, A71*
*W3711, C892, A71*
*W4247, C918, A71*
*W4951, u/s*

Late Roman

50. Body fragment, colourless with some small bubbles; majority of one translucent turquoise oval marvered blob with edge of similar pale blue blob. Slightly convex-curved. Dim 25x13, WT 2; *W2210, C777, A64/66*

51. Applied claw. Green-tinged colourless; some bubbles, including large ones. Claw formed by applying blob of glass to vessel wall, and then drawing tip down and to one side. Claw complete apart from broken tip, side of vessel broken around edge of claw. Dim. of top of claw 24, length of claw 23; *W663, CY43, R1S/15a*

52. Two rim and three body fragments of conical beaker (2 joining). Pale greenish colourless; occasional small bubbles. Curved rim, edge cracked off but not ground; straight side sloping in. One narrow abraded band below rim edge and one similar on upper body, wider band below. PH (joined frags.) 24, RD 95, WT 1.5; *W913 and W2933, C863, A65; W2934, C864, A65; W2957, C865, A65*

53. Rim fragment of conical beaker. Many small bubbles. Curved rim, edge cracked off smoothly but not ground; straight side sloping in. Abraded band on upper body. PH 27, RD 75, WT 1.5; *W2912, C863, A65.*

54. Rim fragment of beaker or cup. Yellowish-green, many small bubbles. Curved rim; edge cracked off smoothly, not ground. Abraded horizontal band below rim. PH 10, WT 2; *W194, F13, A41a* Also four fragments with one abraded band. *W19S and W196 (3 fr.), F13, A41a*

55. Two rim fragments of beaker or cup. Blue-tinged. Curved rim, edge cracked off smoothly but not ground. PH 7, WT 1; *W2913, C863, A65*

56. Base fragment; small bubbles; strain cracks. Shallow concave base. Dim 35x20; *W1540, C715, R17*

57. Body fragment; many small bubbles. Convex-curved side. Shallow diagonal optic blown ribs. Dim 20x12, WT 2; *W2957, C865, A65*

Also one other similarly ribbed body fragment. *W2981, u/s*

Also 16 undecorated light green and greenish colourless bubbly body fragments.
*W224, u/s*
*W1167, C949, R14/15*
*W1185, C948, R14/15*
*W1387, C956, A41a*
*W1541 and W1542, C715, R17*
*W1557, C737, A62*
*W2021, C768, R34/51*
*W2365, C812, R30* (yellowish green)
*W2913, C863, A65* (3 fr.)
*W2962, C867, A65*
*W3646, C868, A65*
*W4245, C918, R44*
*W4489/90, C877, A72*

Bottle glass

58. Rim and neck fragment of bottle. Rim edge bent out, up and in with small triangular profile, inner edge chipped; cylindrical neck. RD *c*35, *W2057, C1002, A66*

59. Rim and neck fragment of bottle. Rim edge bent out, up, in and flattened; cylindrical neck. RD 45, *W678, C958, A41a*

Also three cylindrical neck fragments. *W4213, C847, R44* (2 frs.), *W4243, C918, R44*. One shoulder fragment from a prismatic bottle. *W4216, C918, R44.*

One bottle shoulder fragment *W103, C529, R14.*

60. Handle fragment of bottle. Part of angular reeded handle. Section 48x4; *W4216, C918, R44.*

Also one other reeded handle fragment from a bottle. *W101, C529, R14.*

61. Lower body and base fragment of square bottle. Base design - at least one circular moulding with small circular pellet in the corner; base worn. Base dim. 25x23; *W3700, C868, A65*

62. Lower body and base fragment of prismatic bottle. Base design - one straight moulding parallel to edge with indeterminate triangular moulding, probably fortuitous beyond it. Base dim. 38x14; *W2780, C827, R27.*

63. Base fragment of prismatic bottle. Base design - at least one circular moulding. Base dim. 24x12; *W2057, C1002, A66.*

Also 15 body fragments from prismatic bottles; 5 fragments with 90 deg. angles from square bottles. *W56, u/s, W102 and W104, C529, R14; W1877, C874/758, W2002, u/s*

Ten flat fragments from prismatic bottles. *W253, u/s; W1976, C874/759, A65* (2 frs.); *W2109, C746, A64/66; W2268, C744, A64/66, W2417-20, C854, A67* (4 frs.); *W2878, C855, A67; W2945, C865, A65; W4194, C878, A72; W4489/90, C877, A72* (2 frs.).

## 3.2.2: PERSONAL OBJECTS

### The Brooches
*by S. Butcher*

**Catalogue** (Fig. 23, nos.1-6)

1. The bow and first coil of the spring of a one-piece brooch. The bow is gently arched and plain except for an incised diagonal cross in the centre; the lower part is expanded into a plain rectangular catchplate. Length 50mm. (BZ93, AM.Lab. 732331) *W4181 C786/F21, Area 72, Period 3*

This belongs to the type variously described as a 'Nauheim derivative' or 'poor man's brooch'; it was very common in Britain in the 1st. century AD, with a *floruit* in the middle of the century (*cf* Fishbourne, Cunliffe 1971, II, fig. 37, p. 100), but examples can occur in the earlier or later years. It is also found on the continent in the same period.

2. The upper part only of a brooch with a spring of eight turns held on a lug behind the centre of the head and by the chord threaded through the creast on the head. The crossbar is plain except for grooves at the end and is slightly curved; there are flanges beside the upper bow where it meets the head. Surviving length 25mm. (BZ50, AM.Lab. 673591) *W1866, C739, Area 63, Period ?2*

In construction this is a two-piece Colchester brooch (Camulodunum Type IV, Hawkes and Hull 1947, 310) but the general appearance, with flanged head, is typical of southwestern brooches with the 'Polden Hill' construction (Chew Valley, Rahtz and Greenfield 1978, fig. 114.7, 292). Typologically it should date to the second half of the 1st century AD.

3. The spring of seven turns is secured by a bar which passes through it and is anchored in discs forming the ends of the crossbar; also by the chord passing through a crest on the head. The bow is plain and tapering, with a small moulding continuing the crest and with a very narrow foot marked only by cross-grooves. The triangular catchplate, which has a triangular opening, forms a continuation of the bow. Length 56mm. (BZ32, AM.Lab. 732187) *W674, C655, Area 60, Period ?3.*

The head construction puts this into the 'Polden Hill' group of brooches. It probably belongs to an early stage in their development since it lacks the heavy mouldings of the most typical representatives; there is no direct dating evidence but typologically this may belong to the later 1st century AD. Hull's unpublished corpus Ancient Brooches contains several similar examples from Gloucestershire and South Wales, and the rectangular profile at the head is common on related types from south-western Britain.

4. The pin and spring only from a brooch with an inferior chord; probably a 1st-century type. Surviving length 35mm. (BZ73, AM.Lab. 732187) *W2902, C863, Area 65, Period 5.*

5. A small penannnular brooch. The ring is flattened and crudely faceted and the terminals are coiled upwards. A badly corroded iron pin is fixed to the ring. Diameter 30mm. (BZ1, AM.Lab. 615021) *W67, C554, Area 41, Period 5.*

This belongs to class C of Fowler's typology of penannular brooches (Fowler 1960, 152). It is found in 1st century contexts, e.g. Camulodunum (Hawkes and Hull 1947, fig. 59, 1, 326) and Hod Hill (Brailsford 1962, fig. 11, E8, 12), but also in much later ones, e.g. Rudston (Stead 1980, 95, no. 20). Its distribution in Britain is wide and it also occurs on the continent (cf Riha 1979, fig. 69.1834, 209).

6. A very small penannular brooch. The ring is flat and is crudely cross-grooved at the shoulder; it bears the mark of a now missing pin having been wrapped around it. The terminals are turned back over the ring and cross-moulded. Diameter 26mm. (BZ6, AM.Lab.615026) *W80, F13b, Area 41, Period 5.*

This brooch is type D in Fowler's classification (1960, 167); like type C, above, it occurs on 1st century sites and in much later contexts, and has a very wide distribution.

### Analysis of metals (AM. Lab. Report No. 4932)
*by J. Bayley*

Five brooches were analysed qualitatively by energy dispersive X-ray fluorescence (XRF); the results are given in the following table.

| AML no. | brooch type | alloy |
|---|---|---|
| 615021 | Penannular | bronze |
| 615026 | Penannular | bronze |
| 635032 | Colchester 'B' | leaded bronze |
| 673591 | Colchester 'B' | leaded bronze |
| 732331 | Nauheim derivative | bronze |

About 80% of all two-piece Colchester brooches are leaded bronzes so these two examples are very typical compositions. Some 60% of Nauheim derivatives are bronzes (the others being either brasses or gunmetals) so this example is again typical. Penannular brooches are far more evenly divided between bronzes, brasses and gunmetals so there is no such thing as a typical composition, though the composition of these two brooches falls within the normal range for the type.

## Glass Beads
*by J. Price and S. Cottam.*

Thirty glass beads were found at Witcombe, seventeen of which were from a single necklace retaining many of its copper alloy links and the fastener. Several different types of bead have been identified in this collection, both within the necklace and as single finds, the stylistic and chronological affiliations of which are discussed below:

Bead Necklace from Room 14
The fragmentary necklace *W1003* (Figure 23 no.7), has seventeen complete beads of four different varieties. The beads were strung on individual wires, bent over at each end to form joining loops between each bead. Seven long wound cylindrical beads, in heavily decayed green glass remained. These beads were produced in a similar manner to the wound blue beads described below, with the surface probably smoothed over (Guido 1978, 94). Nine spherical beads, six dark blue and three opaque white, also appear to have been wound. They were probably broken in segments from a wound rod of glass pinched in at intervals. The small square-sectioned bead in dark blue glass, appearing black, is a common type, usually occurring in 3rd and 4th-century contexts, similar in form to *W2211a*, discussed below.

Annular glass beads
Three annular beads, two complete, were found (Fig.23 nos. 8-10). *W2317*, in dark blue translucent glass with an opaque white marvered wave, is a quite common type which originated in the 3rd century BC and survived throughout the Roman Period (Guido 1978, 63-4, group 5A). Many examples are known on Roman sites in Britain including three from Caerleon and single finds from Cirencester (Guido 1978, 129 and 133, fig. 21.1), and Verulamium (Charlesworth 1972, 213, fig. 79.71). *W1582* is a fragment of a colourless annular bead with opaque yellow spots. Colourless beads decorated with opaque yellow spirals, waves, chevrons and other designs are known from many pre-Roman and Roman sites, particularly in western Britain, and a centre of production has been suggested at Meare, Somerset (Guido 1978, 79-89 classes 10-11; Henderson 1980). The earliest examples of the principal form of 'Meare' type bead, decorated with three groups of spirals, appear in the 3rd century BC The variant types such as the Witcombe example, are possibly later. Guido notes only one other example with yellow spots, an unprovenanced find from Derbyshire (Guido 1978, 84, class II type K). It is difficult to suggest a date for this bead, but some examples of 'Meare' type beads are known from Roman sites at South Shields (Guido 1978, 188), Caerwent (Archaeologia 1930, 80, 240, fig. 2) and from near the Roman fort of Newstead (Guido 1978, 192). W658 is a complete very bubbly annular bead with marvered opaque white trails. This is a well known type which existed in the late Iron Age and survived throughout the Roman period (Guido 1978, 66 group 6, 11a). Many beads of this type are known from Roman sites in Britain including examples from Cirencester, Frocester Court villa and Gloucester.

Small glass beads
There is a wide variety of smaller beads from Witcombe (Fig. 23, nos.11-20). W1248a, which retains its copper alloy link, and *W1164* (nos. 11 and 12) are deep blue approximately heart-shaped beads (Guido 1978, 99, fig. 37.17). These belong to a group of beads in a variety of irregular shapes which is very difficult to date with any accuracy, appearing in several colours throughout the Roman period. Dark blue heart-shaped beads have been found in late Roman contexts at Portchester (Guido 1978, 225) and in a burial dated AD 350-70 at the Lankhills cemetery, Winchester (Guido 1979, 299, no. 363).

The small square-sectioned blue bead, *W2211a* (no.13), is also a common type (Guido 1978, 196, fig. 37.7). Examples of a similar size are known from the Roman villa at Colliton Park, Dorset, at the Lankhills cemetery, Winchester (Guido 1979, 300, 560) and on a necklace which probably dates to the 4th century from Verulamium (Guido 1978, 213-4).

*W2964* (no.14) is a small transparent yellow biconical bead. Biconical beads are generally of later Roman date, although blue examples are known from 1st to 2nd century contexts (Guido 1978, 98, fig. 37.12-13). Transparent yellow biconical beads are uncommon, although they have been found on late Roman necklaces from Fordington, Dorset (Guido 1978, 220) and Lankhills cemetery, Winchester (Guido 1979, 298, 248).

Wound beads
Two tapering globular blue beads, *W1248b* and *W2944* (nos. 15 and 16), were probably produced by winding a wire around a rod, which was then withdrawn leaving slightly conical, tapering beads. They may have been made as individual objects or be segments broken from larger beads. *W2211b* (no. 17) is a very small blue spherical bead which does not appear to have been broken from a longer segmented bead. Wound beads are very common in Roman Britain (Guido 1978, 91-3), and are difficult to date with any accuracy.

Green cylindrical beads
Three green beads are cylindrical in section (*W192, W677 and W1490*), a form found commonly throughout the Roman period (Guido 1978, 95, fig. 37.4-5). *W192* (no. 18) is a short opaque green bead, a type known from many sites including; Park Street villa, Hertfordshire (Guido 1978, 212), from a mid 4th-century context at Shakenoak, Oxfordshire (Harden 1968b, 79, no. 38, fig. 26.19), Housesteads (Guido 1978, 212). *W1490* and *W677* (nos. 19-20), the latter slightly flattened, are longer beads of translucent green glass. This type of bead is known from many sites, including a deposit dated AD 160-230 at the bath house at Caerleon (Brewer 1986, 149, fig. 48.35). Barnsley Park villa (Webster 1982, 107, fig. 22.8), and Colliton Park villa, Dorset, post dating the late 2nd century AD (Guido 1978, 209).

**The catalogue (Fig. 23)**

7. Copper alloy and glass bead necklace. One necklace fastener, 15 complete or near complete links and 10 fragments from links - all of copper alloy, and 17 glass beads. Each link originally consisted of a bead threaded onto the centre of a length of wire the ends of which were bent over and wrapped around once forming closed loops articulating with loops of links on either side. Fastener has similar loop with closed hook at either end. Glass beads: seven long cylindrical wound green beads much decayed, also two fragments from a similar bead; six spherical to biconical wound beads of streaky dark blue/turquoise glass appearing opaque; three similar beads in opaque white glass; one long square-sectioned wound bead in very dark blue glass. Two pairs of links with long cylindrical green beads remain articulated with one pair articulated to necklace fastener. One blue spherical and one opaque white bead also remain articulated.
Green cylindrical - section *c*. 4mm, length 8-9mm.
Blue spherical - section 5-6mm, length 4-6mm.
White spherical - section *c*. 5mm, length 6mm.
Blue square-sectioned - section 3.5mm, length 6mm.
Length of links - 13-17mm; *W1003, C953, Room 14, Period 4.*
8. Annular bead, translucent deep blue with opaque white marvered zig-zag trail. 'D' sectioned. Section: 19mm?, length: 9mm perforation diameter: 8.5mm; *W2317, C852, Area 67, Period 4.*
9. Annular bead, colourless with opaque yellow mavered spots. 'D' sectioned. Approximately one quarter extant with parts of three spots. Section: c.?26mm, length: 7mm, perforation diameter: *c*. 12mm; *W1582, C737, Area 62, Period 4.*
10. Annular bead, streaky green appearing opaque with marvered opaque white trail. Several large bubbles appear on surface as voids. 'D'-sectioned. Section: 21mm x 20mm, length: 10mm, perforation diameter: 8mm; *W658, unstratified.*
11. Copper alloy link and glass bead. Approximately heart-shaped, diamond-sectioned, cloudy deep blue, threaded onto length of copper wire, ends of wire bent to form closed loops. Bead - section: 6.5 x 3mm, length: 6mm, length of wire link: 11mm. W1248a, C950, Room 14/15, Period 1
12. Heart-shaped bead, cloudy deep blue; diamond-sectioned. Section: 6.5mm x 3mm, 3.5mm, perforation diameter: 1.5mm; *W1164, C949, Room 14/15, Period 3*
13. Cubic bead, cloudy deep blue appearing opaque, square sectioned. Section: 4mm, length: 5mm, perforation diameter: 2mm; *W2211a, C777, Area 64/66, Period 3*
14. Short biconical bead, translucent yellow. Section: 5mm, length: 3mm, perforation diameter: 1.5mm; *W2964, C868, Area 65, Period 4*
15. Ovoid wound bead, cloudy deep blue. Section: 4mm, length: 5mm, perforation diameter: 2mm; *W1248b, C950, Room 14/15, Period 1*
16. Spherical wound bead, cloudy deep blue. Section: 4mm, length: 3.5mm, perforation diameter: 1mm; *W2944, C866, Area 65, Period 4*
17. Spherical bead, deep blue appearing opaque. Section: 3mm, length: 2mm, perforation diameter: 1.5mm; *W2211b, C777, Area 64/66, Period 3.*
18. Short cylindrical bead, translucent green. Section: 5mm, length: 3.5mm, perforation diameter: 2.5mm; *W192, F13, Period 5.*
19. Long cylindrical bead, translucent green, drawn, circular sectioned. Section: 5mm, length: 11mm, perforation diameter: 2.5mm; *W1490, unstratified.*
20. Long cylindrical bead, translucent green, rectangular sectioned. Section: 7 x 4mm, length: 14mm, perforation diameter: 3.5 x 2.5mm; *W677, C958, Area 41a, Period 4.*

## Jet beads
*by L. Bevan.*

This small group of five beads (Fig. 23, nos. 21-25) contains some unusual examples which are not easily related to common types. However, some design elements are reminiscent of jet beads from Silchester (Lawson 1976) and Colchester (Crummy 1983). The jet cylinder bead with a single transverse groove (no. 21) is a shorter version of the example given in Crummy 1983 (fig. 34:803, 32-3), which 'almost certainly' dates to the 'third to fourth century'. The 'melon-shaped' beads (nos. 24-5), apparently imitating glass beads, are less easily paralleled. The two bands of opposing incisions shown on no. 24 do not meet in the centre in the manner of a true melon bead, but the deep grooving on no. 25 is similar to that shown on the double-perforated hemispherical example from Silchester (Lawson 1976 fig. 1:4, 244-5). Neither of the Witcombe 'melon' beads have been as skilfully turned as Lawson's example, being crudely-shaped and of irregular thickness.

21. Jet bead, cylindrical with single transverse groove and circular section; *W1470, C699, Room 34, Period 2*
22. Jet bead, lozenge-shaped, facetted; *W1520, C768, Room 34/51, Period 2*
23. Jet spacer bead fragment, originally rectangular with two perforations; *W2890, C863, Area 65, Period 5*
24. Jet melon-shaped bead with incised grooves radiating from each side of perforation towards centre of bead without meeting; *W1875, C874, Area 65, Period 5*
25. Jet melon-shaped bead with deep grooves. Like W1875, above, appears to be imitating glass 'melon' bead form; *W4962, unstratified*

# PERSONAL OBJECTS

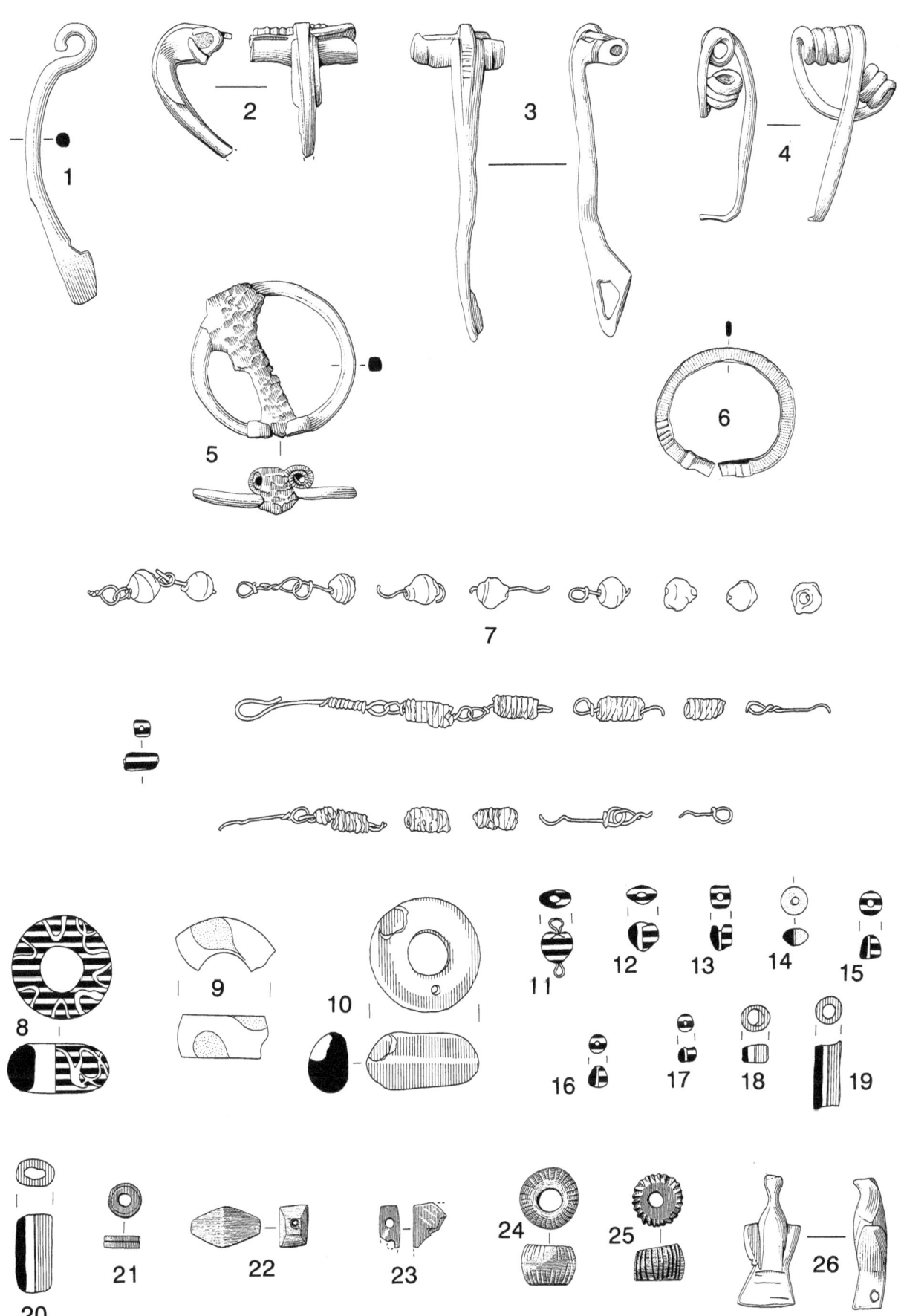

*Figure 23* Brooches, beads and pendant, nos. 1-26 (1:1)

## Bone pendant
*by L. Bevan*

The carved bone pendant in the shape of a stylized bird is unusual for several reasons including the medium used, bone as opposed to copper alloy, which it may have been painted green to imitate, and the mode of suspension from the base of the wide-fanned tail rather than from the head. Although initially the width of the tail would suggest a peacock or dove, from the low shoulders and upright bearing of the small head, it is more likely that the bird was intended to be an eagle, especially when compared with a bronze example from Chesters and a terracotta example from Chester (Green 1978, pls. 62 and 64a-b). A bronze eagle figurine from Fenny Stratford exhibits a similarly wide fanned tail (Green 1976, Pl. VIII:K, 276-7). The eagle of Jupiter, more common than his humanoid representation, has been noted in a variety of materials and forms on several military sites, while a bone eagle-plaque from a civilian context is recorded from Langton villa in East Yorkshire (Green 1978, 12).

26. (Fig.23) Pendant/amulet carved in the shape of a stylised bird with suspension hole drilled in tail. Some green staining, possibly deliberately applied in an attempt to imitate an object of copper alloy; . *W3331, C886, Area 71, Period 2* .

## Bracelets
*by L. Bevan*

Copper alloy (Fig. 24, 1-19)
The assemblage comprises fragments from 34 bracelets, many of which exhibit elaborate decoration including recurring design elements such as 'dot and ring' and notching. Notching has been used to create a beaded effect (nos. 8-12) and has also been used at the edges of bracelets enclosing a central horizontal line (nos. 16 and 17). Both forms of decoration have been combined in no. 15.

Large quantities of bracelets, many with similarly elaborate decoration have also been noted at both the Lydney and Uley shrine sites. Similar styles of decoration between these two sites and Witcombe are probably reflecting regional availability, fashion and chronology, at least. At Lydney, bracelet decoration has been dated to the 3rd and 4th century (Wheeler and Wheeler 1932, 83), At Uley the great majority were deposited in the 4th century or later (Woodward and Leach 1993, 164-166), while the majority of the highly decorated examples from Butt Road, Colchester (Period 2) date from *c.* AD 320-450.(Crummy 1983, 38-45).

The suggested votive function of the Lydney bracelets, where they might have been 'the votive offerings of the poor'(Wheeler and Wheeler 1932, 83), and similarly of the Uley assemblage (Woodward and Leach 1993, 327-8), could in part be significant in the interpretation of the Witcombe bracelets.

Plain bracelets
1. Plain bangle/armlet fragment, 'D'-shaped section; *W209, F13d, Area 41, Period ?5*
2. Flattened bracelet fragment; *W210, F13d, Area 41, Period ?5*
3. Flattened bracelet fragment with pierced terminal, oval cross-section; *W653, C652, Area 60, Period 4*
Not illustrated
Four fragments of plain bracelets; *W451, W2916, W4207, W616*

Wire bracelets
4. Wire bracelet, terminals missing; *W1460, C512, Area 47, Period 2*
5. Complete wire bracelet or necklace with linked twisted terminals and an additional loop of wire (Crummy 1983, fig. 41:1601, 38-39); *W1887, C746, Area 64/66, Period 3*

Cable bracelets
6. Part of double-strand cable bracelet with terminal hook (Wheeler and Wheeler 1932, fig.17:N); *W449, unstratified*
7. Part of large two-strand cable bracelet with one terminal hook (Crummy 1983, fig. 39:1611); *W4465, unstratified*
Not Illustrated
Seven fragments of five-strand bracelet; *W452;* three fragments of cable bracelet; *W460, W2608*; .two fragments of double-strand bracelet; *W2883, W4178*; fragments of three-strand bracelet or necklace, one with terminal loop; *W2598*

Notched bracelets
8. Fragment of flattened bracelet with notched decoration on outer edge (Crummy 1983, 43:57); *W1017, C780, Room 16, Period 2*
9. Fragment of flattened bracelet with notched decoration on outer edge; *W2873, C859, Area 68/69, Period 4*
10. Fragment of flattened bracelet with vertically-incised notches on outer edge (Crummy 1983, 41:1659; Wheeler and Wheeler 1932, fig. 17:S). *W451, unstratified.*
11. Part of a flattened bracelet with notched decoration on outer edge; *unstratified. W223,*
12 Fragment of flattened bracelet with notched decoration on outer edge, *W4170, C871, Area 65, Period 3*
Not illustrated
Fragment, flattened; *W1878*

Miscellaneous decorated bracelets
13. Fragment of intricately-decorated flattened bracelet; *W79, F13b, Area 41, Period ?5*
14. Fragment of cast bracelet with incised cross-hatched and ring decoration to outer face; *W2859, C863, Area 65, Period 5*

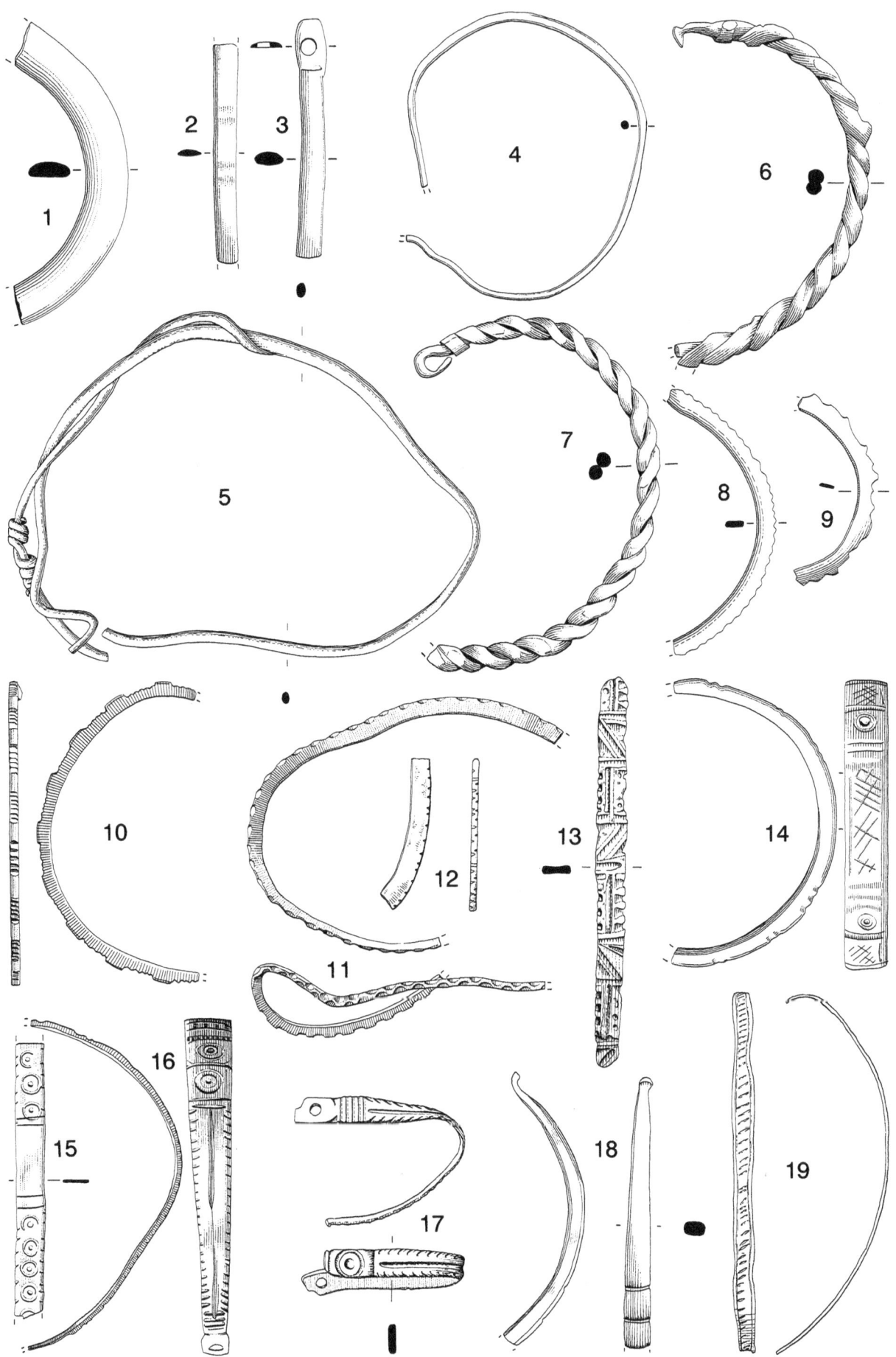

*Figure 24* Copper alloy bracelets, nos. 1-19 (1:1)

15. Fragment of flattened bracelet with alternating bands of incised dot and ring decoration enclosed by notches on outer edges. The dot-and-ring motif is more commonly found on Roman (and later) bone work, but this motif has been used on a copper bracelet in conjunction with a wave motif at Colchester (Crummy 1983, fig. 44:1704), and simple `dot-and-ring' motiffs were common in the Lydney assemblage (Wheeler and Wheeler 1932, fig. 17:E, K); *W2871, C863, Area 65, Period 5*

16. Fragment of flattened bracelet with intricate decoration consisting of incised rings, vertical bands and notching close to pierced terminal. A similar arrangement of design elements is noted at Lydney (Wheeler and Wheeler 1932, fig. 17:H) and at Colchester (Crummy 1983, 47:1725); *W212, F13d, Area 41, Period ?5*

17. Fragment of bracelet with decoration consisting of central incised line, two opposed bands of hatched grooves, ring motif and bands of vertical lines close to one pierced terminal (Crummy 1983, 47:1729; Woodward and Leach 1993, 128:13, 129:4; Wheeler and Wheeler 1932, fig. 17:D, H); *W1015, C673, Area 41a, Period 3*

18. Fragment of oval-sectioned bracelet with one hook terminal and two decorative bands; *W2872, C863, Area 65, Period 3*

19. Fragment of flattened bracelet with transverse scoring between marginal grooves (Crummy 1983, 44:1679; Woodward and Leach 1993, 128:17); *W2919, C865, Area 65, Period 4.*

Shale bracelets
Fragments of nine lathe-turned shale bracelets were recovered, (Fig. 25, nos. 1-9) six of which are from plain bangles of varying thickness (nos. 1-6). The remaining three are decorated with notching from opposing sides (no. 7), with leaf-shaped notching (no. 8) and with incised dot-and-ring motifs (no. 9). A high incidence of plain bangles of varying size and thickness has been noted at Silchester by Lawson (1976, 241-275) whose decorative repertoire has been supplemented by discoveries at Colchester (Crummy 1983, 36-7). Decorated examples from Witcombe have been related to these two studies. With the exception of no. 9, this small group is composed of the more common types identified by Crummy, types which are also represented in the large group from Uley (Woodward and Leach 1993, 166-8).

Plain bracelets
1. Shale bracelet fragment, rectangular section; *W667, C611, Room 11a/12, Period 3*
2. Shale bracelet fragment, 'D'-shaped section; *W1205, C650, Area 61, Period 4*
3. Shale bracelelet fragment, sub-circular section; *W1478, C725, Room 16, Period 2*
4. Shale bracelet fragment, circular section; *W1513, C782, Room 16, Period 3*
5. Shale bracelet fragment, oval section; *W2325, unstratified*
6. Shale bracelet fragment, sub-circular section; *W4459, C862, Area 70, Period 3*

Decorated bracelets
7. Shale bracelet fragment with shallow 'v'-shaped notching from opposing sides, square section. This is a common form of decoration on both shale and jet bracelets (eg. Lawson 1976, 6:52; Crummy 1983, 38:1560); *W1894, C746, Area 64/66, Period 3*
8. Shale bracelet fragment with shallow leaf-shaped notching set in from outer edge, rectangular section (Lawson 1976, 6:54); *W2321, C928, Area 68, Period 3*
9. Shale bracelet fragment with ring-and-dot decoration, sub-circular section. An unstratified example with smaller motifs has been recorded at Colchester (Crummy 1983, 38:1554); *W2930, C867, Area 65, Period 4*

## Pins
*by L. Bevan.*

Most pins were made from animal bone but shaft fragments of one copper alloy pin *(W1719)* and three jet pins *(W458, W1473 and W1501)* were also recovered, none of which have been illustrated.

Thirteen bone hairpins were found (Fig. 25, nos. 10-21), seven of which were complete, and a further 22 fragments of pin shafts. Whenever possible illustrated examples have been related to groups defined by Crummy (1983, 19-25), the most common at both Colchester and Witcombe being Type 3 (nos. 10-16), dated *c.* AD 200 to the end of the Roman period (Crummy 1983, 22). Four examples of Type 5 (nos. 17-20), a 4th-century type (Crummy 1983, 24), were also identified, and two examples of Type 6 (nos. 21-22) dated to the 3rd and 4th-century (Crummy 1983, 24). Five of six pins from Lysons excavations, all of which have been illustrated in Clifford (1954, fig. 21.1-5), can also be related to Crummy's groups. They are as follows; Type 3 (fig. 21.3), Type 5 (fig. 21.2,5), and Type 4 pins with a faceted cuboid head (fig. 21.3,4) dated from *c.* AD 250 (Crummy 1983, 23). The sixth example (fig. 21.6) was the lower part of a bronze human hand-headed pin, a type of pin with possible fertility connotations popular during the second half of the first century, examples of which have been discussed by Cool (1990, fig. 5.1-3, 157-158). Together with the bone pins from Greenfield's collection, the total of all pins and fragments reaches 40 items.

A high incidence of pins (and bracelets and other personal objects) as opposed to other finds categories has been noted on certain temple sites where connections have been postulated with healing cults. At Lydney such objects were offered to the god Nodens, whose healing cult was associated with childbirth (Wheeler and Wheeler 1932, 40-2). The Nodens cult was associated with healing attendant dogs, and canine representations in bronze and stone are present at Lydney, one of which (*ibid.* Pl.XXV) has been compared to the earlier discovery of a bronze dog mount at Witcombe (Clifford 1955, 50 and pl.IX).

PERSONAL OBJECTS

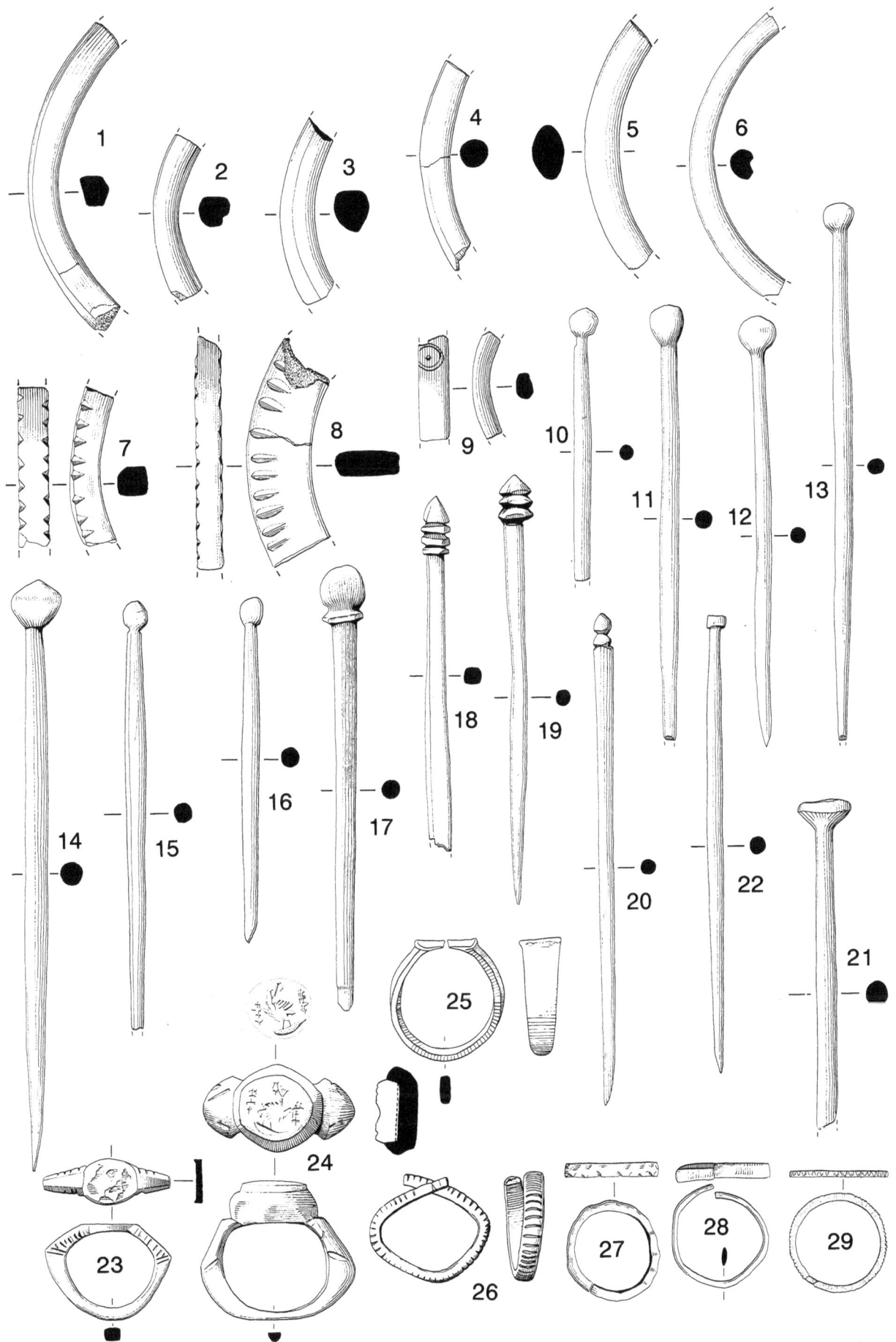

*Figure 25* Shale bracelets, bone pins and finger rings, nos. 1–29 (1:1)

Nodens was also a nature deity with aquatic associations, expressed at Lydney by the mosaic frieze of sea monsters and fish in the cella of the temple (*ibid*, pl.XIX). It is interesting to compare this with the Witcombe mosaic of fish and sea creatures from Room 6 (Clifford 1955, 19-20, plate V1).

10. Hair pin, head and shaft fragment conforming to Crummy Type 3, (1983, fig. 19:275); *W1477, C275, Room 16, Period 2*

11. Hair pin without tip. Crudely-formed head like Crummy Type 3, (1983, fig. 19:275); *W2798, C816, Room 27, Period 3*

12. Complete hair pin, similar to Crummy Type 3, (1983, fig. 19:275); *W2612, C818, Room 27, Period 3*

13. Hair pin, tip missing. Simple rounded head conforms to Crummy Type 3 (1983, fig. 19:275); *W1316, C653, Area 60, Period 1*

14. Hair pin, complete. Head conforms to Crummy Type 3, (1983, fig. 19:268); *W1467, C736, Area 62, Period 4*

15. Hair pin, tip missing, crudely-carved head set in from shaft like Crummy Type 3 (1983, fig. 19:288); *W3715, C893, Area 71, Period .*

16. Hair pin, tip missing, like Crummy Type 3 (1983). *W3332, C886, Area 71, Period 2*

17. Hair pin, tip missing. Closest parallel to this ovoid, poppy-shaped head is Crummy Type 5 (1983), although this form is more bulbous than Crummy's examples; *W1874, C758/874, Area 65, Period 5*

18. Hair pin, lower shaft and tip missing, with three carved rings beneath conical head, similar to Crummy Type 5, (1983, fig. 21:411); *W2951, C865, Area 65, Period 4*

19. Hair pin, complete, with two carved rings beneath a conical head, similar to Crummy Type 5 (1983); *W1514, C782, Room 16, Period 3*

20. Hair pin, complete. Closest parallel is Crummy Type 5 (1983) but in this instance the characteristic 'reel' shape beneath the ovoid head is also oval and only slightly smaller than the first; *W1482, C725, Room 16, Period 2*

21 Hair pin, shaft fragment with crudely-formed large reel-shaped head similar to Crummy Type 6 (1983); *W2622, C819, Room 27, Period 3*

22. Complete hair pin with single 'reel' top, a crudely carved version of Crummy Type 6 (1983, fig. 22:420); *W1497, C771, Room 51, Period 3*

Fragments not illustrated:
*W996, W1483, W1514, W2639, W2339, W2963, W1795, W1461, W429, W676, W1295, W795, W1876, W2905, W3697, W4174, W4176, W4185, W2336, W2337, W2338, W4201*

## Finger rings

### Silver (Fig. 25)
*by M. Henig*

23. Silver finger ring (SIL 1) with expanded triangular shoulders, notches cut into sides as decoration, flat oval bezel from which the setting is missing (Woodward & Leach 1993, fig.132.17). Found with SIL 2, below; *W1503, C781/F26, Room 41 ?Period 3.*

24. Silver finger ring (SIL 2) with sexagonal bezel and triangular sloping shoulders decorated with a foliate design. The bezel, which was made separately from the ring and then soldered on to it, contains an intaglio cut in orange cornelian. Condition good, although the ring has suffered some wear, particularly on the shoulders. The intaglio is a little pitted and there is a chip by the eagles' head. Crystaline impurities on the stone itself spoil its appearance but the impression of the intaglio is almost perfect. Probably manufactured in the second half of the 3rd century, although from the wear sustained by both ring and intaglio it need not have been lost for some time after that; *W1852, C781/F26, Room 41, Period 3?*

Three similar silver rings have been found at Lydney Park (Wheeler 1932, 82 and fig. 16 nos. 53-55; especially no. 54 which retains its bezel with intaglio), and another possibly found with a collection of early 4th century coins from Grovely Woods, Wiltshire (Numismatic Chron. 6, 1906, 345, fig. 1)

The intaglio represents an eagle standing left and looking right; it holds a wreath in its bill and stands upon a low pedestal. On either side is a legionary standard. Other examples of the 'Eagle and Standards' type from Britain are Hod Hill (Brailsford 1962, 20 and pl.XIVA.M2), cornelian, mid-1st century AD; Great Casterton (Todd 1968, 53 no. 18 and pl.IV), nicolo, mid-1st century AD; and Caerleon (Boon 1963, 334-5), onyx. The last is not dated but may be later and is very like the Witcombe gem in style, with its head turned to the right holding a wreath in its beak. A number of similar specimens have also been recorded on continental sites. The device clearly has a direct relevance to the Roman army (and particularly the Legions), and not surprisingly the majority of intaglios bearing it have been found on military sites.

At first glance, this find from a Gloucestershire villa is somewhat unexpected. However, there is no reason why the ring could not have belonged to an army veteran - possibly from the nearest legion to Witcombe, II Augusta stationed at Caerleon. The considerable wear on its shoulders suggests that its owner had worn it for many years (or that the ring had had a succession of owners) before its loss or deposition with the other ring? (above) at the villa.

A number of other gems show at least one standard and must likewise have belonged to soldiers; examples come from Wanborough, Aldborough and Verulamium in

Britain. Other eagles, represented without standards on intaglios, are not specifically legionary for the eagle was the sacred bird of the Roman state, par excellence, and the attribute of its chief deity Jupiter Optimus Maximus.

### Copper alloy
*by L. Bevan*

This small group of finger rings (Fig. 25) includes decorative parallels of common types known from Colchester (Crummy 1983, 45-49).

25. Ring, bezel and intaglio missing; *W211, F13d, Area 41, Period 5?*
26. Ring, pennanular with transverse grooves and 'D'-shaped section (Crummy 1983, fig. 50:1770); *W427, C508, Area 47, Period 4*
27. Ring with one break, faceted decoration, worn condition; *W1468, C736, Area 62, Period 4*
28. Ring, flattened with interrupted registers of shallow transverse grooving on outer surface; *W2884, C863, Area 65, Period 5*
29. Ring, flattened with alternating notches on the outer edges forming a wave design (Crummy 1983, fig. 50:1766); *W3689, C793, Area 65, Period 2*

Other rings (Fig. 26)

Two other copper alloy rings were recovered, the form and size of which suggests their use other than as finger rings. These two cast circular rings closely resemble examples from the large assemblage of votive 'tokens' from Uley (Woodward and Leach 1993, 135-140).

1. Ring, heavy plain triangular cross-section, diameter: 90mm; *W3690, C868, Area 65, Period 4*
2. Ring, circular, roughly-cast with sub-circular cross-section, diameter 42mm; *W1013, C656, Area 60, Period 4?*

### Glass (Fig. 26)
*by J. Price and S. Cottam*

Three fragments (nos. 3-4) come from two finger rings of dark yellow/brown glass (appearing black). These rings are uncommon, and examples in deep yellow/brown glass have not frequently been noted. A similar example with a flat oval bezel and a tolled shoulder comes from the late Roman site at Poundbury (Charlesworth and Price 1987, 109 no. 9 fig. 78), a small fragment with a band scored across was found at the temple site at Thistleton (unpublished), and two examples are known from Malton, which have a grooved band and a flat oval bezel (1927-31 excavations). There is very little dating evidence for these objects, although the example from Poundbury may indicate a late Roman date.

3. Finger ring, deep yellow-brown appearing black. 'D'-sectioned hoop expanding near bezel; pinched rib across hoop at side of flattened bezel. Approximately two-thirds of hoop and most of bezel missing. Internal diameter of hoop: c. 15mm, hoop section: 5 x 4mm; *W1903, C746, Area 64/66, Period 3*
4. Finger ring, two joining pieces, deep yellow/brown appearing black. 'D'-sectioned hoop expanding at bezel which is pinched flat with uneven upper surface. Approximately half hoop and most of bezel missing. External hoop diameter: 21mm, hoop section: 2.5 x 1.5mm; *W1904, C746, Area 64/66, Period 3*

### Toilet accessories (Fig. 26)
*by L. Bevan*

Toilet articles of copper alloy include a complete, highly-decorated manicure set (no. 5), a nail cleaner and a probe (no. 6 and 7). Previous finds included an ear probe and a spoon probe (Clifford 1954, figs. 13:1 and 16:3), the latter double-ended and more elaborate than the example shown here (no.7).

5. Complete manicure set comprising tweezers with a poppy-shaped terminal decorated with a double band of transverse grooves, upon which are pivoted a probe, nail cleaners and an ear scoop. Some additional linear decoration on the implement shafts; *W1902, C746, Area 64/61, Period 3*
6. Nail cleaner with suspension hook, shaft decorated with incised bands, tip missing; *W2898, C863, Area 65, Period 5*
7. Complete probe; *W4208, C919, Room 44, Period 3*

Chains

Seven lengths of copper alloy chain were recovered, three of which are illustrated. The possible functions of chain, both utilitarian and ornamental, have been discussed by Crummy (1983, 163).

8. Six double links of 'S'-shaped flattened copper alloy chain. *W74, F13a, Area 41, Period 5?*
9. Nine double links of 'S'-shaped flattened copper alloy chain; *W2929, C866, Area 65, Period 5?*
10. Four double links of fine figure-of-eight copper alloy chain; *W3696, C893, Area 71, Period 2*

Not illustrated: *W68, W82, W83, W1888*

Spoons

One fragment of a copper alloy silvered spoon bowl was found, the condition of which precludes illustration. Previous finds have included four spoons (Clifford 1954, fig. 16:1-4); *W660, C620, Trench A, Period 3*

### Buckles and buttons (Fig. 26)
*by L. Bevan*

11. Copper alloy 'D'-shaped buckle or strap end with square section; *W207, F13d, Area 41, Period 5?*
12. Copper alloy button, centrally perforated disc with looped wire pin and ring attachment; *W3695, C893, Area 71, Period 2*
13. Copper alloy stud, hexagonal with a raised oval boss with central indentation and single rivet on reverse. This common type is associated with horse harness (e.g. Allason-Jones 1984, 3.1870, 237), and the grooving on an example from Uley has been interpreted as a representation of the female pudenda and accorded a possible votive function (Woodward and Leach 1993, fig. 97:3). 'Pudenda' bosses of this type are usually associated with leatherwork (Woodward and Leach 1993, 111 for references); *W3333, C886, Area 71, Period 2*

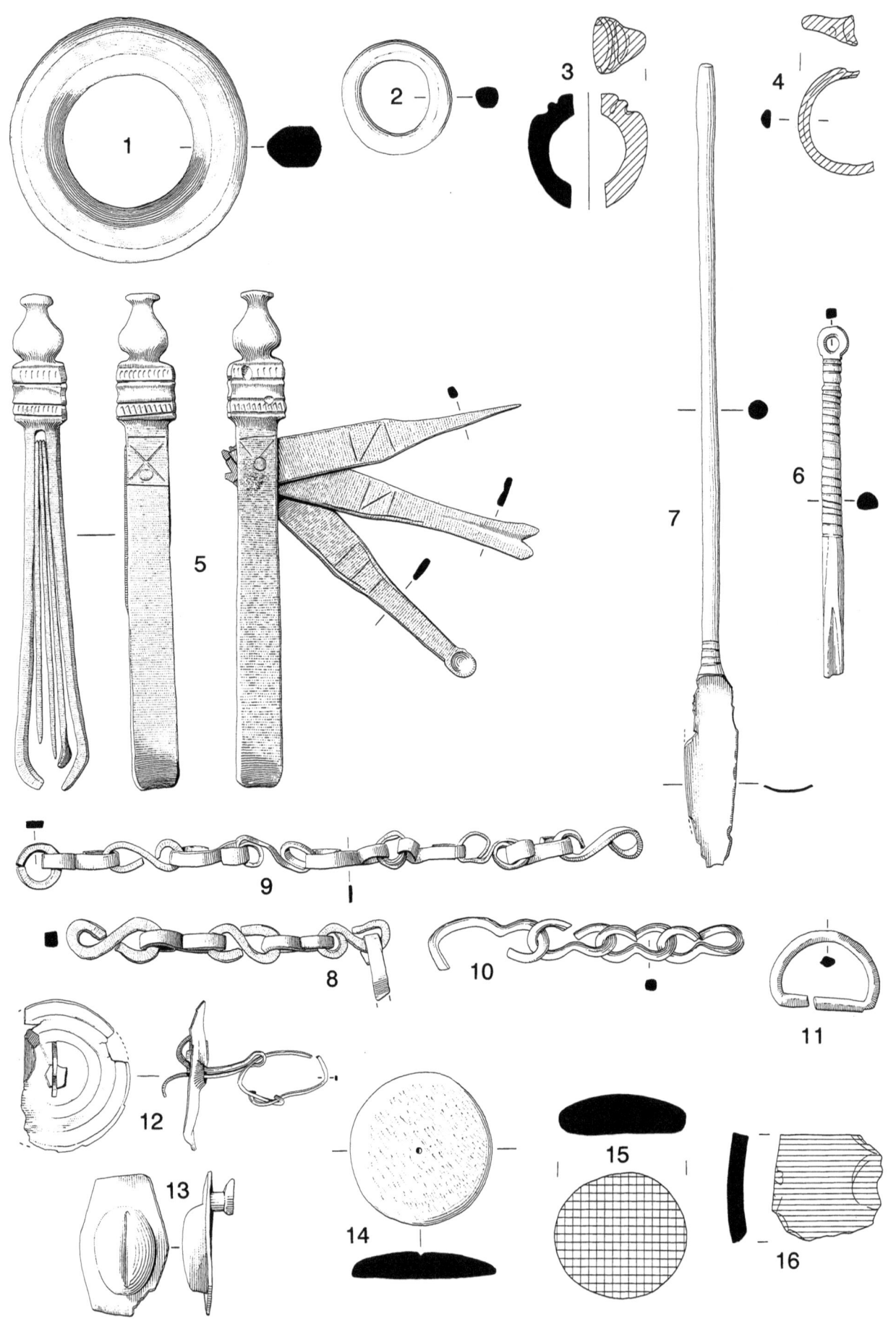

*Figure 26* Rings, toilet implements, dress accessories and counters, nos. 1-16

## Counters and gaming pieces (Fig. 26)

### Bone and pottery
*by L. Bevan*

At least five gaming pieces/counters were identified, in bone, pottery and glass. The bone example is a complete lathe-turned circular counter with a central indentation (Crummy 1983, fig. 94:2247)
14. Bone counter; *W1859, Rooms 16/41, unstratified*
Two ceramic counters are not illustrated:
Pot fabric D1, *W1673;* Pot fabric A1, *W4426*

### Glass
*by J. Price and S. Cottam*

Two gaming pieces or counters were found. Number 15 is a plano-convex counter, slightly larger and flatter than is usual, in dark purple glass, appearing black. The counter had a smooth lower surface, with occasional linear scratches, suggesting that it had been worn through use. Undecorated plano-convex counters are commonly found on Roman sites, and occasionally sets of plain or decorated pieces are found in burials. Examples are known from Lullingstone Villa (Cool and Price 1987, 139 no. 391 fig. 57), at Lankhills cemetery, Winchester (Clarke 1979, 252, 50 pl. 1b), Grange Road, Winchester (Biddle 1967) and from a burial at Ospringe (Whiting 1925, 95.XXXVII). Number 16 is a blue/green body fragment from a household flask or bottle which has been grozed on at least two sides to form a roughly square shape, possibly for use as a counter.
15. Counter, deep purple appearing black. Plano-convex with smooth undersurface. Diameter: 25 x 23mm; *W4467, C841, Room 29, Period 2*
16. Counter, slight convex-curved blue/green body fragment grozed to sub-square shape. Diameter: 20 x 20mm; *W1247, C950, Room 14/15, Period 1*

## Shoe fittings
*by L. Bevan*

A number of hobnails and shoe cleats were recovered. The largest concentrations of hobnails came from Area 65 (42) where five shoe cleats were also found, and from rooms 27 (30) and 29 (31). There were no significant concentrations which might signify footware formerly *in situ*, and the quantities and distributions suggest no particular patterns of deposition. A flue tile fragment with part of a hobnailed boot impression was found in Area 72, *W4721, C882* (not illustrated).

### 3.2.3.: THE COINS
*by J. A. Davies*

A total of 225 coins was recovered from the excavations by Ernest Greenfield; 222 of which are Roman and 3 are post-Roman issues. Full details of all the coins are provided in an accompanying coin list (in archive). A summary catalogue of the Roman issues present is published with this report. The Roman coins comprise an appreciable assemblage for a villa, although it is not exceptionally large for this category of site. It should, however, be noted that a further 49 coins were recorded by Mrs Clifford, deriving from her excavations in the West Wing of the house and from Lysons' collection at Witcombe Court (1955, 52-6); the latter possibly only part of a larger number likely to have been recovered by Lysons and Hicks. Other Cotswold villas, from this area of rich Roman settlement, have also turned up large numbers of coins, including those at Barnsley Park (653), Chedworth (309) and Frocester Court (557) (Reece 1995). In Table 5 the chronological distribution of the coins recovered by Clifford and Greenfield has been summarised within the twenty one issue periods used by Reece (1972). Figure 27 represents the Greenfield assemblage in diagrammatic form.

The earliest coin present dates to AD 194-5. Three earlier issues were recovered in the excavations of 1938-9 (Clifford 1955, 52-6) which recorded a further 74 coins (see Table 5). The subsequent small numbers representing the early and mid-3rd century reflect the low volume of coin lost on British sites at that time. As the *aes* coinage, which had been in circulation during the 2nd.century, gave way to silver during those years, less coins were subject to casual loss. Coin loss at Witcombe subsequently picked up sharply after AD 260, when large numbers of debased *antoniniani*, and their copies, entered circulation. It is the copies, popularly known as barbarous radiates, which dominate the coin total during the last quarter of the 3rd century. However, it is to the 4th century that the greatest coin numbers belong. Reece has pointed out that later 4th-century coins outnumber issues of the late 3rd century on rural sites in Britain (1979). Coins issued between AD 330 and 402 outnumber those of the years AD 259-294 by more than 2:1 at Witcombe. This is a typical trait of Romano-British villas, in contrast to urban sites, which tend to turn up roughly equal numbers of these two groups (Reece 1979). The overall pattern of coin loss recorded for the site is completely normal for a villa until the years AD 364-78, when the proportion of Valentinianic coin present is seen to be slightly high by comparison with

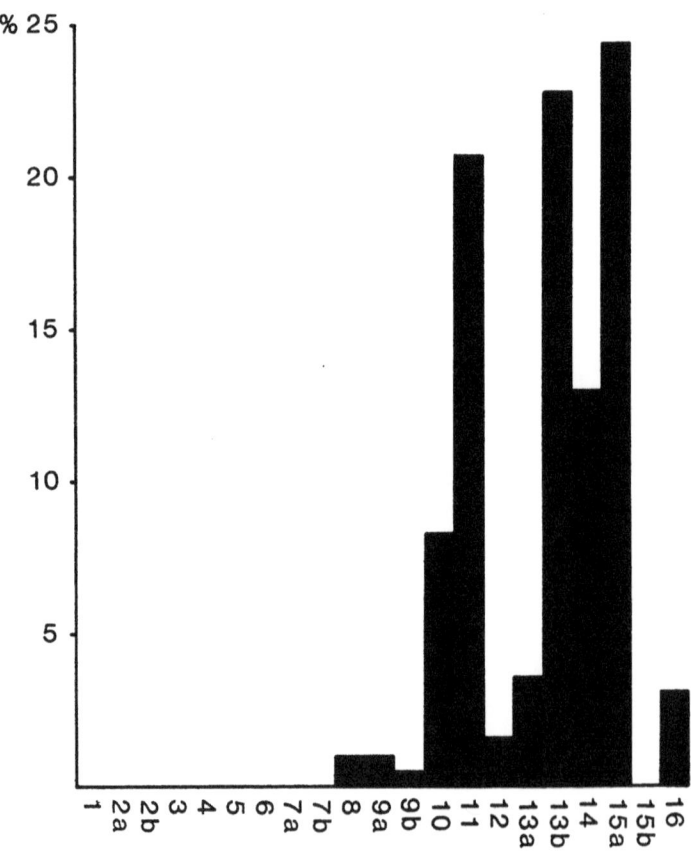

*Figure 27* Roman coins; representation by coin issue periods (after Reece 1972)

other rural sites. This trait is further emphasised by Mrs Clifford's published assemblage (1955, 52-6). Coin loss then continues through to the end of the 4th century.

A high proportion of mid 4th-century imitations have been recorded at Witcombe. Coins minted between the years AD 330 and 364 are outnumbered in a ratio of of 4:3 by irregular types. Imitations are found to predominate in this way generally on British sites (Boon 1974). The irregular coin types present have been quantified in the summary catalogue. Eighty-five genuine coins of the 4th century were present, of which 64% possess legible mint marks. These coins have been listed under their relevant mints in the summary catalogue. Trier is seen to have produced 76% of the legible coins struck between AD 317 and 364, after which Arles took over as the main source, accounting for 63% of the AD 364-78 total.

To summarise, the Witcombe coin list shows continuous, steady coin loss from the end of the 2nd century through to the very late 4th century. The heaviest period of coin loss belongs to the years from AD 330 to 378, but with particularly high loss during the third quarter of the 4th century. Overall, the assemblage from Great Witcombe can be considered to be a typical Romano-British villa group.

**Table 5: Chronological distribution of coins (issue periods 1-16 of Reece 1972)**

|  | GREENFIELD | | CLIFFORD 1938-9 | |
|---|---|---|---|---|
| Coin period | No | % | No | % |
| 1 (to AD 43) | | | | |
| 2 (43-69) | | | | |
| 3 (69-96) | | | 1 | 1.6 |
| 4 (96-117) | | | | |
| 5 (117-38) | | | | |
| 6 (138-61) | | | | |
| 7a (161-80) | | | 1 | 1.6 |
| 7b (180-92) | | | 1 | 1.6 |
| 8 (192-222) | 2 | 1.0 | | |
| 9a (222-38) | 2 | 1.0 | | |
| 9b (238-59) | 1 | 0.5 | | |
| 10 (259-75) | 16 | 8.3 | 8 | 12.5 |
| 11 (275-94) | 40 | 20.7 | 4 | 6.3 |
| 12 (294-317) | 3 | 1.6 | 1 | 1.6 |
| 13a (317-30) | 7 | 3.6 | | |
| 13b (330-48) | 44 | 22.8 | 7 | 10.9 |
| 14 (348-64) | 25 | 13.0 | 14 | 21.9 |
| 15a (364-78) | 47 | 24.4 | 25 | 39.1 |
| 15b (378-88) | | | | |
| 16 (388-402) | 6 | 3.1 | 2 | 3.1 |
| Total identifiable | 193 | | 64 | |
| Illegible C3-C4 | 12 | | | |
| Illegible C4 | 17 | | 10 | |
| Post-Roman | 3 | | | |
| Totals | 225 | | 74 | |

**Summary catalogue of Roman coins (Greenfield)**

Coins struck from AD 193 to 222
1 Septimius Severus  RIC 4: 411
1 Geta              RIC 4: 61a

Coins struck from AD 222 to 238
2 Severus Alexander  RIC 4: 178, 250

Coins struck from AD 238 to 259
1 Salonina  RIC 5: 26

Coins struck from AD 259 to 275
1 Gallienus  RIC 5: 193
2 Salonina  RIC 5: As 21, Illeg. *antoninianus*
4 Claudius II  RIC 5: 14, 19, 36, illeg. *antoninianus*
1 Postumus  Illeg. *antoninianus*
4 Victorinus  Elmer 654, 699(2) *Virtus Aug*
1 Tetricus I  Elmer 770
2 Tetricus II  Elmer 778, Illeg. *antoninianus*
1 Uncertain Gallic Empire *antoninianus*

Coins struck from AD 275 to 294
9 Carausius  RIC 5, London: 20, 98, illeg. RIC 5, 'C mint': 439; Uncertain mint: illeg. *antoninianus* (4), irreg. *antoninianus*
1 Allectus  RIC 5, London: 55
31 Barbarous radiates, individually listed in full catalogue

Coins struck from AD 294 to 317
2 RIC 6, London: 85, 125
1 Irreg. As RIC 7, Lyons: 17

Coins struck from AD 317 to 330
4 RIC 7, Trier: 316, 341, 429, 441
2 RIC 7, Lyons: 148, 198
1 Irreg. As Trier, Constantine I, *Beata Tranquilitas*

Coins struck from AD 330 to 348
5 RIC 7, Trier: 527, 530, 540, 543, 591
4 RIC 8, Trier: 111(2), 195, 206
5 Other Trier: GE1(4); Constans, *Victoriae DD Augg Q NN*
1 RIC 8, Arles: 78
1 RIC 8, Antioch: 116
4 Uncertain mint: GE2; Constantius II, GE2; GE1 x2
24 Irregular: GE2(4); Constantinopolis (5); *Urbs Roma* (5); GE1 (7); *Victoriae DD Augg Q NN* (2); Constantius II, *Victoria Augg*

Coins struck from AD 348 to 364
1 RIC 8, Amiens: 12
4 RIC 8, Trier: 220, 227, 232, 234
1 RIC 8, Arles: 219
1 RIC 8, Rome: 140
2 Illeg.mint: Magnentius/Decentius, *Salus DD NN Aug et Caes*; *FTR, FH*
16 Irregular: *FTR*, Galley: Magnentius/Decentius, *VDN Aug et Cae* (2); Magnentius, illeg.; *FTR, FH* (12)

Coins struck from AD 364 to 378
2 RIC 9, Trier: 32b, SR (uncertain emperor)
2 RIC 9, Lyons: 20a, 20c

15 RIC 9, Arles: 7d, 7/16, 7d/16b/17b, 9b(2), 9/17, 9a/17a, 9b/17b, 14a, 15(2), 16a, 17b(2), GR (uncertain emperor)
 1 RIC 9, Rome: 23c
 2 RIC 9, Aquileia: 9b,(2)
 2 RIC 9, Siscia: 5a/14a, GR (uncertain emperor)
20 Uncertain mint: Valentinian I, GR; Valens, GR(2); Valens, SR(2); Gratian, GR; Gratian, SR; Gratian, GNS; Others - GR(7), SR(2), Illeg. House of Valentinian (3)
 3 Irregular: Valentinian I, GR; Valentinian I, SR: Valens, SR

No coins struck from AD 378 to 388

Coins struck from AD 388 to 402
 1 RIC 9, Arles: 30d
 5 Uncertain mint: House of Theodosius, As RIC 9, 86 (Trier); Valentinian I, *Victoria Auggg*, Arcadius, *Victoria Auggg* (2); *Victoria Auggg* (uncertain emperor)

Other 3rd. - 4th. century coins
12 Illegible

Other 4th. century coins
17 Illegible

**Abbreviations**

| | |
|---|---|
| Irreg. | Irregular |
| Barb.rad. | Barbarous radiate |
| H of C | House of Constantine |
| H of V | House of Valentinian |
| GE2 | *Gloria Exercitus*, 2 standards |
| GE1 | *Gloria Exercitus*, 1 standard |
| 2 victories | *Victoriae DD Augg Q NN* |
| VDN Aug et Cae | *Victoriae DD NN Aug et Cae* |
| FTR | *Fel Temp Reparatio* |
| FH | Fallen Horseman |
| GR | *Gloria Romanorum* |
| SR | *Securitas Republicae* |
| GNS | *Gloria Novi Saeculi* |
| RIC | Roman Imperial Coinage, Spink 1923 |
| Elmer | Bonner Jahrbucher 146, 1941 |

## 3.2.4.: BUILDING MATERIALS, FIXTURES AND FITTINGS

### Building stone
*by L. Bevan*

As a result of previous disturbances in the area of excavation, most finds of building materials (carved stone blocks and columns, fragments of wall plaster, *tesserae* and roof and floor tiles) tend to have been re-deposited away from their place of origin and, as such are of limited value in the reconstruction of rooms.

The most common building stones were the locally-available tufa, Jurassic oolitic and Lias limestones, and sandstone, both Devonian Old Red and Carboniferous Pennant - probably from the Forest of Dean. Coarse-grained oolitic limestone was used for ashlar building blocks and slabs, some with carved decoration, and also for balustrades, doorsteps and door jambs. Finer Oolitic limestone was also used for columns and mouldings. Tufa was 'used in the core of the walls' and 'for wall facing' (Clifford 1954, 24) and possibly also for vaulting, as in the bath houses. Sandstone was used for doorsteps and door jambs, for floor paving slabs, and Clifford suggests that a finer variety resembling marble, and often painted?, was used for facing walls. A few pieces of marble were recovered; six fragments of cornice and two fragments of shelving. Microscopic examination of a piece found by Lysons identified an Italian origin as Carrara marble (Clifford 1954, 25).

Grey-blue and buff-coloured Lias limestone was also used for floor tiles, together with Old Red and Pennant sandstone from the Forest of Dean. The Lias tiles are divided almost equally between triangular and square shapes, with the occasional circular example. Old Red sandstone was also used occasionally for circular tiles. Lysons records the remnants of a floor of this type in the *triclinium* (Room 15), and the gallery (Room 14) may have been similarly floored. Settings of alternating lighter and darker tiles, probably in a chequer pattern, can be expected in these rooms. No further mosaic or tesselated floors were located by Greenfield but some loose tesserae and small mortared settings were collected.

In contrast to the high incidence of floor tiles, roof tiles known from earlier excavations to occur in 'earthenware' and, less commonly, 'Old Red Sandstone' (RCHM 1976, 61) were under-represented in Greenfield's assemblage. Ceramic tile (see below), common in the 1938/9 excavations, was apparently most widely used for roofing the villa buildings, but some rooms may have had stone tiled roofs. Pennant sandstone tiles, with triangular terminations and nail holes, are present, and were evidently popular in the region, occurring in Gloucester and Cirencester as well as at sites such as Frocester, Kingscote, Lydney or Uley.

The bulk of the material in this assemblage was collected from the South Courtyard, where substantial deposits undisturbed by previous excavators still remained. The content of many surviving layers here however suggest that they incorporated material derived from collapse or destruction of immediately adjacent portions of the villa. The presence of so many stone floor tiles, column bases and fragments, as well as stone and ceramic roof tile in Areas 41, 41a, 61, 65 and 72, is almost certainly a reflection of the former character of the Central Range and its interiors.

The material has been listed and identified with its provenance in the archive, and a selection of pieces are illustrated (Figs. 28-30), supplemented by some unprovenanced examples of column fragments housed in the building over Room 6 on the site at Witcombe, which probably came from Lyson's excavations (Figs. 28 and 29, nos.8a, 8b, 9, 10 and 11).

Fig. 28
1. Limestone column moulding; *W356, C548, Area 41*
2. Limestone column shaft moulding; *W1288, C652, Area 60*
3. Limestone column base fragment; *W1289, C652, Area 60*
4. Limestone column shaft moulding; *W1255, C650, Area 61*
5. Limestone column shaft with moulding; *W2927, C864, Area 65*
6. Limestone column shaft with moulding; *W3673, C864, Area 65*
7. Limestone column moulding; *W4455, C880, Area 72*
8a, 8b. Limestone moulded shaft and capital from a single column; *Room6 store*
9. Limestone moulded column base; *Room 6 store*
Fig. 29
10. Limestone moulded column capital; *Room 6 store*
11. Limestone moulded column base; *Room6 store*
12. Limestone column shaft with scratched grafitti; *W1855, Room 41 south-west wall*
13. White Carrara marble shelf fragment, plain; *W1760, C781, Room 41*
14. Fragment of dressed sandstone with maroon paint; *W1287, C652, Area 60*
15. Fragment of moulded limestone cornice; *W929, C658, Area 60*
16. White Carrara marble moulded cornice fragment; *W1000, C652, Area 60*
17. White Carrara marble moulded cornice fragment; *W3691, C868, Area 65*
18. Fragment of Blue Lias panel with moulding; *W3513, C867, Area 65*
19. Two fragments of moulded limestone arcade; *W935, unstratified*
Fig. 30
20. Lias limestone roof slate with fixing nail; *W1916, unstratified*
21. Old Red sandstone roof slate; *W2328, C859, Area 68/69*
22. Old Red sandstone circular floor tile; *W850, u/s,*

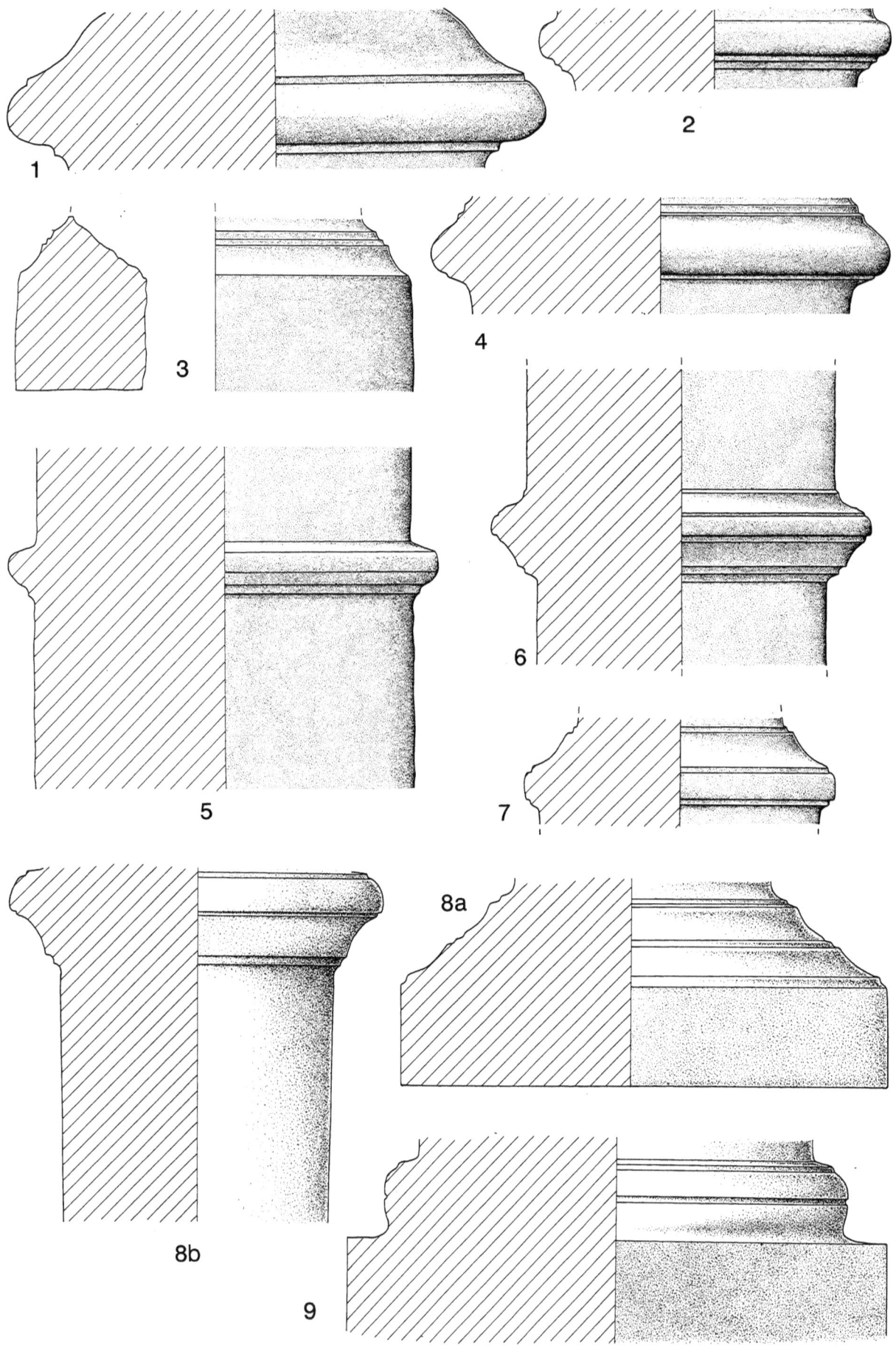

*Figure 28* Column shaft, bases and capitals, nos. 1-9 (1:4)

# BUILDING MATERIALS, FIXTURES AND FITTINGS

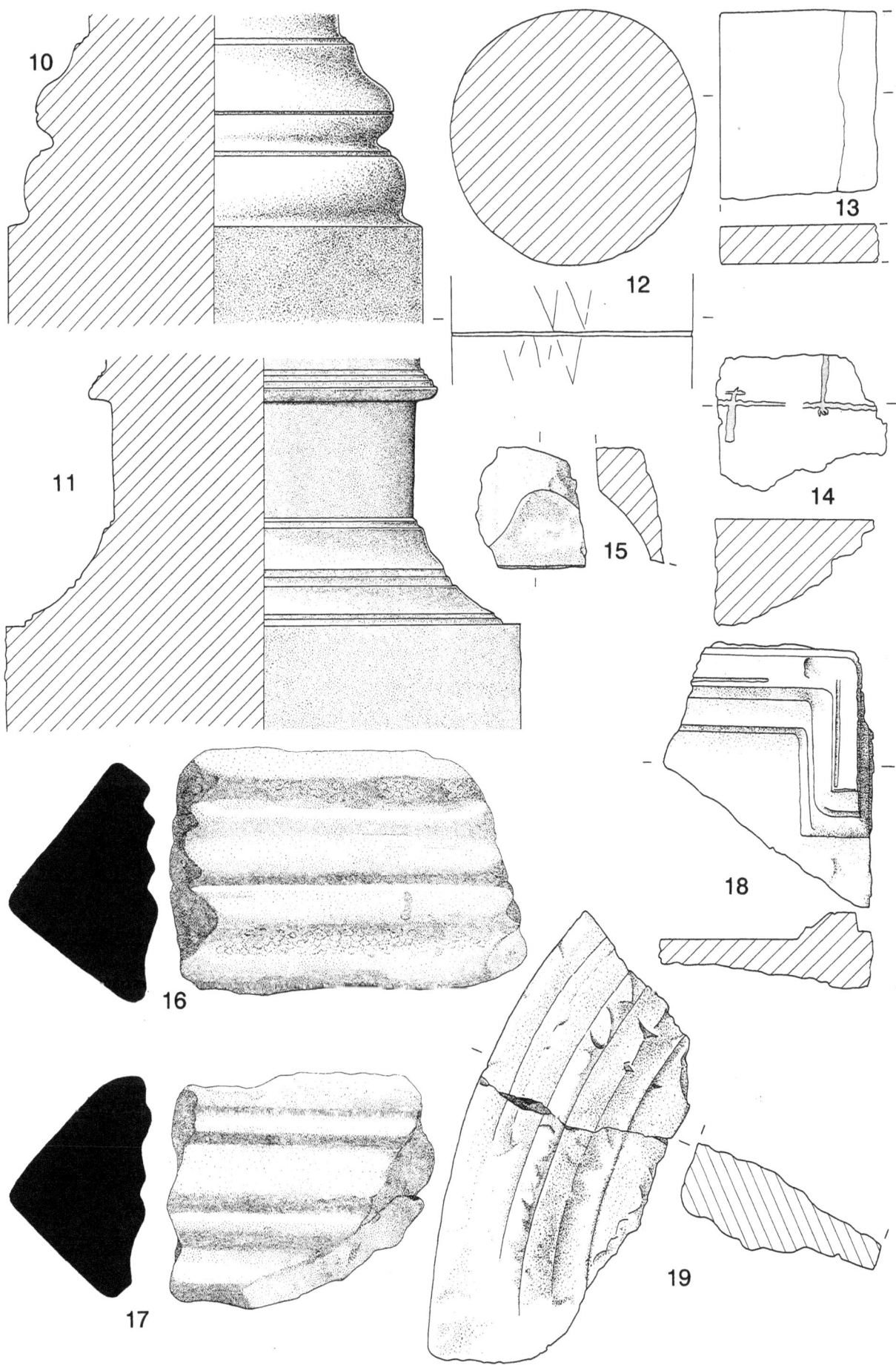

*Figure 29* Column bases and architectural fragments, stone and marble, nos. 10-19 (1:4)

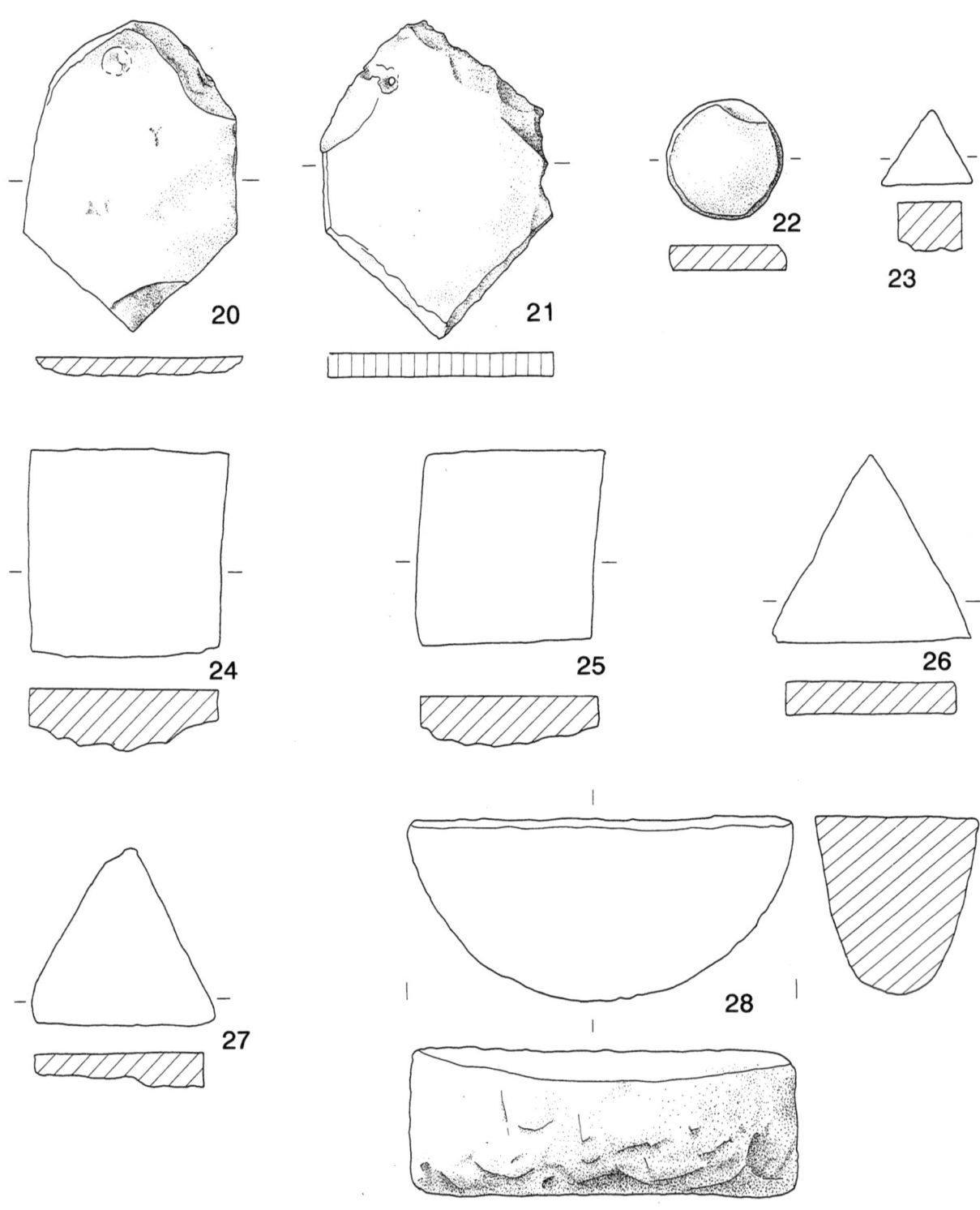

*Figure 30* Stone tiles and architectural fragment, nos. 1-9 (1:4)

*Trench A*
23. Lias limestone triangular floor tile; *W835, C620, Trench A*
24. Old Red sandstone square floor tile; *W263, F13, Area 41*
25. Lias limestone square floor tile; *W4438, C877, Area 72*
26. Old Red sandstone triangular floor tile; *W1035, C639, Area 60*
27. Lias limestone triangular floor tile; *W1034, C639, Area60*
28. Dressed, semicircular limestone block, voussoir?; *W263, F13, Area41*

## Ceramic tile and brick
*by L. Bevan*

Fired clay tile was used extensively throughout the villa and was probably the most widely used material for roofing (Clifford 1954, 24). Only a sample of *imbrex* and *tegula* roofing tile was retained by Greenfield. These tiles, particularly *imbrex*, were also commonly used to line drains. *Tegula* were used as bases for the square brick tiles forming the *pilae* supports for hypocaust floors, notably in the Lower Baths. These, and box flue tiles are still found *in situ* there, although the latter (often with combed or scored decoration) were found more widely over the site. Other roof furniture comprised one fragment of roof finial with crested decoration and a fragment of possible chimney pot (not illustrated). A tile with the imprint of a dog's paw (Area 65), and a second with the imprint of a hobnail sole (Area 72) were found. The occurrence of *tegula* wasters (Room 31 and Area 65) suggests that a tile production site may not have been far distant.

Fig. 31
1. Fragment of roof finial with crested decoration; *W4835, C856, Area 67, Period 2*
2. Fragment of imbrex with scored surface; *W3021, C859, Area 67/68, Period 4*

Not illustrated
Fragment of ?chimney pot, *W723;* roof tile fragment, *W1176;* fragments of possible roof furniture, *W3765* and *W3766*.

Two distinct kinds of surface treatment were noted on the box tile fragments; combed and scored. Combed designs include linear cross-hatched (nos. 3-5) and curvilinear examples (nos. 6-8), sometimes combined (no.9). Scoring is restricted to lattice patterns of various sizes (nos. 10-12) with the exception of one example which has two scored lines and an area of smaller 'labyrinthine' scoring (no.13).

Fig. 31
3. Box tile with combed cross hatch, two joining fragments; *W717, u/s, Area 60*
4. Box tile with combed cross hatch, two joining fragments; *W1141, u/s, Area 41a*
5. Box tile with combed cross hatch, three fragments; *W4250, C930, Area 65/72*
Fig. 32
6. Box tile with combed curvilinear design; *W939, unstratified*
7. Box tile with combed curvilinear design; *W4861, unstratified*
8. Box tile with combed curvilinear design; *W1141, u/s, Area 41a*
Fig. 33
9. Box tile with combed curvilinear designs enclosed within a cross hatched border, three joining fragments; *W3228, C865, Area 65*
10. Box tile with scored lattice decoration; *W1848, F22c*
11. Box tile with scored lattice decoration; *W1694, C725, Room 16*
12. Box tile with scored lattice decoration; *W1695, C725, Room 16*
13. Box tile with scored linear decoration; *W1006, C653, Area 60*

## Plaster and mortar
*by P. Leach*

A substantial quantity of unattached painted wall plaster was recovered during Greenfield's excavations, of which a basic record was made, but at the time of reporting the bulk of this could not be located. In consequence, no detailed analysis of this material was undertaken, but some assessment of its distribution and potential significance is made on the basis of the excavator's record. One exception was a group recovered from a drain in the South Courtyard and held by the Ancient Monuments Laboratory, English Heritage. This was restored as part of a decorated plaster ceiling (below), and is published separately (Davey and Ling 1982, 199-200, XCIX and fig. 54). Very little wall plaster remained *in situ* by the time these latest excavations took place, although Lysons recorded substantial portions, notably in the West Wing, most of which was subsequently destroyed by weathering. The walls of Room 1 were covered in pink stucco and different coloured panels, while in Room 2 panels outlined in orange/yellow and pale blue on a white ground were divided by intervals decorated with ivy leaf candelabra (Davey and Ling 1982, 218-9). Many rooms of the Lower Bath Suite were also plastered, some of which still survives where protected by the covering buildings. The hot bath Room 10 was plastered dark red, while the cold plunge baths in Rooms 7 and 7a were lined by grey-blue and pale green-buff plaster, respectively. In the latter, fragments of plaster painted with fish and recovered from cracks in the floor, may represent the decoration on the walls above. Rooms 5 and 6 also had plastered walls painted in panels and the other rooms in this bath suite were probably similarly decorated. Mrs. Clifford found parts of two pottery vessels used as paint pots and an oyster shell used as a palette beneath the floor in Room 1, all with traces of paint adhering (Clifford 1955, 17 and 60).

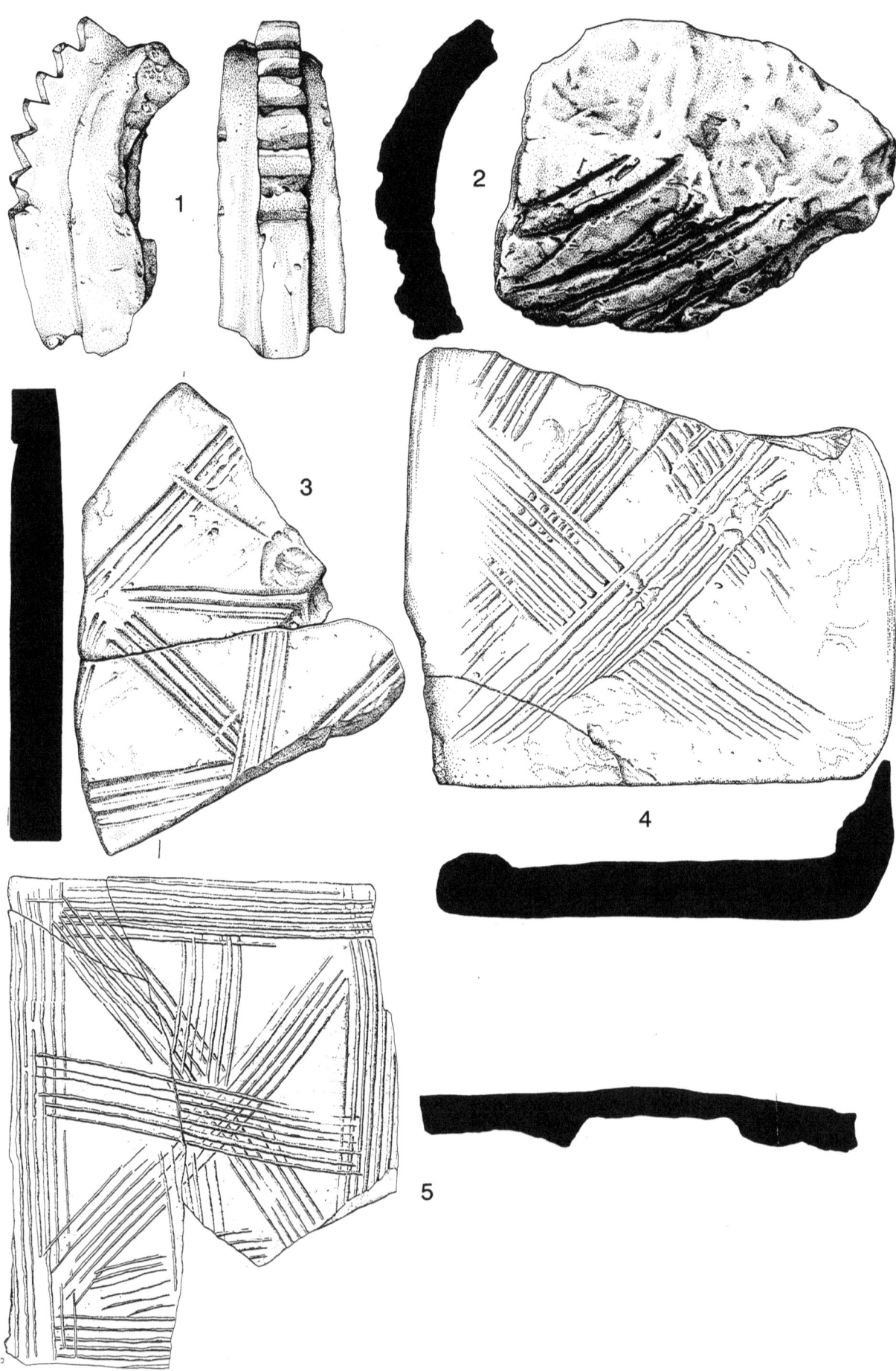

*Figure 31* Clay roof tile and incised box tiles, nos. 1-5 (1:2)

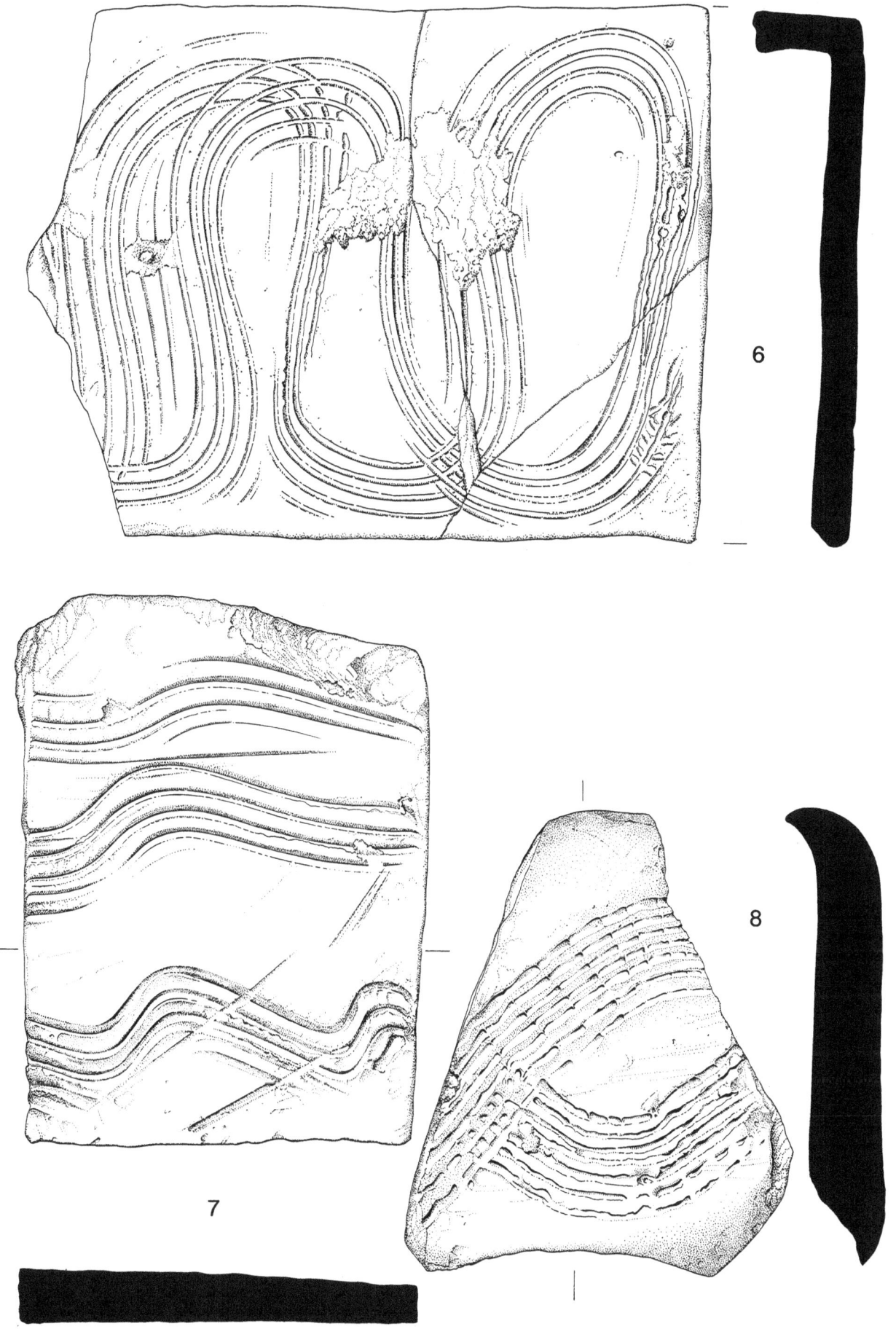

*Figure 32* Incised clay box tiles, nos. 6-8 (1:2)

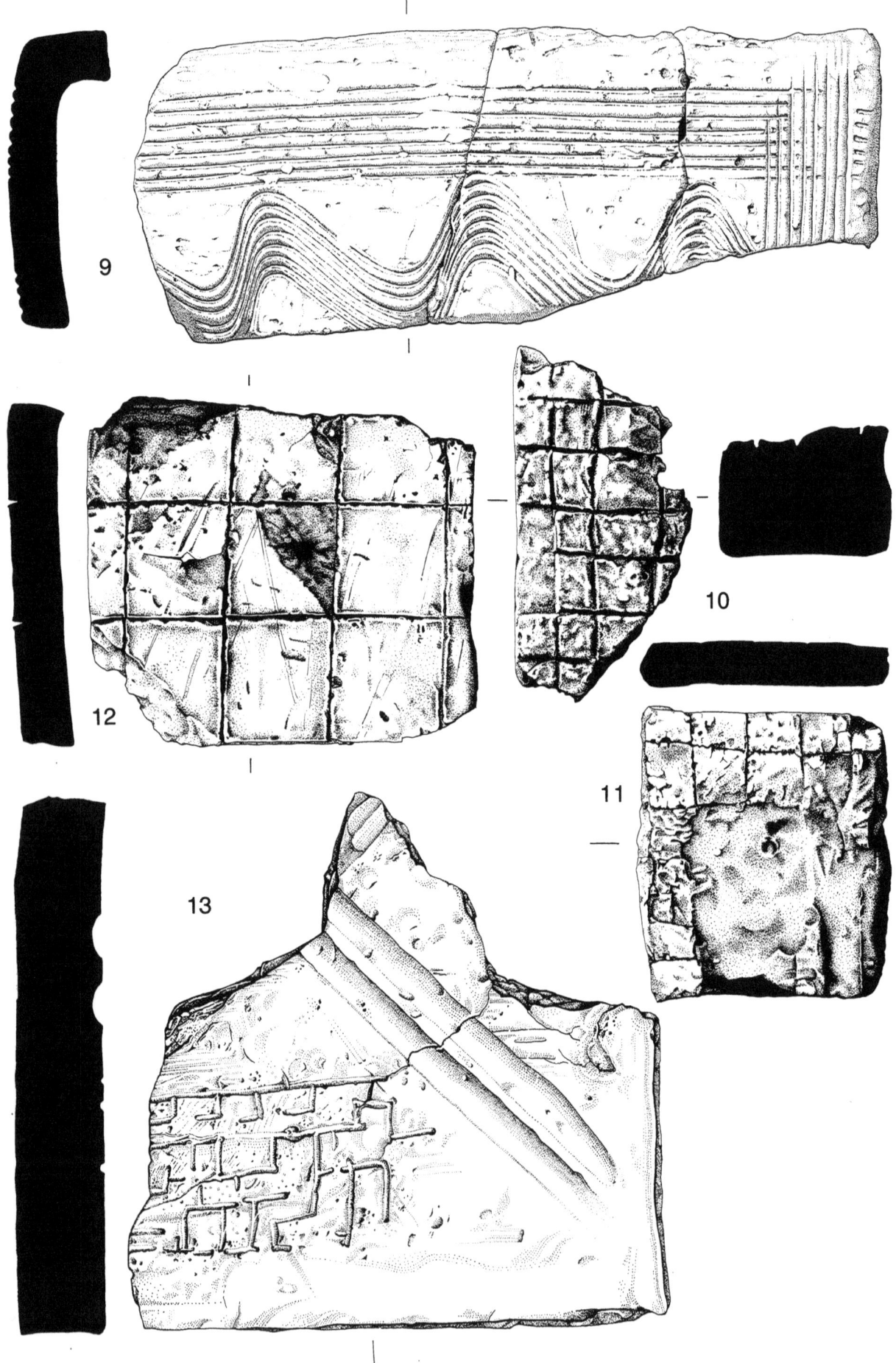

*Figure 33* Incised clay box tiles, nos. 9-13 (1:2)

The extent of painted wall plaster and its design elsewhere within the villa is less certain. No other portions are recorded *in situ*, but some inferences can be made from surviving detached fragments, particularly when associated with rooms. The Upper Bath Suite was almost certainly decorated with painted plaster, and though less well preserved than the Lower, the plunge bath in Room 45 was lined with cream and grey plaster, while Clifford recorded pink plaster from Room 34. Wall painting on plaster can be anticipated in at least some rooms of the Central Range and was recovered by Greenfield. Fragments of maroon red plaster and some moulded corners from Room 15/15a may hint at one of the colours and the decoration used in this dining room. Nothing was recorded from the corridor or verandah (Room 14), but a substantial quantity of plaster survived in Room 16, some of which may derive from the corridor above or the adjacent entrance rooms (Rooms 41-43 and 52). This collection included fragments of painted panels, speckled decoration, leaf decorated friezes and some moulded pieces.

Some of the largest collections of plaster came from the South Courtyard, notably from Areas 41, 41a and 65, and to a lesser extent Area 72. One collection from the drain F11 has been restored (above) as part of a decorated ceiling of square panels on white, framed by garlands with sprigs and berries, alternately pale green and ochre. Alternate panels contain double roundels painted purple (outer) and pale green (inner), surrounding plant whorls or rosettes. The panels without roundels contained central ornamentation representing a bowl or shield in one case, and possibly a *ballista* in another. The original location of this ceiling is uncertain, although a similarly decorated fragment recovered by Mrs. Clifford suggests a room somewhere in the West Wing. Other pieces from the South Courtyard area included panel borders and larger areas in pink, pale blue, green, red, purple, yellow and blue/black, as well as cream or white and speckled designs. Much of this probably derived from the Central Range, mixed with other architectural fragments of stone and tile. Concentrations of plaster in Trench A and Area 61 may have come from the Lower Baths, but the density of fragments generally decreases away from the Central Range. The sparsity of wall plaster recorded in the East Wing suggests that few of these rooms were so decorated, and no significant amounts were recovered from adjacent exterior areas to the south or east. The only substantial quantity was recovered from Room 29, but here wall plaster and mortar was evidently reused as floor foundation, presumably deriving from some other room in the villa. Although many of the rooms in the South East Range were well preserved when cleared by Lysons, his failure to mention wall plaster surviving *in situ*, as well as the remains of industrial activity there, is probably good negative evidence.

A catalogue of the wall plaster in the archive lists its recorded contexts by Room or Area and Period. None is illustrated here.

## Window glass
*by J. Price and S. Cottam*

Approximately 33% of the total glass assemblage from the excavations is window glass (104 fragments). Eighty of these came from cast matt/glossy window panes of 1st-3rd century date in blue/green, pale green and colourless glass. The predominance of this form of window glass when compared to the small number of bottle fragments among the vessel glass is hard to explain, as these glass items are broadly contemporary.

Cast panes were probably produced by pouring molten glass into wooden trays, forming the characteristic matt/glossy surfaces (Boon 1966, 43-4). Several of the edge fragments show tooling marks where the molten glass was pushed to the edge of the tray. One fragment has a grozed edge where the pane has been shaped, possibly to fit a frame. Cast panes with grozed edges were found at the bath house at Garden Hill, Hartfield, Sussex (Harden 1974, 280). Only 24 fragments came from blown window panes (Harden 1961), indicating that very few 4th-century window panes were in use.

None is illustrated but a summary catalogue lists the material by type, with reference to site find number and location.

Blue/green cast matt/glossy (54 fragments)
Area 41: *W192-7*; Trench A: *W731*, *W766* (x3, 1 with rounded edge), *W837*, *W849* (x5, 1 rounded edge); Area 41a: *W930*, *W1352*; Room 14/15: *W879 and W1165* (1 rounded edge); Room 15/15a: *W1091* (1 rounded edge); Room 14: *W1309 and W1339* (x4); Room 16: *W1506* (x3), *W1659*, *W1867*; Room 53: *W1813*; Room 27: *W2605*, *W2790*, *W2815*; Room 11a: *W3716* (rounded edge); Area 65: *W1994*, *W2910* (x2, 1 rounded edge), *W2961*, *W2978*, *W3702* (worn rounded edge), *W3703*, *W3708*, *W4107-8*, *W4188*, (1 edge grozed), *W4192*, *W4680*; Area 66: *W2057*; Area 64/66: *W2109*, (x3), *W2268* (x2, 1 rounded edge); Area 67: *W4826*; unstratified: *W2914*, *W4223*, *W4989*.

Clourless cast matt/glossy (8 fragments)
Room 14/15: *W1191*; Room 29: *W2915*; Room 44: *W4246*; Area 62:, *W1618*; Area 65: *W2961*, *W4175*; Area 67: *W2417-20* (rounded edge); unstratified: *W4226*.

Pale green cast matt/glossy (18 fragments)
Room 15/15a: *W780*; Room 27:, *W2604* (x2); Room 27/29: *W2753*; Trench A: *W599*; Area 41a: *W709*; Area 41a/72: *W1424*; Area 61: *W893*; Area 62: *W1584*, *W1618*; Area 65: *W1994* (x2); Area 64/66: *W2109* (x2); Area 68/69: *W2524*; Area 72: *W4196*; unstratified: *W613*, *W2757*.

Pale green blown double glossy with elongated bubbles (24 fragments)
Room 14/15:, *W1166*; Room 16: *W1517* (x2); Room 34/51: *W1935*, (1 rounded edge); Room 26: *W2600*; Room 27: *W2781*; Area 64/66: *W2109*; Area 65: *W2901*

(1 rounded edge), *W2910* (x2), *W2913* (1 rounded edge); *W2934* (x3); *W2956* (x3, 1 rounded edge); Area 67: *W2417-20* (1 rounded edge); Area 68/9: *W2877*; Area 72: *W4194, W4196, W4230,* W4479.

## Door furniture
*by L. Bevan*

Two keys and part of an iron barrel padlock were recovered (Fig. 34). The copper alloy key (no. 1) probably originated from a small lock for a box or cupboard (Crummy 1983, 123). The iron key and padlock part (nos. 2-3) were from heavier, probably external, doors to dwellings or storage areas. Two complete iron keys were found during earlier excavations (Clifford 1954, fig. 15, 1-2).

1. Copper alloy lever-lock key with cut-out decoration on suspension loop; *W1474, C725, Room 16, Period 2*
2. Iron lift key, originally 'T' or 'L' shaped, terminal missing. Short handle ends in eye like Manning 1985 (pl. 40:O36); *W3722, C879, Area 71, Period 3*
3. Central component of iron barrel padlock; *W290, F13, Area 41, Period 5*

## Nails and miscellaneous iron fittings
*by L. Bevan*

All ironwork associated with structures and building works has been grouped in this category and includes a variety of clamps and brackets, plates, pins and spikes, collars and ferrules, and nails. Whilst no detailed discussion is attempted here, all items have been included in the archive catalogue and a small selection are illustrated (Figs. 34 and 35). All the nails examined will have been used for masonry and heavy timber and most conform to Manning 1985, Types 1a and 1b. Types 7 and 9 were also present in small numbers, both categories 'probably used in upholstery work' (Manning 1985, 135).

Fig. 34
4. Pipe joint collar; *W926, C658, Area 60*
5. T-shaped clamp; *W4198, C878, Area 72*
6. Pipe joint collar; *W2322, C928, Area 68*
7. Looped band; *W2215, C777, Area 64/6*
8. Split pin with link; *W3720, unstratified*

Fig. 35
9. Clamp; *W463, C666, Room 7*
10. L-clamp used in building (Manning 1985, pl. 62.R73); *W596, C622, Trench A*
11. Hinge plate; *W322, C548, Area 41*
12. Linch pin (Manning 1985, Type 2b, pl. 31.H41/H42); *W596, unstratified*
13. Hasp plate with nail; *W2216, C777, Area 64/66*

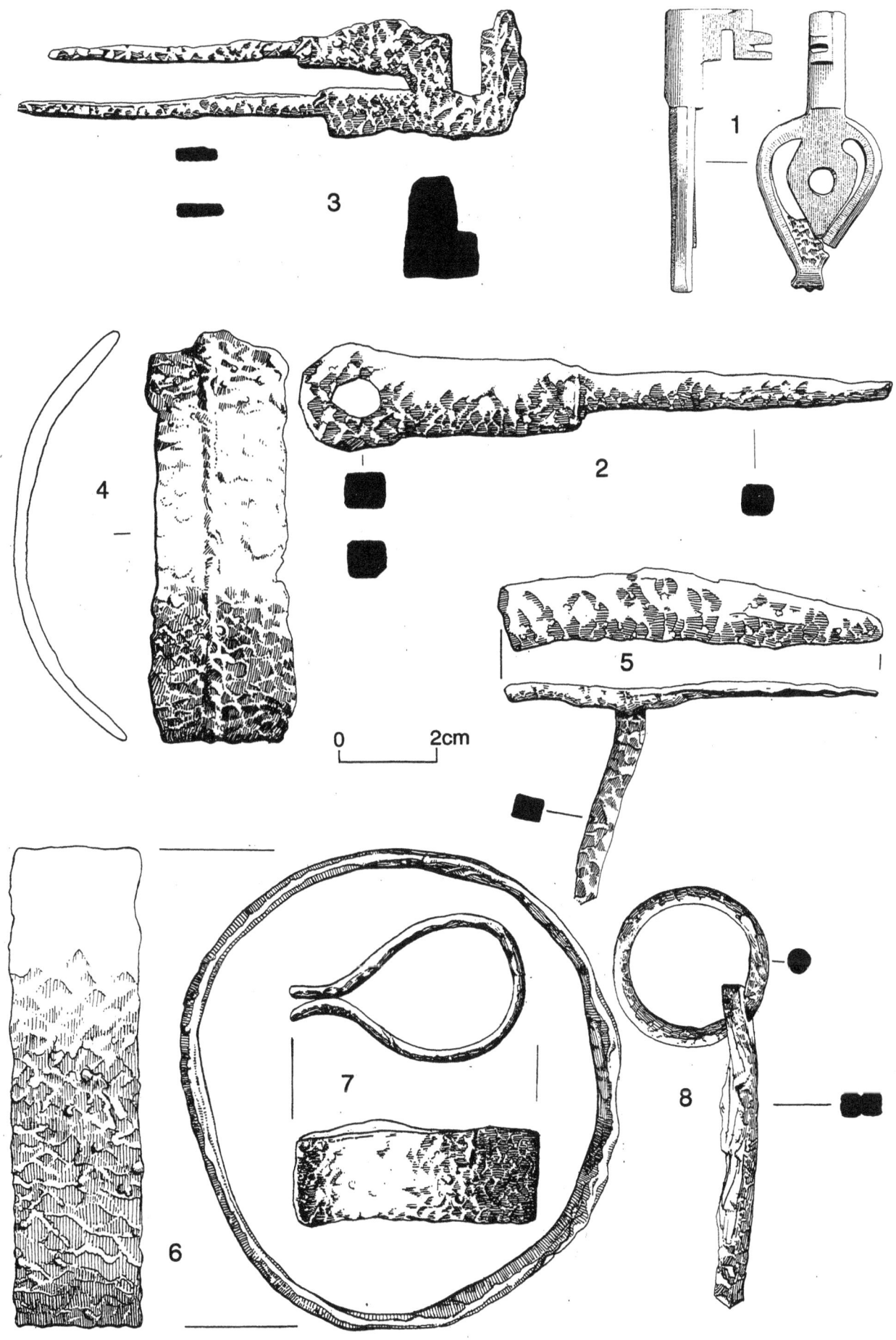

*Figure 34* Keys, lock and iron building fixtures, nos. 1-8

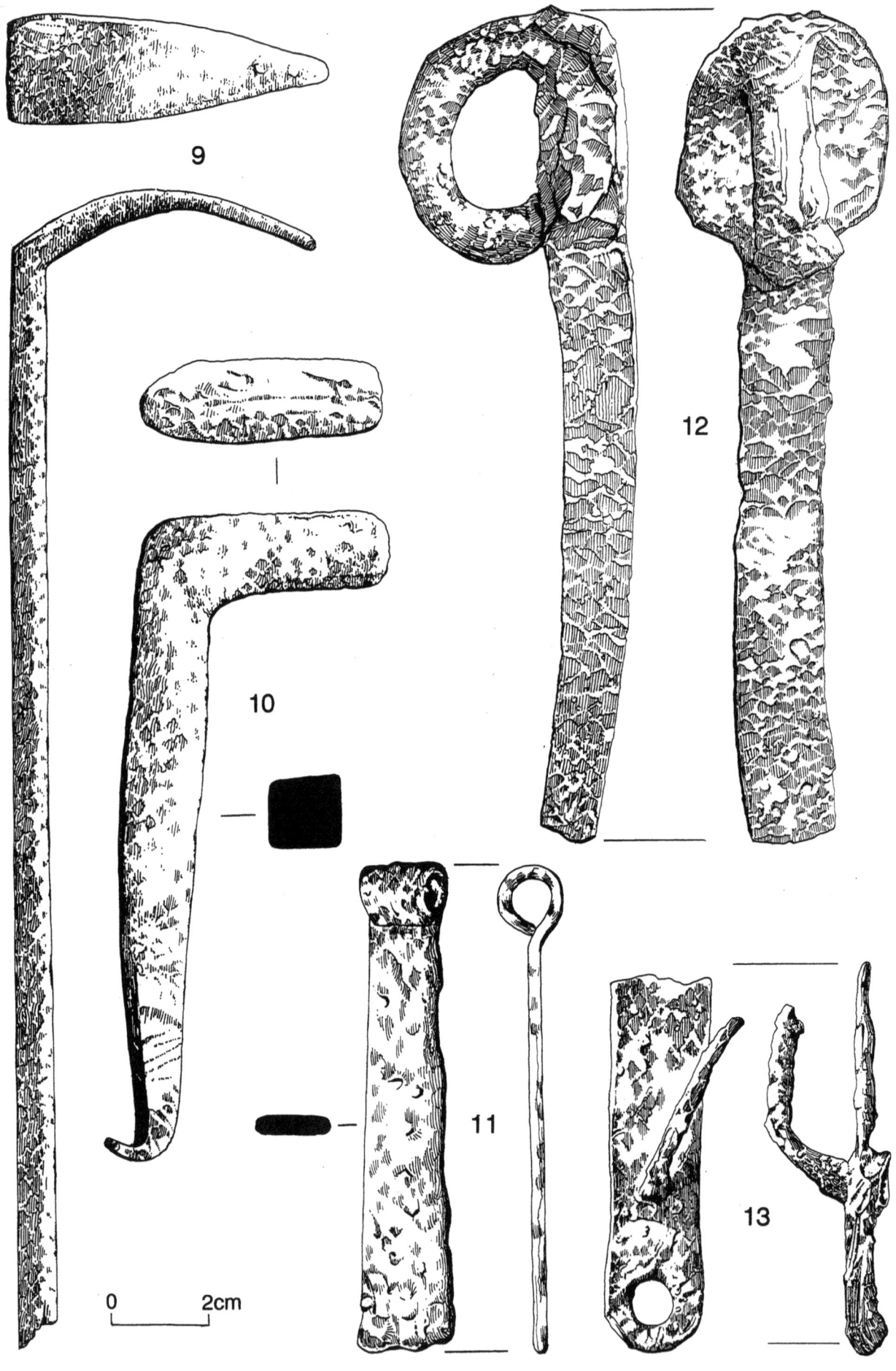

*Figure 35* Iron Building fittings and fixtures, nos. 9-13

# 3.2.5.: DOMESTIC TOOLS, UTENSILS, FITTINGS

## Whetstones
*by L. Bevan*

Nine whetstones, including three fragmentary examples, were found, eight of which have been illustrated (Figure 36). All appear to correspond with the 'waterworn pebbles' and 'slab'-shaped whetstones identified at Uley made from Palaeozoic sandstone (Roe 1993, 197-8). At Witcombe there is a single example of the slab-shaped type, probably made from the same type of sandstone as the Uley examples (no. 5); the remainder of the collection are either wide rectangular or narrow rod-shaped pebbles. With one exception, a waterworn pebble of siltstone with quartz veins (no. 2), the remainder are made from a fine-grained micaceous grey-green sandstone, possibly from the Forest of Dean.

1. Whetstone made from rectangular pebble. ?Pennant sandstone; *W749, C621, Trench A, Period 2*.
2. Pebble whetstone of ?Pennant siltstone with quartz veins, waterworn; *W2623, C879, Room 27, Period 4*.
3. Rod-shaped pebble whetstone, half extant, fine grey micaceous sandstone ?from the Forest of Dean; *W4878, C918, Room 44, Period 3*
4. Whetstone of ?Kentish Rag; *W708, C655, Area 60, Period 3*
5. Slab-shaped whetstone of ?Palaeozoic sandstone; *W3526, C867, Area 65, Period 4*
6. Rod-shaped whetstone of ?Kentish Rag, two joining pieces; *W2889, C863, Area 65, Period 5*
7. Half whetstone with rectangular section, fine grey-green micaceous sandstone ?from the Forest of Dean; *W3795, C891, Area 71, Period 4*
8. Half whetstone with rectangular section, fine grey-green micacious sandstone ?from the Forest of Dean; *W3706, C891, Area 71, Period 4*
Whetstone fragment; *W1634, C746, Area 64/66, Period 3* (not illustrated)

## Querns, millstones and rubbers
*by L. Bevan*

This group comprises one complete bottom rotary quernstone, another almost complete in two joining pieces and 57 fragments; the majority from rotary querns, although at least one fragment of a millstone can be identified (Figs. 36-7). The largest concentration was from Room 27 where one almost complete quern, the millstone and 34 other fragments were found; the majority reused as paving. No precise geological identifications have been made, but the millstone and possibly all of the other querns were made of a medium pink-red conglomeritic sandstone with quartz pebbles; probably derived from Old Red sandstone formations in the Forest of Dean. The measurable rotary quern fragments, from upper and lower stones, varied between c 350-520mm in diameter. The millstone fragment could not be measured exactly but may have had a diameter of 680mm. The following selection are illustrated, the remainder are catalogued in the archive according to their locality and context.

A small collection of stone pebbles with signs of secondary use were probably utilised as rubbers/polishers or pounders, one of which is illustrated (no. 11)

Fig. 36
9. 1 lower rotary quernstone in two joining pieces, diam. 400mm.; *W2839, C817, Room 27*
10. 1 half of a lower rotary quernstone, diameter 420mm.; *W2840, C817, Room 27*
11. 1 circular sandstone rubber, one face smoothed; *W2112, C746, Area 64/66*

Fig. 37
12. 1 damaged half of an upper rotary quernstone, diameter 520mm.; *W2841, C817, Room 27*
13. 1 segment of a millstone with bands of parallel grooves on the grinding surface, diameter approx 680mm.; *W2842, C817, Room 27*
14. 1 complete lower rotary quernstone reused as a coverstone for drain F23, diameter 420mm.; *W1519, C770, Room 51*

## Knives, handles, projectile heads, iron tools, utensils and implements
*by L. Bevan*

Knives and handles (Figs. 38-9)
1. Iron blade and tang, almost complete, Manning Type 11a (1985, 114), similar to an example from Hod Hill dated to the mid-first century (Brailsford 1962, pl. 54: Q34); *W1495, C726, Room 16, Period 2*
2. Iron, with long tang, tip of blade missing, Manning Type 11a (*ibid*); *W1633, C746, Area 64/66, Period 3*
3. Iron, with leaf-shaped blade and long tang (Manning 1985, Type 21, 116), similar to an example from Uley with a bronze terminal ferrule (Woodward and Leach 1993, fig. 144:4, 192-3); *W1912, C776, Area 64/66, Period 3*
4. Complete iron blade and tang, conforms to Manning Type 18b (1985, pl. 55:Q57, 117); *W2333, C854, Area 67, Period 3*
5. Iron blade and tang fragment, possibly Manning Type 24 (1985, pl. 56 ?Q79), characterised by 's' curvature still visible in this incomplete fragment; *W2214, C777, Area 64/66, Period 3*
6. Two fragments of a complete iron knife, tang bent into a loop; *W2979, unstratified*
7. Cleaver blade fragment, a generally convex type suggestive of Type 2a (Manning 1985, 122); *W1183, C648, Area 61, Period 2*
8. Iron blade (tip missing) with tang; *W2334, C854, Area 67, Period 3*
9. Part of an iron blade attached to a fragment of antler bone handle by a rivetted copper alloy ferrule with notched decoration on one edge; *W1872, C758, Area 65, Period 5*
10. Bone knife handle fragment, lathe-turned with bands of grooved decoration (*cf* Woodward and Leach 1993, fig. 144.8); *W1657, C726, Room 16, Period 2*

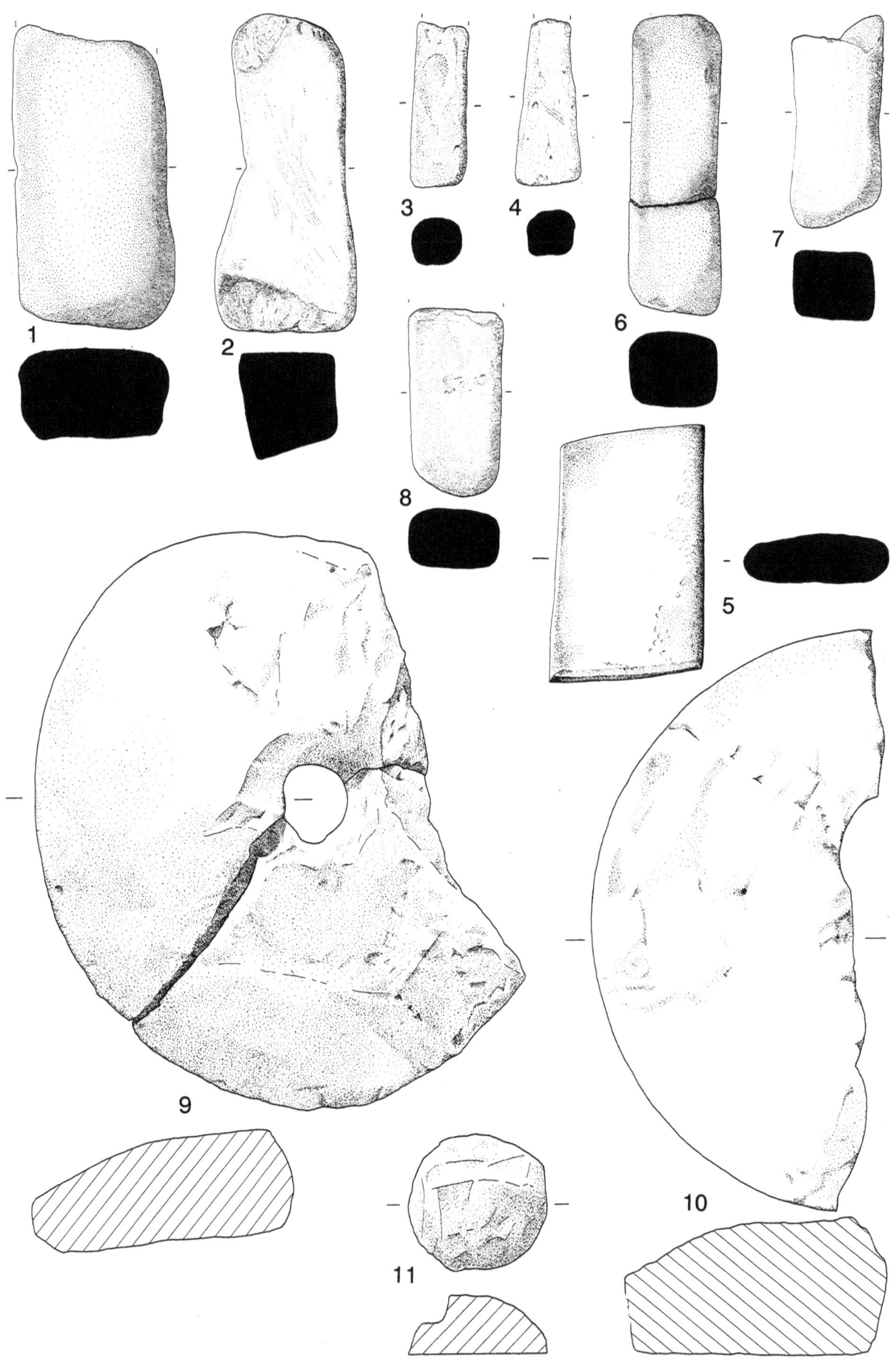

Figure 36 Whetstones (1:2), rubber and quernstones (1:4), nos. 1-11

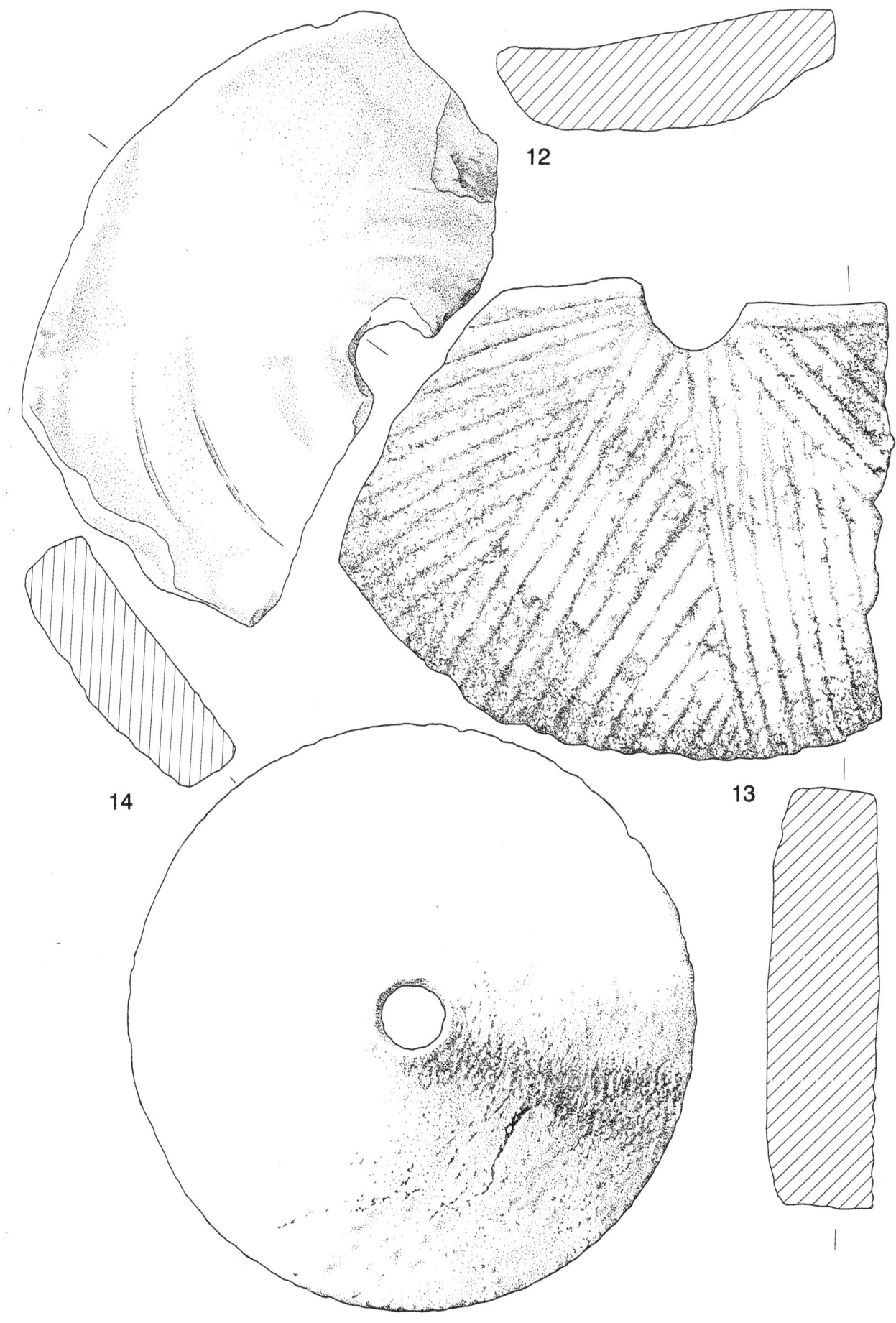

*Figure 37 Quern and millstones, nos. 12-14 (1:4)*

11. Bone knife handle, large plain fragment retaining part of socket; *W4400, C871, Area 65, Period 3*

Projectile heads (Fig. 39)
12. Bolt or arrowhead, with a long socketed shank and triangular head; probably Manning Type 1 (1985, V281, 177-8, pl. 85); *W218, F13d, Area 41, Period 5*
13. Spear or arrowhead, socketed, with narrow elongated barbs close to the shank. Similar to Manning's Type 1 but the excessively long barbs are unusual (1985, 177); *W1885, C1002, Area 66, Period 4*
14. Arrowhead, trilobate head with short tang conforming to Manning's Type 11 (1985, V282, 177-8, pl. 85). A barbed example from Hod Hill, Dorset dates to the mid-first century, but both barbed and unbarbed examples may continue in use as late as the fourth century; *W4165, C864, Area 65, Period 4*

Iron tools, utensils and implements (Figs. 39-40)
15. Hammerhead; *W1346, C654, Area 60, Period 5*
16. Punch, a common form used by smiths (Manning 1985, pl. 6: A31, A32, 10); *W2212, C777, Area 64/66, Period 3*
17. Punch, a blunt form used in leatherworking (Manning 1985, pl. 16: ?E29, 41); *W2104, C746, Area 64/66, Period 3*
18. Firmer chisel, a general-purpose type used by carpenters (Manning 1985, fig. 4:4, 22); *W1883, unstratified*
19. Paring chisel, characterised by a wide, thin blade and used by hand or shoulder pressure (Manning 1985, fig. 4:1, 21); *W1577, C737, Area 62, Period 4*
20. ?Wedge, badly corroded; *W2701, unstratified*
21. Ox goad fragment, spirally-socketed; *W2107, C746, Area 64/66, Period 3*
22. Socket of reaping hook or sickle, pierced for attatchment to handle; *W501, C578, Room 9, Period 3*
23. Implement shaft, ends missing, possibly an awl; *W884, C649, Area 61, Period 4*
24. Skillet or ladle, part-bowl/handle fragment; differs from example given in Manning 1985 (pl. 50, 33) in having a plain rather than a 'twisted' handle; *W927, C658, Area 60, Period 4*
25. Small ?spatula, ends of blade and stem missing. Similar to Manning 1985 (pl. 70: S134a/b) but without a 'twisted' stem characteristic of ?hearth implements. Alternatively, this is the eraser and shaft of a stylus; *W652, C646, Area 60, Period 4*
26. Hook, possibly part of ?meat suspension hook or fish hook. Similar in shape to a possible fish hook found in earlier excavations (Clifford 1954, fig. 19:2). *W78, F 13a, Area 41, Period 5*
27. Flesh hook with two tines, plain undecorated stem; *W2666, unstratified.*
28. ?Flesh hook, thick central shaft largely missing, with three tines arranged in 'trident' form; *W3734, C856, Area 67, Period 2*

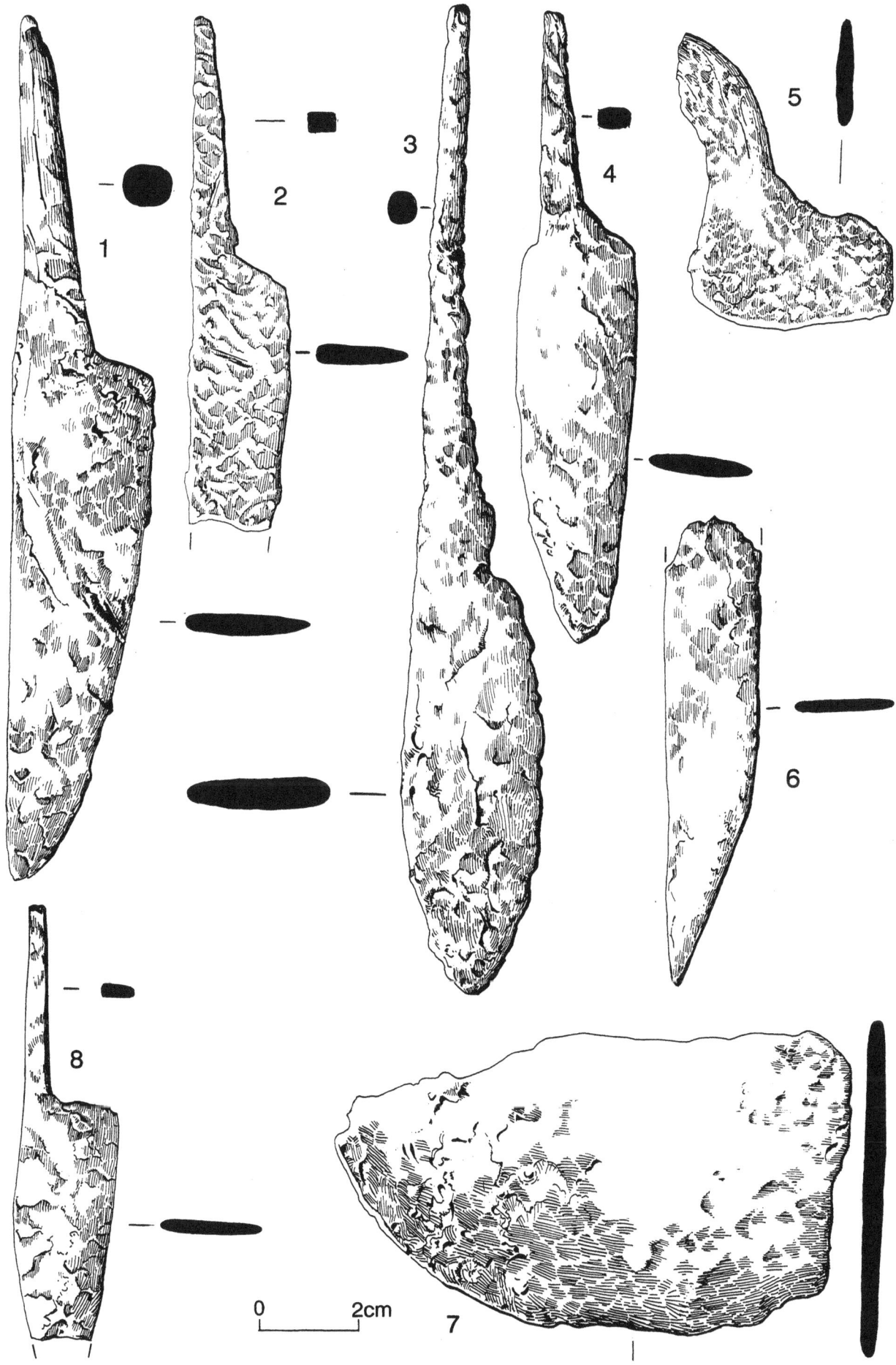

*Figure 38* Iron knives and blades, nos. 1-8

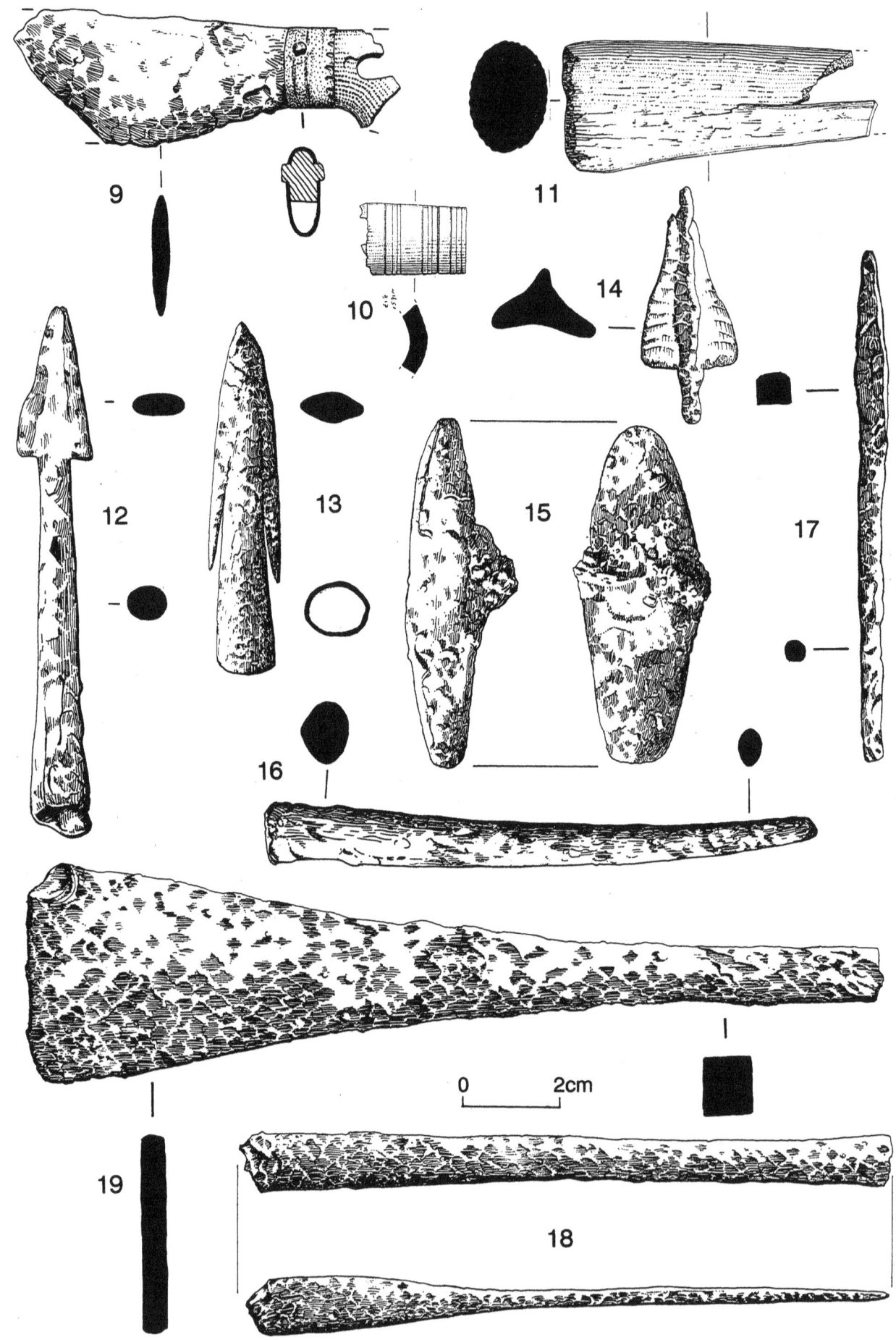

*Figure 39* Knife handles, projectile heads and iron tools, nos. 9-19

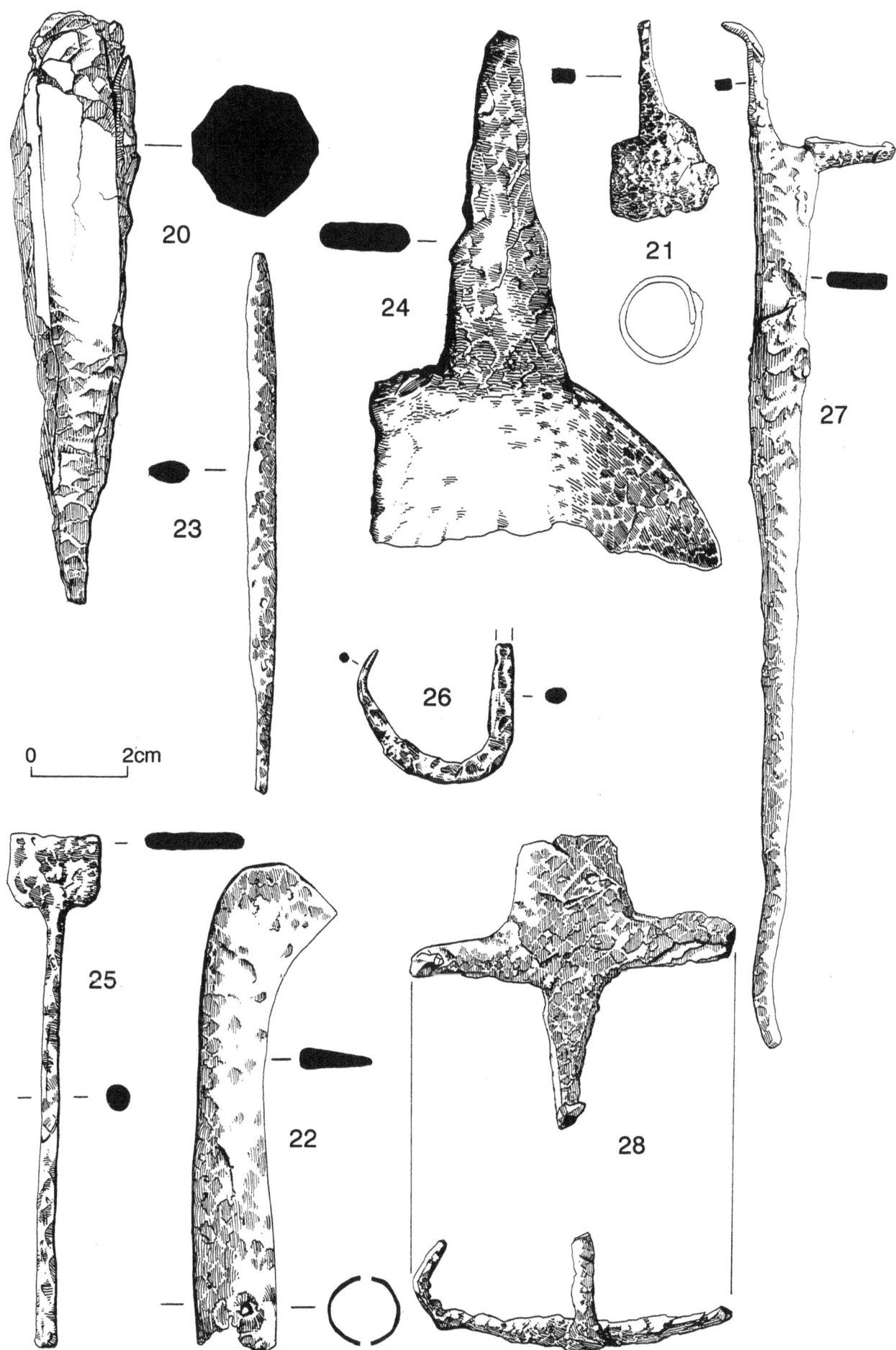

*Figure 40* Iron tools and utensils, nos. 20-28

## Spindlewhorls and miscellaneous fittings and furnishings
*by L. Bevan*

Spindlewhorls (Fig.41)
Evidence of weaving comes in the form of spindlewhorls, some fragmentary, made from a variety of materials, of which three are illustrated. Some are common types, e.g. the shale example (no. 1), a late 3rd-century type (Lawson 1976, 271-2). Lathe-turned bone counters are also common (e.g. Crummy 1983, fig. 94, Allason-Jones 1984, 2.145-214), many decorated with concentric grooves, but bone spindlewhorls (no. 2) with a wide central perforation are much less common, although a similar example has been found at Uley (Woodward and Leach 1993, fig. 143:8). An even more unusual example is the idosyncratic adapted fossil (no. 3). Reused potsherds are frequently the most common material for spindlewhorls, five examples occurring in this assemblage (not illustrated).

1. Shale spindlewhorl, circular, lathe-turned. A slightly distorted version of the more regular-shaped examples in Lawson (1976, fig. 14:107) and Crummy (1983, fig. 71: 2002); *W2318, C854, Area 67, Period 3*
2. Bone spindlewhorl in two pieces, circular with lathe-turned concentric groove decoration; *W1504, C781, Room 41, Period 3*
3. Stone half-spindlewhorl made from a fossil echinoid; *W888, C649, Area 61, Period 4*

Miscellaneous fittings and furnishings (Fig.41)
A number of pieces of bone and copper alloy which, in common with the copper alloy key (Fig. 34.1), probably originated from either boxes or small furniture, are illustrated (nos. 4-11). Strips of bone, both plain and decorated, usually with ring-dot motifs like the example shown (no. 4), 'were used principally as casings for wooden boxes or caskets' (Crummy 1993, 82). Further material, principally of copper alloy, is catalogued in the archive but is not illustrated.

4. Bone inlay fragment with incised ring and dot decoration and one rivet hole; see similar examples from South Shields (Allason-Jones 1984, 2.232-235, 61-2); *W2952, C865, Area 65, Period 4*
5. Fragment of rectangular bone plate with two rivet holes; *W454, unstratified*
6. Copper alloy sheet with silvered surface and repoussee decoration (three fragments); *W680, C620, Trench A, Period 3*
7. Copper alloy plate retaining three out of four rivets *in situ*; *W2102, C746, Area 64/66, Period 3*
8. Copper alloy sheet fragment with nail hole; *W217, F13d, Area 41*
9. Copper alloy stud or tack, as used in upholstery (see also Manning 1985, Types 7-9); *W1100, C676, Room 15/15a*
10. Small copper alloy stud, as no.9; *W1881, C1001, Area 66*
11. Copper alloy domed terminal or stud head; *W2687, unstrat., Room 29*
12. Copper alloy handle with flattened, pierced terminals and one nail *in situ*; *W1458, C512, Area 47, Period 2*
13. Part of a cast copper alloy handle or ring; *W2776, C826, Room27, Period 5*
14. Iron handle with loop attached, possibly from a bucket; or alternatively part of a two-link snaffle bit (Manning 1985, 66-7); *W1236, C650, Area 61, Period 4*
15. Part of an iron tub or bucket handle with one suspension loop; *W1825, C768, Room 34, Period 2*
16. Iron box/furnishing handle or fitting; *W885, C649, Area 61, Period 4*
17. Spiralform decorative iron fitting from a candlestick, see parallels at Uley (Woodard and Leach 1993, 201, fig. 149:1, 206-7, Figure 153:26); *W656, C646, Area 61, Period 2*

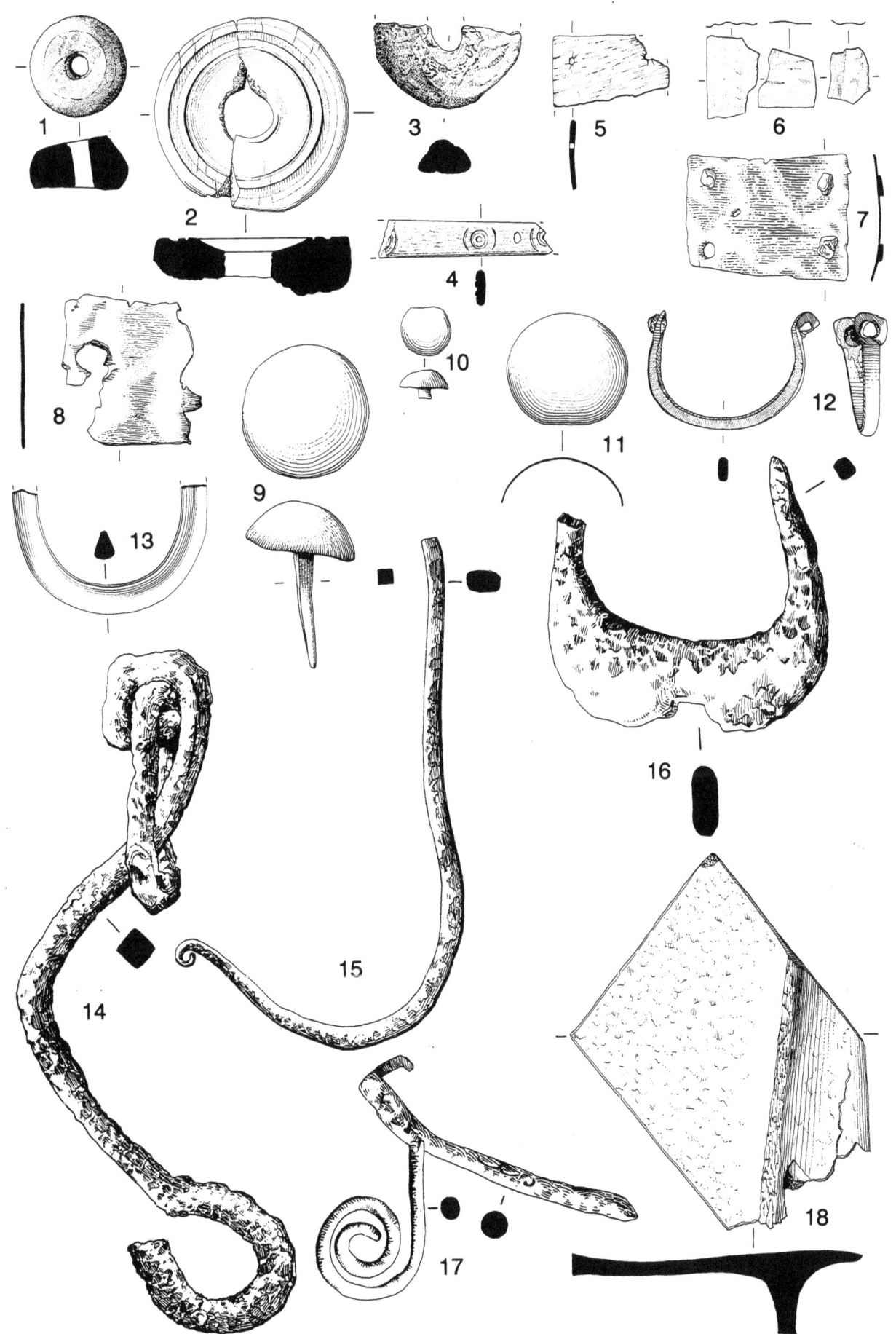

*Figure 41* Spindlewhorls, furnishings and handles, nos. 1-18 (1:1)

## 3.2.6.: INDUSTRIAL BY-PRODUCTS

### Industrial Debris
*by T. Finney*

**Assessment of industrial debris**

A small quantity of industrial debris (3712g.) was recovered by Greenfield and submitted for examination to the Ancient Monuments Laboratory, English Heritage. The following is an extract from A.M.L. Report 50/95.

All the debris from Witcombe was individually weighed, visually examined and classified to type. It is not known to what extent this category of material was selectively sampled by the excavator, nor what may have been lost in previous excavations, and thus how representative this assemblage is.

Visual examination of metalworking debris allows it to be classified into various categories based on its morphology, density, colour and vesicularity. Of these categories only a small proportion are diagnostic of a particular metal working process. Others can only be assigned to the working of a particular metal, whilst many can be produced by a wide range of high temperature processes.

Table 6 Summary of industrial debris from Witcombe Roman villa

| Summary of industrial debris from Witcombe Roman villa | | | | | |
|---|---|---|---|---|---|
| Context | Area | Phase | Weight (g) | Interpretation | Comments |
| F13 | 41a | 5 | 31 | Iron object | |
| 584 | 41 | 4 | 100 | Vitrified hearth/furnace lining | Brick? |
| 548 | 41 | 4 | 184 | Vitrified hearth/furnace lining | Roman type tile |
| 647 | 1.b. | 2 | 37 | Mineral block | Geological |
| 620 | 1.b. | 3 | 1 | Vitrified material | Green glaze |
| 649 | 61 | 4 | 26 | Vitrified hearth/furnace lining | Green glaze |
| 651 | 61 | ? | 17 | Vitrified hearth/furnace lining | Green glaze |
| 639 | 61 | 3 | 161 | Vitrified hearth/furnace lining | Roman type tile |
| 944 | 15a | 3 | 523 | Smithing hearth bottom | Dense |
| 650 | 61 | 4 | 14 | Vitrified material | Green glaze |
| 650 | 61 | 4 | 395 | Vitrified hearth/furnace lining | Roman type tile |
| 653 | 60 | 1/2 | 37 | Vitrified material | Green glaze |
| 653 | 60 | 1/2 | 18 | Vitrified material | Green glaze |
| 654 | 50 | 5 | 18 | Vitrified material | Green glaze |
| 700 | 34 | 2 | 8 | Dense slag | small run |
| 700 | 34 | 2 | 202 | Vitrified hearth/furnace lining | |
| F22 | 39 | 3 | 140 | Vitrified hearth/furnace lining | Green glaze |
| F22a | 34 | 3 | 39 | Undiagnostic ironworking debris | |
| 759/864 | 65 | 5 | 41 | Vitrified material | Black glaze |
| 777 | 64/66 | 3 | 21 | Vitrified material | Green glaze |
| U/S | U/S | U/S | 48 | Vitrified hearth/furnace lining | Green glaze |
| 797 | 28 | 3 | 87 | Undiagnostic ironworking debris | |
| 747 | 64/66 | 1/2 | 129 | Smithing hearth bottom | |
| 747 | 64/66 | 1/2 | 128 | Smithing hearth bottom | |
| 868 | 65 | 4 | 221 | Smithing hearth bottom | |
| 864 | 65 | 4 | 67 | Undiagnostic ironworking debris | |
| 866 | 65 | 4 | 4 | Cinder | |
| 885 | 71 | 4 | 8 | Vitrified material | Green glaze |
| 893 | 71 | 2 | 404 | Smithing hearth bottom | |
| 893 | 71 | 2 | 27 | Vitrified hearth/furnace lining | Green glaze |
| 898 | 71 | 5 | 48 | Dense slag | |
| 868 | 65 | 4 | 3 | Vitrified material | Green glaze |
| 793 | 65 | 2 | 105 | Vitrified hearth/furnace lining | |
| 793 | 65 | 2 | 50 | Vitrified hearth/furnace lining | Green glaze |
| 793 | 65 | 2 | 60 | Vitrified hearth/furnace lining | Green glaze |
| 878 | 72 | 4 | 148 | Undiagnostic ironworking debris | |
| 865 | 67 | 2 | 140 | Unidagnostic ironworking debris | |
| ? | ? | ? | 30 | Vitrified material | Green glaze |
| ? | ? | ? | 57 | Fired clay | |

Table 7 Quantities of the various type of debris from Witcombe

| Slag type | Total Weight (g) |
|---|---|
| smithing hearth bottoms | 1405 |
| undiagnostic ironworking debris | 481 |
| dense slag | 56 |
| cinder | 4 |
| iron object | 31 |
| vitrified hearth/furnace lining | 1515 |
| geological mineral block | 37 |
| fired clay | 57 |

Three selected samples were analysed qualitatively by X-ray flourescence to investigate the possibility of them being related to non-ferrous metal working.

Table 8 XRF analysis of selected debris from Witcombe

| Context | Lab. Number | Object | Elements Present |
|---|---|---|---|
| 548 | 615045 | Vitrified type tile | Si Ca Ti (Mn) Fe Zr |
| 647 | 635007 | Mineral block | (Ca) (Mn) Fe |
| 868 | 732274 | Vitrified material (green glaze) | Si K Ti (Mn) Fe |

Key:
**XX** elements strongly detected*
XX element moderately detected*
(XX) element weakly detected*

* Based on the peak height in the flourescence spectrum, and not necessarily proportional to concentration of the element in the original sample.

Mn = Manganese, present in soil or sample fabric.
Fe = Iron, present in soil or sample fabric.
Ti = Titanium, from sample fabric or soil contamination.
Ca = Calcium, from sample fabric or soil contamination.
K = Potassium, from sample fabric or soil contamination.
Si = Silicon, from sample fabric or soil contamination.
Zr = Zirconium, from sample fabric.

## Discussion

The quantity of debris recovered is small, and only a fraction is diagnostic of a particular industrial process. Smithing hearth bottoms area evidence of smithing, and one would expect smithing to have taken place on or near the villa site. However, the amount of slag recovered could have been produced in a single day's blacksmithing, so does not necessarily represent evidence for a smithing industry. Like other metalworking debris, smithing hearth bottoms are often found used as hardcore, and these examples may have been transported to Witcombe for this use.

Other iron slags are present in such small quantities that they do not support a case for any ironworking industry at Witcombe. They could have come from either smithing or smelting of iron, and may have been brought to the site as hardcore. If they were produced at Witcombe then smithing is their most likely origin, as there is no diagnostic evidence for smelting.

The hearth lining and vitrified material with green glaze seems to have originated from the same high temperature process. XRF analysis did not show the presence of non-ferrous metals which might have indicated the working of copper alloys.

The mineral block, although being iron rich, is unlike any iron slags encountered before. Given that only one example was recovered, its origin is likely to be geological rather than industrial.

## Conclusions

Overall, it is difficult to identify solid evidence for any industry at Witcombe. The sample available is very small, only a fraction of which is diagnostic of a particular activity. The amount of smithing slag recovered, together with its temporal and spatial distribution, does not indicate that iron smithing was an activity regularly carried out on the site. It may be that smithing was carried out infrequently, or that the origin of the slag is outside the excavated area.

The vitrified material could have come from ferrous or non-ferrous metalworking, or another high temperature process. The lack of traces of non-ferrous metal on the samples examined by XRF does not support a non-ferrous metal working origin, although this cannot be ruled out.

In conclusion, the evidence neither supports nor rules out industry at Witcombe. All the debris is of a kind that could have been brought in as building material (iron slag), or have been produced by a non-industrial high temperature process (vitrified material). Thus, while some of the evidence is diagnostic, none is conclusive.

## Metal and bone working waste
*by L. Bevan*

The most convincing evidence for the on-site working of copper alloy comes in the form of a collection of melted globules and offcuts found together within the remains of a small hearth (F91) which may also have been used for lead smelting in Room 28 (*W648, C805, Period 2?*). Single waste globules were also recovered from C801, also in Room 28, and from C508 in Area 47.

Evidence for lead working was obtained from Room 28, where the remains of two small smelting hearths (F55 and F91) contained pieces of lead melt with ash and coal (the latter presumably used as fuel) The hearth F91 may also have been used for bronze working (see above), but had been partly destroyed by Lyson's original clearance. Although recorded by Greenfield, no samples from these hearths appear to have been kept, although small quantities of lead, mainly in the form of offcuts and molten globules, occur in adjacent rooms or areas around the South East Range. Some of this material may have originated from Room 28, although not all is necessarily the product of metalworking. This and other fragments from the site were found in Rooms 27, 29 and 44 and in Areas 65, 71 and 72.

The only evidence of possible boneworking is the unstratified find *W1465* from Room 34 (Fig. 41 no. 18), a lozenge-shaped offcut of cattle scapula which may have been intended to be used as decorative inlay in the manner of Fig. 41 nos. 4 and 5.

## 3.2.7.: ENVIRONMENTAL EVIDENCE

### Animal bone and shell
*identified by R.Jones and J.G.Evans*

A small assemblage of animal bone was collected throughout the course of the excavations, amounting to a few hundred pieces (identified originally as BO1-BO110, archive). From the site notebooks it is evident that not all the animal bone was kept, and it is not clear upon what basis the surviving material was collected. A report from the Ancient Monuments Laboratory (100/75) by Roger Jones in 1975 provides a species list for *c.* 25-30% of the material (in archive); a sample considered then to be too small for further interpretative comment.

The sample is insufficient to present the data chronologically or even quantitatively. With the exception of the dog burial from Area 64 (F39), there is no evidence in the site record or from the material itself for substantial articulated portions of birds or animals, although evidence for butchery is occasionally noted. Animals such as Cattle, Sheep/Goat, Pig and Domestic Fowl were presumably brought to or kept in the vicinity of the villa, both for food and other products. The same might apply for Horse, although these animals could equally have been used for traction or riding. Dogs may have been present both as pets and as working animals. Very few wild species of animal or bird are recorded, but include the Short-tailed Vole, Jackdaw, Duck and Goose; the latter possibly domesticated.

A very small collection of Mollusca was retained in the course of the excavations (identified as SH1-SH21, archive), although once again it is clear from the site records that this represents only a sample of what was encountered. It is not possible to determine on what basis this was collected, or what proportion of an originally surviving assemblage it represents. The material was submitted by the excavator to the Ancient Monuments Laboratory, and a species list was provided by Dr. John Evans (University of Wales, Cardiff).

With the exception of *Helicigona lapicida* and *Pomatias elegans*, which were probably living incidentally on the site, all the shells should represent human food debris. Oyster, Mussel, Whelk, Dog Whelk and Great Scallop are marine species found on many Roman sites, although scallop shells are unusual and could have had secondary uses. *Helix aspersa* is an edible land snail which is not thought to have entered Britain until early in the Roman period.

### Human Remains
*by J. D. Henderson*

Three small samples of human bone were examined in the Ancient Monuments Laboratory and reported upon by the author in 1986 (A.M.L. Report 9/86). Observations were made for information on sex and age, and any skeletal anomalies or abnormalities. Details of the methods used and the results obtained by individual are given in the attached catalogue. Very little may be said and few inferences made from such a small and incomplete sample of these individuals. The two samples of adult skull fragments (HB.1 and 2) both came from the south-east corner of the South Courtyard, among deposits which relate to abandonment and dereliction of the villa buildings here. The third sample (BUR.1), an incomplete infant burial, was recovered from a late? 4th-century occupation deposit in the north corner of Room 27 in the South East Range; presumably the site of its original deposition.

Catalogue
HB 1 (AML no. 732158)
A very small sample of human skull weighing only 28g. The bone was fragmentary but it is suggested that all the pieces come from one parietal bone. Probably a young adult of undetermined sex, although the appearance of the sutures indicate the possibility of a large juvenile or sub-adult; *W3037, Context 861, Area 70, Period 4*

HB 2 (AML no. 8140831)
Five small fragments of human skull, total weight 15g, only two of which could be identified as parietal. An adult, based on bone thickness and the appearance of the suture on one fragment; sex undetermined; *W4542, Context 878, Area 72, Period 4*

Burial No.1 (AML no. 860274)
Partial skeleton in fair condition (approximately 25%), representing the skull and lower half of the body (skull fragments, R + L *ilia*, R *ischium*, R + L *femora, tibiae, fibulae*, fragments of *tarsals* and *metatarsals*). Infant, birth-6 months; sex undetermined. This estimate was based on the size of the *femora, tibiae* and *fibulae* (see below), using the standards of Ubelaker 1978 and Stewart 1979. On the basis of these it is suggested that death may have occurred sometime after birth but within the first six months of life; *W2651, Context 818, Room 27, Period 3*

| Maximum diaphyseal length: | Right | Left |
|---|---|---|
| *Femur* | 79mm | 79mm |
| *Tibia* | 71mm | 72mm |
| *Fibula* | 68mm | 68mm |

## Carbonised Plant Remains
*by A.M.L.*

Samples of charcoal (CH1-CH32) and a small group of carbonised grain samples (CG1-CG5) were submitted by the excavator to the Ancient Monuments Laboratory. These were identified by species (authors unknown) but no formal reports were prepared. In addition to the species list (below), attention is drawn to the significance of particular samples by virtue of their site associations. The charcoal was apparently collected as pieces rather than in soil samples, and precise weights or quantities are not usually recorded. As far as is known none of the samples were sieved or floated.

The charcoal samples derived almost exclusively from species of trees and woody shrubs, and included *Acer* (Field maple), *Alnus* (Alder), *Betula* (Beech), *Carpinus* (Hornbeam), *Crataegus* (Hawthorn), *Corylus* (Hazel), *Fraxinus* (Ash), *Malus* (Apple), *Pinus* (Scots pine), *Populus* (Poplar), *Prunus* (Blackthorn/Plum), *Quercus* (Oak), *Rosa* (Dog rose), *Salix* (Willow) and *Tilia* (Lime). All these species could have been growing locally in the hedgerows or be components of woodland on the surrounding hills, as they are today. Many of the smaller samples were obtained from deposits exterior to the building and are not particularly informative. By far the largest were collected from deposits associated with a series of hearths and drain fills in Room 27. The most common species for fuel used in the oven F56 were Alder, Blackthorn/Plum, Hawthorn, Hazel and Oak; Blackthorn/Plum and Hawthorn in hearth rakeout from F57; and Blackthorn/Plum and Ash with the oven F62. Charcoal washed into the drains F52 and F53 within this room, presumably derived from the hearths, included Hazel, Beech, Lime and some Willow and Alder. Charcoal associated with the oven F61 in Room 28 was predominantly kindling of twigs and bark, some of which could be identified as Willow or Poplar. In Room 29, fuel residues associated with firing of the large corn drying oven F54, included Beech and Apple charcoal.

Carbonised samples, predominantly of grain, were also obtained from the corn-drying or malting oven in Room 29 and its immediate environs. The exact size of the samples or their proportion relative to the entire volume of deposits is unknown, and only a species list and quantities of grains identified is recorded by the A.M.Lab. By far the most common was Spelt (*Triticum spelta* L.; 119 grains), along with a few grains of suspected bread wheat (*T. aestivium* or *T. compactum*; 8 grains) One sample also contained a few grains of oats (*Avena sp.*) and barley (*Hordeum vulgare* L.), and another, the common weeds curled dock (*Rumex crispus* L.) and sorrel (*Rumex acetosa* L.). Together, all these samples may represent only a small residue of one or more firings associated with this kiln. The preponderance of spelt presumably reflects the most common crop for drying or malting, although there was no information recorded which positively signified the latter process. The presence of other grains may be accounted for as weeds within the main spelt crop, as undoubtedly were the dock and sorrel. However, oats and barley, as well as different wheat species, may well have been grown locally in fields belonging to the villa and brought in for processing.

## Coal
*by P. Leach*

Ten samples of coal were recovered (CO1-CO9), one of which was submitted by the excavator to the Ancient Monuments Laboratory for further examination. This specimen (*CO 1, W418*) was identified as coal type Clarain/Vitrain, and on the basis of its palynological assemblage, as of Carboniferous age from a horizon near the Westphalian C/D boundary. A likely local source would be the Woorgreen or Coleford High Delf coal seams, whose closest outcrops are found some 20 miles from Witcombe in the Forest of Dean.

Several specimens were collected from deposits around the exterior of the villa, but perhaps the most significant were found in and around the South East Range. In Room 28 samples from a Period 3 hearth (F55) associated with the smelting of lead suggest that coal was used as a fuel in that process. Other fragments not associated with hearths were found in Rooms 26 and 44, and in Area 67 just outside the building to the south east. In the North East Range a coal sample from the oven F24 in Room 34, may be another specific indication of the use of coal as fuel at Witcombe in the 4th century. A full list of the specimens collected and their site location is in the archive.

A recent review of the occurrence of coal in Roman Britain indicates a particular concentration of sites in the Lower Severn/Bristol Channel region (Dearne and Brannigan 1995). Doubtless, to a great extent this is a reflection of its local availability from outcrops in the Bristol area and the Forest of Dean. In this instance the latter coalfield is suggested by the analysis as the most likely source, from where other raw materials, notably stone, were being imported for use on the site.

Chapter 4

# REVIEW AND DISCUSSION

## 4.1: Dating

Evidence for the origin and chronological development of the main villa building at Great Witcombe is dependant on associations between datable finds and depositional and structural sequences. Necessarily, previous excavation strategies on the site have not always been conducive to answering these questions. This problem is perhaps most acute in respect to origins, since retention of the most durable structural elements, notably walls, has normally taken precedence over excavation and recording to determine their foundation or development. Despite this, it was evident to Greenfield in particular that a structural sequence could be determined from the surviving building remains, although the evidence was not thoroughly or systematically documented. Greenfield discerned two principal building phases within the main villa but there is no evidence that he ever developed this beyond a basic interpretative site plan (Fig. 4). In attempting to redefine this scheme, can a more precise chronology of events be proposed?

Discounting the slight evidence for some transitory early prehistoric human presence here, the origins of settlement at this locality may well lie within the Iron Age (Period 1). The only direct evidence was the ditch 708 and its pottery contents below the North East Range. No other features and hardly any more Iron Age pottery was found elsewhere, but the location of this east-west aligned ditch could allow its interpretation as a boundary to activity further north. The ground rises immediately north from the villa site to a short promontory which slopes down eastwards from the present site of Coopers Hill Farm (Fig.3). This location has the potential for a small Iron Age settlement, better drained than the later villa site but adjacent to a good water supply from the springs.

On the villa site itself it is clear that Greenfield frequently excavated down to the old ground level, both within and around the ranges of rooms. There is no hint of any coherent structural remains predating the earliest phase of stone building in Period 2. Clifford (1955, 25-6) interpreted finds from her excavations, in particular the pottery, as indicating a primary construction date 'towards the end of the first century'. Given the much larger assemblage of finds recovered by Greenfield, can this hypothesis be upheld? Samian wares are not well represented and are dominated by later Antonine and East Gaulish products. For a site of this status founded before the third century, such an impoverished assemblage would be inconceivable. Oxidized Severn Valley wares (Fabrics D1, D2 and D4) are the most abundant ceramic group on the site. Believed originally to have been produced primarily in the 1st and 2nd-centuries, this pottery is now well known from 3rd-century and even later contexts (Webster 1976 and 1993). The ceramic assemblage otherwise is dominated by 3rd and 4th-century British products, earlier types or other imports being rare. Among the vessel glass very few pieces can be dated to the 1st century (possibly heirlooms), the most notable material belonging to the 2nd and 3rd centuries. Datable small finds, mainly of non-ferrous materials, are almost exclusively 3rd and 4th-century types; 1st and 2nd-century brooches being poorly represented. As might be expected, the coin assemblage is dominated by later 3rd and 4th-century issues, with only one 1st-century coin (Domitian) and a handful of the later 2nd century. Thus, the structural evidence combined with that of the finds provides little support for significant development on the villa site before the early 3rd century.

The core of the main villa building comprises an 'H' shaped layout of equal-size wings (east and west) linked by a central range of rooms around a courtyard to the south (Fig.42, Period 2). Its primacy was evidently first recognised and defined by Greenfield, who was able to demonstrate the secondary structural relationships of other rooms and features to it. Evidence for a construction date is harder to come by. Where such occasional excavation opportunities arose (as beneath Rooms 15/15a or in the East Wing) the few diagnostic finds do not contradict a post AD 200 origin for this building in Period 2. The only element at obvious variance with the primary layout is the bath building (Rooms 9, 10 and 11) of the South West Range. Conceivably, this reflects an even earlier building layout, or at least an originally separate bath house (Neal 1977, 31). There is no evidence for a direct link here between the bath house and the main building, although remains of any Period 2 arrangement could have been obliterated in Period 3.

On the presently available evidence the main courtyard villa building was laid out sometime during the first half of the 3rd century, possibly closer to AD 200 than later.

From its plan and layout (the building terraced into the hillside and commanding panoramic views) this was evidently a grand design, probably planned and executed within a relatively short period (contra Hingley 1989, 51-3). Evidence for the function and development of the villa - its rooms and close environs - thereafter, is discussed at greater length below. The courtyard villa building of Period 3 (Fig.42) was evidently a more organic development, its plan probably evolving as a progressive series of additions and modifications to the original structure between the later 3rd century and the last decades of the 4th, although an episode of major remodelling, possibly during the first quarter of the 4th century, is likely.

The final years of the 4th century saw a marked change in the apparent continuity of status and use which the villa had enjoyed since its early 3rd-century foundation. The clearest evidence for this came from the West Wing, where the lower bath suite was decommissioned and rooms of the upper baths and Central Range adapted for reuse. This episode is dated to *c* AD 380 or later, when a short break in the representation of coins from the site from then (after AD 378) may also be significant, although a phenomenon observed in many villa coin assemblages (Reece 1989). The duration of what is probably then the final phase of occupation at Witcombe is more difficult to estimate. The reappearance of the latest coin issues (between AD 388 and 402) on the site suggests activity continuing into the 5th century, one from occupation debris in Room 27 indicating that the South East Range was also still being used in this period. The villa site lies remote from the later medieval focus of settlement at Great Witcome (Fig. 2), and there is nothing beyond a handful of medieval pottery sherds (signifying much later agriculture) to show that occupation continued for long into the post-Roman era.

## 4.2: Function and Reconstruction

Period 2

As is apparent both from the layout of Period 2 and the terracing of the site, the Great Witcombe villa was planned early in the 3rd century as a unified structure, on what seems to all intents and purposes to have been a virgin site (Fig.42). This was an ambitious project at a location carefully chosen, no doubt, to exploit the fine views to the south east, a good water supply on site and the shelter provided by higher ground to the north and west. Both the slope of the ground and the on-site springs posed considerable problems for the builders, who terraced or embanked different sections of the villa to ensure its stability. This appears to have been generally successful, although additional strengthening was required in some places, and rooms at the southern extremities of the East and West Ranges were eventually affected by major subsidence. Located on a moderate slope, the building operated on several levels, as is amply demonstrated by Neal's perceptive reconstruction (1977, 27-40). The primary 'H' plan has a symmetry which was evidently intended to make a strong visual impression, and doubtless the main villa building was an imposing edifice, viewed either from below or from across the combe. The plan is somewhat unusual and not closely matched elsewhere in Britain, though based essentially upon the winged courtyard style. Unusual also was its approach, the main entry being from the north rather than via the courtyard, as is almost always the case in other British villas of this type.

Inevitably, the most complete reconstruction of the building, its rooms and their functions, relates to its fullest development in Period 3 (Fig. 42). It is nevertheless still possible to get some impression of the original Period 2 layout. Although virtually equal in proportion, the two wings of the building always seem to have had very different functions. The west wing is dominated by the two sets of baths; the lower originating as a separate establishment, while the upper of almost identical form (Rooms 1a, 49 and 50) appears to be integral with the primary structure of the North West Range. It is no longer possible to determine the original function of the two most southerly rooms (3/4/5 and 6) in the west wing, although the *caldarium* Room 5 may have been converted from an earlier *apodyterium*. Despite their incorporation into the developed bath suite of Period 3, it is equally possible that these rooms were initially part of the living accommodation. Neal's suggested reconstruction (1977) favours an upper storey to Room 1; an arrangement which could well have extended above Room 5, though given the fall in natural ground levels here perhaps not over Room 6. Room 1 was positioned centrally in the West Wing, and Lyson's original suggestion that it functioned primarily as a shrine (1821, 180) is still an attractive hypothesis. A potential ceiling height in excess of 3m and its restricted entry from the rest of the villa also accords well with such a function, as do finds made within the room or nearby, e.g. a fired clay pine cone from Area 41 (Clifford 1955, 16-7 and pl.XI).

The presence of a second upper bath suite in the North West Range requires some explanation, if both suites are indeed contemporary. The upper baths appear to have been an original Period 2 feature and were evidently well positioned to serve most conveniently the requirements of the household. Although far less well preserved, Rooms 34a, 50, 1a and 49 all appear to have been heated; the latter in all probability the site of a sunken hot bath similar to that in Room 11 - which would explain its lower floor level. In their primary form the better preserved lower baths were a separate establishment, at variance with the main building alignment and conceivably of earlier origin. It has been suggested (Neal 1977, 33) that the lower baths were intended for use by estate workers, which may well have been the case in Period 2, although this does not rule out an even earlier origin. In this respect it should also be noted that there are enigmatic references in Greenfield's records to

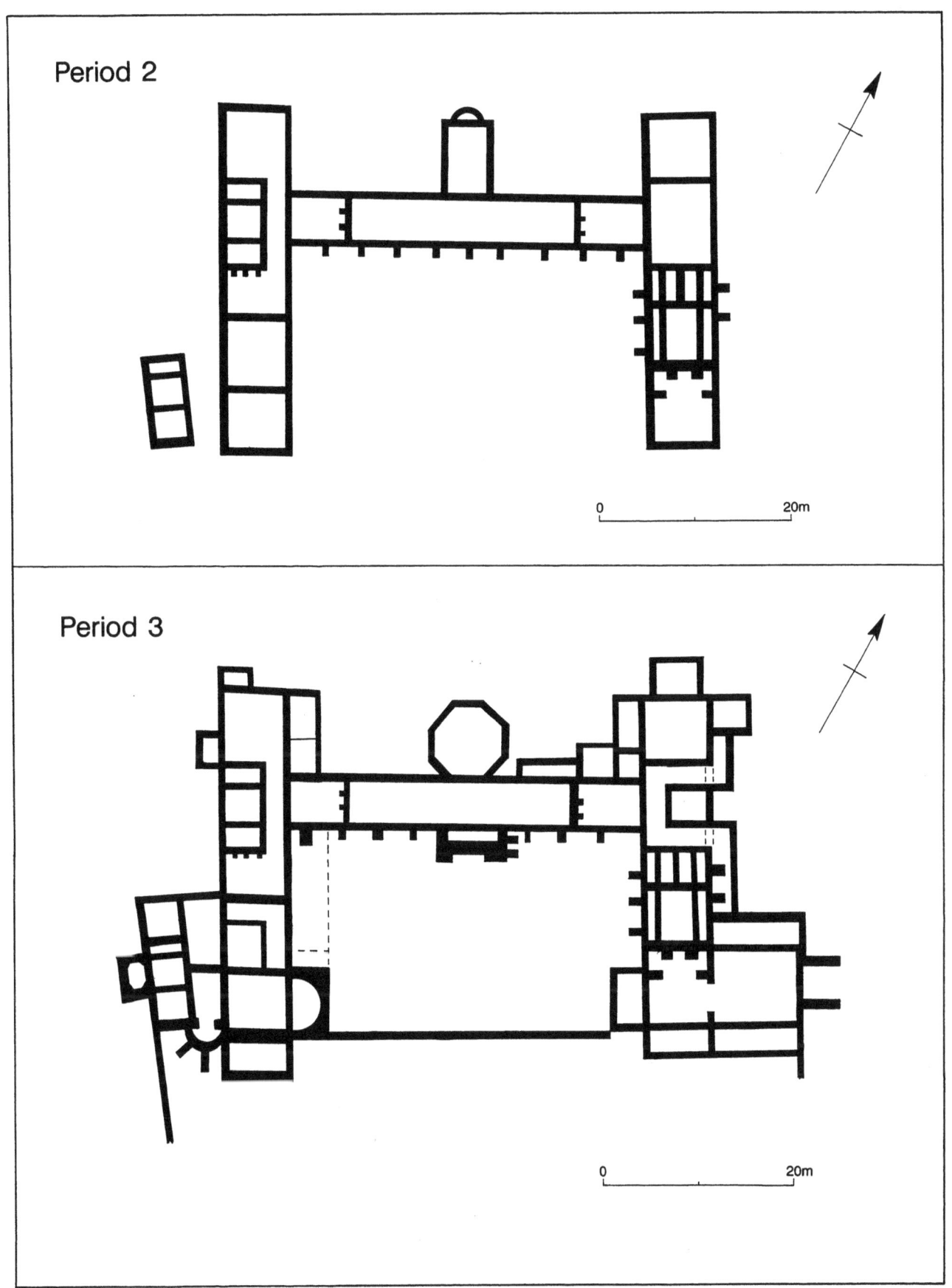

*Figure 42* Villa layout, Periods 2 and 3

structural foundations beneath Rooms 6 and 7a. There is possibly some confusion here with the Period 3 boundary wall to the South Courtyard, but the potential for an earlier building cannot be wholly discounted (RCHM 1976, 60).

Rather less evidence of the original function of rooms in the East Wing survived, though clearly planned on a scale equal to its western counterpart. Evidence for the subsequent use of Room 34 and hearths within the adjoining later Rooms 17 and 51, suggest that both northern rooms may have been kitchens; while at the same level the linked basement room below Room 16 could also have been for food storage or preparation. Both rooms may have had a second storey, an arrangment which possibly continued above Rooms 19-25. The latter were supported on a strongly buttressed platform standing out from the hill slope, suggesting an upper storey, but may in reality have comprised no more than two sets of two rooms one above the other - most probably private living quarters. The East Wing terminates to the south at Room 27, whose floor is significantly lower (up to 6m), in conformity with the natural fall of the ground, than those of the other rooms. While this room may also have had a second storey, it would have required the addition of a third to continue the roof line at the same level as that above Rooms 19-25 to its southern extremity. Given the relative instability of the site and the absence of buttresses against the outer walls of Room 27 this seems unlikely. An alternative reconstruction could allow the second floor building level of Rooms 19-25 to terminate at the position of two large opposed buttresses within Room 27. This is exactly in line with the wall separating Rooms 5 and 6 in the West Wing and would result in a more symmetrical building design, each wing then terminating with a single room of equivalent size (6 and 27) one floor lower than the remainder to the north west. Building symmetry would have been enhanced further through an equality of roofline heights between both wings, requiring on the one hand only a single storey to be built for most of the West Wing (except above Rooms 1 and 5) and on the other the addition of another floor above the East Wing rooms (Figs. 42 & 43).

Linking the two wings The Central Range comprised a long corridor or gallery sub-divided into three rooms. The largest (14) gave access to a centrally-placed rectangular room (15a), with a small apse to the north which appears to have been a later addition. This is likely to have been a reception and/or dining room (*triclinium*), to which the apse could have been added later in the 3rd century prior to a complete 4th-century remodelling as the polygonal Room 15 in Period 3. The adjacent gallery rooms in this range could also have had a more public function. Access to the kitchens may have been via stairs from the gallery down into Room 16 or into the corridor 15/18 beyond. At probably the same level as the central corridor, direct access would then have been possible to the suite of second floor private rooms occupying much of the East Range. Also at this level would have been the principal public access to the house from the north, suggested by exterior metalling in this area. Nothing survived of the building to this level but an entry via the upper gallery levels above Rooms 16 or 13 is possible. Alternatively the blocked doorway in the north-west wall of Room 16 was part of the original entrance, access to the gallery and rooms in the East Wing at a higher level being via a staircase. The present remains of Rooms 13 and 16 almost certainly represent basements or store rooms below the extremities of the main gallery (Room 14), where there is no evidence for a lower room. Room 16 also gave access to the lower East Wing kitchen complex. Built across the natural slope, it was necessary from the first to buttress the Central Wing against movement down the hill. This tendency was likely to be exacerbated by the springs which emerged just above this point, and a complex system of stone-lined drains was planned to accommodate the water, evolving with the progressive development of the villa. Water was channeled for functional reasons into both wings, primarily for the baths and the kitchen. A proportion also passed through the South Courtyard, where it may well have played a more decorative role. There is little clear evidence for the use of this area as a garden, as might have been expected, some of the area at least being metalled in Period 2.

Period 3

The subsequent development of the villa building may have been a more piecemeal affair, although at least one other major development scheme could have involved a remodelling of the lower baths, the Central Range facade and dining room, and possibly the South East Range. No very precise dating evidence was obtained from structures or deposits associated with these developments, although the late 3rd or very early 4th century is the most likely context. Previous attempts at reconstruction have depicted the villa at its maximum stage of development (de la Bedoyere 1993, 63 and pl.3; and Neal 1977, 27-40). David Neal's study still provides the best working model, although certain modifications can now be suggested (Fig.43).

Whatever the original scheme for baths in the West Wing, Period 3 saw a major redevelopment of the lower suite which linked the original bath house to the southern rooms of the South West Range (Figs.5 and 42). This involved not only the addition of further rooms and baths (Rooms 7, 7a, 8/8a, 11a, 11b and 12), but also the conversion of the two southern ground floor rooms in the main building. The original northern room was now subdivided into a *caldarium* (Room 5), with access via a slype through a new *tepidarium* (Room 8/8a) to the original bath house; and a latrine and corridor (Rooms 3 and 4) in its north and eastern part. If, as previously suggested, this room was originally of two stories, Room 4 may also have functioned as a stair well, giving direct access from the upper levels of the main house to the

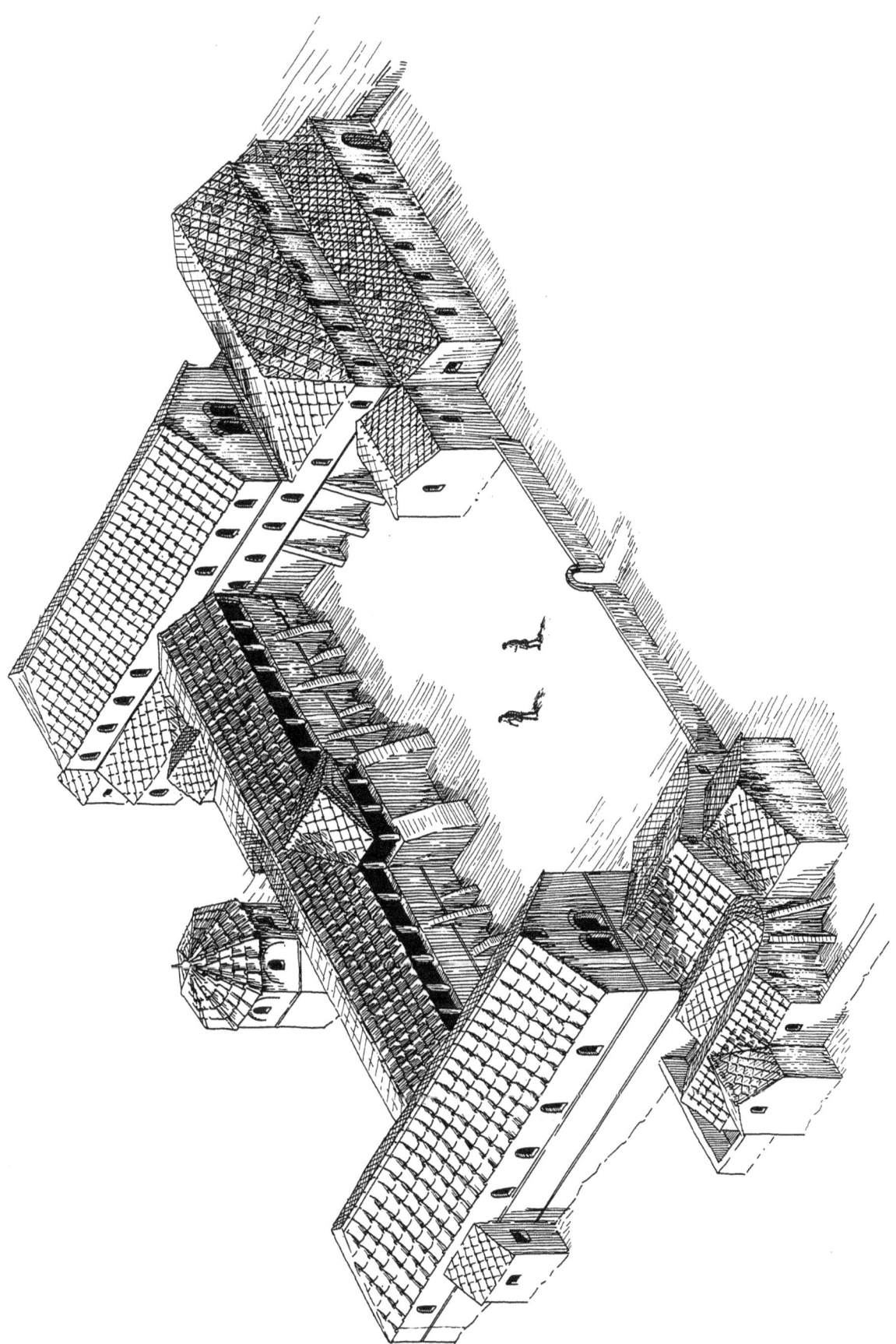

*Figure 43 Great Witcombe Villa in the 4th century, an isometric reconstruction view from the south*

lower baths via the doorway into the single story Room 6 - now a *frigidarium* with new cold plunge baths (Rooms 7 and 7a) opening off it. An alternative access arrangement might have involved stairs descending from the upper level of Room 13 to a corridor or covered verandah in Area 41a, which led alongside the West Wing rooms to an outer doorway in Room 4. The presence of an especially large end buttress against the outer wall of Room 13 could also be interpreted as part of a stair support here. Both Lysons and more especially Clifford document the presence of this additional room, although it is not clearly depicted on any plan (Figs. 4 and 42). Whatever the access arrangements or its earlier status it is difficult not to interpret this greatly expanded bath suite, with its fine decorated mosaic floors, as primarily serving the villa's owners and their guests, although this need not rule out a shared use with other members of the estate's community.

More problematic is the status and history of the upper bath suite in Period 3 (Figs. 6 and 42). The clearest evidence for its continued use is the addition of two baths (Rooms 45 and 48) to Room 34a. Clifford (1955, 23) cites two late 3rd-century coins from prime construction contexts in each, providing *terminus post quem* dates for their addition; the succession of floors in 48 suggesting that this room at least was in use well into the 4th century. This evidence implies that both bath suites were in contemporary operation, although the location of the upper baths would still favour their use by the villa household rather than by estate workers. Given the size and layout of the main villa building it is difficult to postulate two separate households as an explanation for these arrangements. The addition of Room 46 may have allowed easier access to the upper baths, since direct access from the rest of the house through the upper Room 13 would only have been possible via a passage to the left over Room 2 and into an upper Room 1. However, Room 46 could also have functioned as corridor and vestibule to another entrance into the building here, since a second phase of exterior cobbling approaches the North West Range from the north east. In these circumstances the allocation of this bath suite for use by other members of the villa estate becomes a more viable proposition; effectively perhaps a reversal of the relative positions of the two bath suites in Period 2. Another option would link the suggested religious function of Room 1 with ritual bathing, for which the upper baths were well located, although they seem rather too elaborate for such an exclusive role. Clearly there are several options or combinations possible here to account for these arrangements.

It could be argued that the remodelling of the Central Range was part of a plan which included the expansion of the lower baths, but this cannot be physically demonstrated. The principal works involved a new octagonal dining room, an entrance complex to the north east, and changes to the southern facade (Figs. 6 and 42). Some of the latter work may have been necessitated by structural weakness, since a new series of supporting buttresses were added to the outer walls of Rooms 13, 14 and 16. Of arguably more importance however, was the opportunity taken to enhance the appearance of this frontage by the addition of the central portico structure (Room 32). The associated drainage suggests that it may have been combined with a water cistern, perhaps even as a *nymphaeum*. Whatever its precise function this feature will have provided a central focus to the main southern villa elevation, the impact of which, as a grand classical facade, was almost certainly emphasised by the reconstructed dining room behind (Room 15), whose roof probably dominated the Central Range. The form of this dining room/ audience chamber is paralleled by a small number of such polygonal rooms in late Roman Britain and further afield (Ellis 1995), and is doubtless a further reflection of the status of Great Witcombe and its owners. The main entry to the villa living quarters was probably always at the east end of the range. This appears to have been elaborated in Period 3 by the provision of a first floor corridor (above Rooms 42 and 43) from an entrance at the higher ground level to the north west, which led to a landing (over Room 41) with stairs down into Room 16, and another corridor (Room 52) giving direct access to the gallery (Room 14). The ground floors of Rooms 42 and 43 (as well as 41) were terraced into the hillside and may have been stores connected with the kitchens to the east.

As part of the original Period 2 layout it has been argued above that the East Wing may have had two stories, at least as far as Room 27. Subsequent developments in the North East Range evidently expanded the kitchen premises with the addition of Rooms 35, 53 and probably the lower floors of 42 and 43 (Figs.8 & 41b). Room 34 with its drains and hearths continued as the main kitchen, but the adjacent room to the south was modified through the insertion of a corridor (Rooms 18 and 51) which gave access ultimately to an upper floor of the South East Range. It has been suggested (Neal 1977, 35) that the insertion of this corridor implies demolition of Room 17 (and thus any upper storey), possibly to enhance the view north east from the gallery. Against this is the evidence for a continuation of activity in the reduced core of Room 17 and the apparent retention of its north east wall, as well as the problem of access from the Central Range into first floor rooms of the East Wing which its removal would create. More likely is the retention intact of the upper floors in this wing; that over Room 17 being carried by arches across the breeches in its outer eastern wall created by the corridor (Rooms 18 and 51).

The most substantial addition to the villa in Period 3 affected the South East Range, the greater part of which was created then. This comprised a large but relatively short aisled structure with the original Room 27 at its core (Figs. 9 and 42). Whatever the original Period 2 character of Room 27, it was now linked eastwards via a broad ?arched opening with the two-storey open aisled hall - Room 28 - having its large entrance porch (Room

31) to the north east. Whether or not Room 27 retained an upper floor, this addition to the main building almost certainly necessitated the removal of that part of the upper floor of Rooms 19-25 which it was suggested (above) overlay the north end of Room 27 at a second floor level in Period 2. The access from the main house into this range via the corridor Room 18 implies an upper floor in the north aisle (Room 26), although stairs from the corridor could have descended straight down to ground floor level here. The southern aisles (Rooms 29 and 30) and an extention to the south west (Room 44) are more likely to have been single storey. Their character and the remains documented from these rooms suggest rather different uses and status for this part of the villa. Such buildings are more often associated with activities relating to the running of an agricultural estate, and probably also combined use as living accommodation for workers or household servants. Evidence for some food storage, processing and small scale manufacturing in its later phase of use is indeed found here, and it is interesting to compare the layout and contents of Rooms 27 and 44 with Rooms 34/53 of the North East Range kitchens. A recent suggestion that aisled halls incorporated into villa buildings may sometimes have served as feasting halls (Black 1994, 106-7), could be supported by the location of a second kitchen suite here in the South East Range, if not by the direct corridor (Room 18) access from the upper kitchens into the north aisle room (26). In reality, a multiplicity of uses for the South East Range should be anticipated throughout its life. It is perhaps also significant that this was the location of the only recorded infant burial from within the villa.

As noted previously, there was little clear evidence for the layout of the South Courtyard, either in Period 2 or 3. The records suggest that some if not all the area was metalled for much of the time, presumably sealing the sequence of drainage systems carrying water from the North West, Central and North East Ranges (Fig. 10). The most prominent feature seems to have been the wall built in Period 3 to close off the courtyard to the south cast. This probably abutted the south-east corner of Room 7 but looks to have been planned with an opening to the east before this was blocked by the addition of Room 44 to the South East Range. Alternatively the wall was built later, to abutt Room 44, and may have had a central opening, although there was no evidence for this. The remains of walls continuing south east down the hillside from the two outer southern extremities of the villa, may have been contemporary additions, designed to create a much larger enclosure - possibly a walled garden - immediately in front of and below the main villa building (Fig.42).

Period 4

The scale of early 19th-century excavation was such that relatively little evidence survived within the villa interiors to document its final occupation and subsequent abandonment. Some of the best evidence survived in the West Wing: deliberate infilling of hypocaust chambers in the lower baths and remains of Clifford's 'squatters economy' (post holes, hearths and ovens, rough paving of reused stone), from the upper baths area (1955, 26-7). Allied to this is similar evidence from the South East Range; re-use of stone for paving, hearths and a 'corn-drying' oven, and occupation deposits. The Southern Courtyard wall may also have been removed at this time; thoroughly robbed out to its bottom foundations before the ditch was completely infilled again.

All of this evidence suggests a major change in the function and status of the villa building towards the end of its existence, probably after $c$.AD 380, whether or not there was a short break in its occupation. It is not now possible to document the full extent of this change, but the surviving evidence implies that either the estate owner was no longer resident and that the premises were now being utilised within a late 4th and 5th-century rural economy by subordinates, or that it was no longer possible to maintain the quality of life indicated by pre-existing remains. The infilling of the hypocausts beneath rooms of the lower baths suggests a need for greater support for their floors. Was this area of the villa now being utilised for the storage of agricultural produce?, possibly because other rooms were already used to capacity or unavailable for other reasons. Suspected 'corn-drying' ovens in Rooms 34a and 29 demonstrate that crop processing was being undertaken within two extremities of the building, although no great change of use or status need be implied for the South East Range, where such activities may always have featured. The creation of floors using reused building materials, other occupation debris and the presence of post holes, suggests that parts of the building were also still lived in.

In the absence of finds datable to the 5th century or later it is impossible to estimate the duration of this ultimate phase of use. Doubtless the building will have begun to deteriorate soon after its vacation by a wealthy estate owner, a process exacerbated by the natural instability of the site and a lack of materials and probably resources to effect any major repairs. Several rooms at the south extremities of both wings eventually suffered major subsidence, although the core of the house seems to have survived well at ground floor level. Upper stories and roofs will have deteriorated first, and their collapse was no doubt represented in the substantial deposits of building debris which were still present over much of the South Courtyard. Little evidence for stone robbing had survived, although some is to be expected. By the 19th century the remains were evidently quite obscured by hillwash and soil formation, prior to their accidental rediscovery in 1818.

## 4.3: Status and Economy

Unlike the majority of villas so far investigated in Roman Britain the house at Great Witcombe was built from the first as a grand design, in the early decades of the 3rd century. Utilizing what was seemingly a virgin site, its original plan and foundation represented a considerable investment over what must have been a relatively short period. Although overlaid somewhat by later modifications and remains, it is apparent that the first building was designed primarily as a well appointed residence for a wealthy landowner and his family. With the possible exception of the detatched lower bath house, there is no sign of humbler agricultural structures or other estate buildings in the immediate vicinity. Admittedly, the potential for such remains has barely been explored, but the overall impression is of a country house designed at first to stand alone, exploiting its splendid hillside position and the panoramic views around.

The wealth of Roman Britain and its predominantly native aristocracy was based above all upon agriculture and the ownership of land. We are unlikely ever to know the name of the builder of this house or of his family, but the reason for and ability to build such a house is surely to be found in such a context. Many Romano-British villas appear to have evolved from relatively humble beginnings, from simple and modest adoptions of Roman building style replacing native in the early years, to sometimes quite large and elaborate complexes by the later 3rd and 4th centuries. No such process is evident here, although there is just the hint that a pre-Roman native settlement may have been located nearby to the east. Should we perhaps look elsewhere in the locality for a predecessor, possibly lying at some distance from this new building? Other remains are indeed suspected quite close to the site, although for reasons discussed below, none seem strong candidates for an early villa predecessor. Known sites further afield like Hucclecote or Dryhill (Figs. 1 & 2) should represent separate estates, and so the question of a forerunner for the Great Witcombe villa and an original focus for its estate remains open for the time being.

The plans and layout of villa buildings and their compounds are sometimes quoted as evidence for multiple ownership, or more likely, extended family ownership of estates. This may be manifested through paired villas in a single compound, as at Halstock or Gayton Thorpe, or the division of single buildings as at Rockbourne or Marshfield (Smith 1978; Hingley 1989). At Witcombe, only the main house is available upon which to base any such assessment, and even here the evidence is conflicting. The original unitary planned house of Period 2 certainly favours a single dominant family, although the developments of Period 3, and in particular the two bath suites, could reflect two later households of roughly equivalent status. Aisled houses attatched to or closely associated with villa buildings can also be interpreted as living quarters, perhaps for family members of lower status. This may be another explanation for the South East Range extention, although from the surviving evidence of its more utilitarian use occupation by estate workers is perhaps most likely.

Much of the evidence for the character and lifestyle of the occupants relates to later phases of use, but seem to imply the maintenance of high standards of comfort and sophistication at Witcombe right through until the final decades of the 4th century. The position and successive modification of the dining/reception room implies occupation by senior and influential members in society, whose continuing wealth and position evidently permitted major expansion and remodelling of the house in Period 4. The operation of two substantial bath suites may be another status indicator, although apart from postulated first floor living rooms above, these appear to be the only heated rooms in the villa. The positioning of the house, exploiting an extensive view, has already been noted, but could other aspects have been influential? The water supply and its management was a major factor here, both as a benefit but also as a potential hazard to the stability of the building. The significance of water, and in particular its sources, features prominently in celtic religion, as in many others. The springs which emerge from the hillside at Witcombe may well have had just such a status, further influencing the positioning of the house. This is perhaps the context for the suggested shrine in Room 1, its central cistern receiving water directly from the spring via drains or conduits to the north. Although integral with the house, this religious focus probably had significance for a wider spectrum of society, at least within the villa estate, who may thus also have had access to it. The possibility that this feature was in some way connected with the second, upper bath suite, has already been mentioned.

Apart from the layout and suggested functions of the building and its major spatial components themselves, further qualitative detail is supplied by the array of more portable finds recovered from among the remains. Not only was the original building carefully planned and well founded on its hillside site, but the quality of materials used in its construction was often of the best. Today, surviving sections of well dressed and evenly coursed walls support this, as do the finer architectural pieces of dressed oolite recovered from among the debris of building decay and collapse. These include fragments of door and window casements, balustrades, pediments, roof finials and coping stones, and numerous sections of columns (Figs. 28-9). Some of the latter are still preserved on the site (though not *in situ*), while the recovery of many others from deposits above the South Courtyard suggests that most originated from the Central Range. Where full reconstruction is possible it is evident that the columns were little more than one metre high but of two sizes (RCHM 1976, pls. 28-9), and it has been suggested that many of the larger and more weathered examples were used as colonnade supports for the roof above the central gallery (Room 14); part of a grand classical facade which was open to the south and must have been designed both to enhance the whole building and thus its owner's status (Fig. 43). Columns were perhaps also used in window openings, while the smaller unweathered columns were presumably employed for internal openings within rooms of the bath suites and/or of the Central Range.

Both Clifford and Greenfield found large quantities of clay roof tile, but much was discarded without detailed record and it is difficult now to reconstruct the character of individual roofs. There are indications in this region that ceramic roof tile was most commonly used in the 1st and 2nd centuries, being progressively replaced by a variety of stone slates in the later Roman period (Williams 1972, 105-7). Although the chronology at Witcombe is uncertain, it is tempting to suggest that the first phase of the villa was roofed almost entirely with locally-made clay tile, while later additions used the less abundant stone slates which were also found on the site. Other architectural details of the upper storeys to the house are harder to come by, but the rare discovery of collapsed wall elevations on sites elsewhere in Roman Britain (e.g. Meonstoke, King and Potter 1990) hints at the potential for their embellishment on buildings of the status of Great Witcombe. Below ground the extensive drainage system was designed both to supply parts of the building (notably the baths and kitchens), and to lead water away from it. Springs rising immediately to the north east and north west of the villa were the main source, channeled originally in stone-lined and capped conduits. The system was evidently modified in accordance with the development of the villa and its requirements over time. Smaller drains sometimes reutilised clay *tegula* or *imbrex* tiles, iron collars attest the presence of wooden water pipes, while a lead pipe survives *in situ* within Room 48 of the Upper Bath Suite.

Within the building tufa was widely used within wall cores and as interior wall facing material. In all probability it was also used to roof the heated bath houses. A fine sandstone was also used widely to line walls, and seems to have been painted for decoration. More familiar as a wall and ceiling covering was painted plaster, some of which survived *in situ* in rooms of the West Wing when first uncovered by Lysons. From its known distribution this wing and the Central Range were the most highly decorated, at least in the later phases; its relative absence from the East Wing perhaps a reflection there of more utilitarian functions and status. Cornice fragments of imported white Cararra marble were also found by both Lysons and Greenfield (Fig. 29, 7-8), though none can be identified as originating from specific rooms. The surviving mosaic floors of the lower baths are perhaps the most striking status indicators, although some and possibly all belong to Period 3 (RCH.M 1976, pls. 11-12). Whether such floors were originally a feature of the upper baths or other rooms in the Central Range is unknown. Room 1 has a floor of Old Red Sandstone flags, while the corridor rooms 41 and 46 may have had plain tesselated floors. The central gallery and dining rooms (13-16) seem to have been floored by a variety of stone tiles, probably laid in chequer patterns or other designs (Fig. 30). More elaborate mosaics could have been laid here as part of the original design, but are less likely to have featured in the East Wing of the house, from which indeed no such remains are recorded.

Window glass was moderately abundant, the majority originating from the Period 2 structure since 4th-century glass was far less common. Most was recovered from exterior contexts, but its presence in the Central Range and both bath suites suggest glazed windows there, although it was much rarer in the East Wing.

In circumstances where previous excavation has been extensive and many surviving contexts with large artifact assemblages were residual, the results of detailed distributional analysis are of limited value (see archive). Pottery was the most abundant artifact retained by the excavator and, despite certain drawbacks of the assemblage and its recording, was capable of a fairly detailed analysis. Identification of the sources for the pottery revealed a relatively restricted range; dominated by products from the Severn valley, south Midlands and Dorset, with imports (notably Samian) poorly represented. This typifies many later Roman assemblages in Britain, as here, an attribution confirmed by most of the datable forms and conforming with the suggested chronology for the villa. A coarse analysis of the principal form types suggests virtually a 3:2 split within the assemblage between kitchen and storage vessels, and tablewares; the first two represented in roughly equal proportions. The relatively high proportion of finer tablewares would, once again, be consistent with a higher status site, although there are still all too few similar analyses to confirm this. At Uley, a site of comparable status, if rather more diverse function in the same region, the proportions of these basic categories are similar overall, though tablewares make up almost 50% of the assemblage in the later periods (Woodward and Leach 1993, 241-3). Recent data from rural sites further down the Severn Valley and in Somerset indicates smaller proportions of tableware and greater representation of coarsewares on what should be settlements of lower social status (Evans 1996). The finest tableware at Witcombe was represented by vessels of glass, among which the range of 2nd and 3rd-century types was notable. Less than 20% of the assemblage were 4th-century types, although doubtless some earlier material continued in use as heirlooms long after its period of origin. Much of the earlier material was imported, and overall the assemblage appears to reflect a household of some sophistication.

Other categories of smaller personal objects, including beads, rings, bracelets, pins, toilet articles, etc. were relatively well represented and typify the range of such material to be found commonly in the wealthier and more developed sites and settlements of later Roman Britain. This assemblage supplements a comparable group recovered by Lysons and Clifford (1955). Brooches were poorly represented, as is to be expected on a site which seems not to have been in occupation before the 3rd century. Later 3rd and 4th-century coinage was relatively abundant and typical of assemblages from most other Romano-British villa sites; demonstrating that in its heyday the villa was operating well within the money economy of the province. Overall, there are few items of especial note, although several suggest links with the temple complex at Lydney Park on the other side of the Severn (Wheeler and Wheeler 1932). Among these a silver ring with an intaglio is notable also in hinting at one of the occupants of Great Witcombe and his possible connections with the army in Britain.

The more utilitarian aspects of life at the villa are reflected in a range of tools and utensils as well as by the residues of other activities. Many objects had a connection with food processing, including a range of knives and cleavers (Fig. 38), kitchen utensils such as skillets and fleshooks, querns, millstones and whetstones, some rubbers and pounders (Figs. 36-7), and of course the range of pottery vessels used for cooking, preparing and storing food and drink. The hearth and ovens and the drainage system centred upon Room 34 in the North East Range surely identify this as the heart of a kitchen complex which functioned throughout Periods 2 and 3, serving the needs of all its occupants. Although another kitchen centred upon Room 27 in Period 3 may have served the South East Range and perhaps other communities on the estate. Other activities in and around the villa are reflected by implements associated with spinning, wood and metalworking, and perhaps bone, leatherworking and stone dressing (Figs.39-41). More direct evidence of leadworking was associated with small hearths in the South East Range, and other hearths in these rooms and occasionally elsewhere around the villa could reflect further small scale industrial processing or cooking operations. Charcoal for fuel was probably produced locally from timber on the estate, but it is interesting to note the presence of coal imported from the Forest of Dean for use in both the kitchen and for small-scale industrial smelting. All this evidence probably reflects no more than localised activities, servicing the villa and its maintainence and operating requirements.

Our view of Great Witcombe villa, its contemporary setting and environs, is restricted almost exclusively to evidence from the main house itself. With its prosperity resting upon land ownership and the produce of its estates, glimpses of the latter and associated activity may relate more to the later periods when such matters begin to impinge upon the main building. This is apparent at first in the South East Range, but ultimately through an evident change of status for the villa building in its final phase of use. This was the context for the location of Period 4 corn drying ovens in Rooms 29 and 34a. Though by no means a thorough analysis, examination of residues from the oven in Room 29 suggest that spelt was being cultivated locally; while the much rarer presence of bread wheat, barley and oats could signify other grain crops. The discovery of an iron knife-coulter in the 19th-century excavations, possibly belonging to a coultered ard, is further indirect evidence for cultivation (Clifford 1955, 33-4). A wide variety of wood charcoal was identified in samples from hearths, ovens and drains, almost certainly reflecting a varied local environment of hedgerows, coppicing, mature woodland and possibly orchards. Another element of the economy will surely have involved livestock, whether reared for food, subsidiary products or used for other purposes. Unfortunately, the sample size and level of its recording allow little more than the demonstration that animals such as sheep, cattle, horses, pigs, dogs, and domestic fowl, geese and ducks were present and probably part of the estate. These scraps of evidence are supplemented by occasional artifacts such as reaping hooks or ox goads (Fig.40), or arrow/spear heads (Fig.39) as reflections of local hunting - most probably for sport.

We have no accurate knowledge of the bounds or detailed character of the Great Witcombe estate, although it should not necessarily be envisaged as a single large holding focused almost exclusively upon its principal residence (Todd 1989). Modern landscapes frequently preserve vestiges of their earlier origins, though whether anything significant of the Roman pattern still survives here (as demonstrated at Barnsley Park, RCHM 1976) has not been researched. The more general characteristics of the local environment and its exploitation however, are probably still to be perceived today. Behind the villa to the south and west, and continuing to the east, the steep scarp slopes of the Cotswold Hills are for the most part thickly wooded; a circumstance which may well have pertained in the Roman period and earlier. Management of these woodlands, hedgerows and any smaller coppices or stands of trees would have supplied most, if not all of the timber and charcoal requirements of the estate. Above *c.* 200m the dissected Cotswold plateau had long been clear of trees and was predominantly a pastoral landscape. It might reasonably be anticipated that some share of these lands fell within the estate, supporting mainly cattle and sheep, though perhaps also growing some grain crops, as today. The broad combe of Great Witcombe is now a patchwork of fields, hedgerows and copses, dominated by pasture on the heavier clays but with some arable areas, and more rarely today, orchards. Most, if not all of the combe probably fell within the core of villa estate, and its present appearance and mixed agricultural economy may differ little from its Romano-British character.

The apparent isolation of the main villa building today is misleading. At the time of the original uncovering of the villa in 1818-19 another stone building was discovered approximately 100m to the south east beside a small stream here (Fig. 3). This was a rectangular suite of at least seven rooms, some with plastered walls and floors, ?stone roof tiles and an exterior drain. Its size was not recorded although it may well have exceeded 30m in length, and it appears subsequently to have been destroyed (Clifford 1955, 13-15). In 1965 Greenfield excavated a series of test pits down the slope south east from the villa towards the site of this building. The lowest of the series evidently relocated its remains but added little more information relating to its size, character or context. The absence of evidence for occupation between the villa and this building is probably a consequence of the relatively steep and broken ground there, which might however have been utilised as terraced gardens. Without some further investigation of the lower structure and its environs no firm interpretation is possible, although its resemblance to the plans of certain early villa buildings in Britain, such as Ditches, North Cerney, Gorhambury or Park Street could be significant. Either this is the predecessor to the main building, abandoned or more probably adapted when the former was planned early in the 3rd century, or it belongs to a discrete range of ancillary buildings more closely linked with the operation and functions of an agricultural estate and contemporary with the main villa building. From what little is known of this structure it appears to have been primarily a dwelling of moderate sophistication, which could have accommodated a tenant or estate manager and his household. If this interpretation is correct it could provide a context for the separate lower bath house which is postulated for the first phase of the villa layout (Fig.42). The addition of an aisled building to the South East Range in Period 3 conceivably signifies replacement of the lower house and the amalgamation of its household into the main villa range, although one alternative suggestion for the primary use of that addition is offered above, while both are as likely to have continued in contemporary use.

The separate building beside the stream was probably set within a system of enclosures containing and adjacent to the main house at Witcombe, as seen where more extensive excavations have taken place around villas (e.g. Gorhambury, Neal *et.al.* 1990; or at Rockbourne, Hants.). A range of further structures should be anticipated in the vicinity, including barns, workshops, animal byres and dwellings for humbler estate workers. Another attempt to locate such evidence was made by Greenfield in 1966 through a series of test pits along the hillside to the south of the villa. This area is crossed by the watercourse of a spring emerging higher up the slope, which may have fed the baths, but there was no other evidence of contemporary structures in this direction (Fig. 3). A more likely position for ancillary buildings is below the villa and associated with the known building there, or perhaps upon the spur to the north, where the potential for a prehistoric settlement location has already been suggested. Further afield there are two sites recorded along the foot of the scarp slope below Witcombe Wood to the east (Fig. 2, A and B). Surface finds of stone, roof tile and pottery suggest the location of separate buildings (RCHM 1976, 61-2), in all probability the farm settlements of tenants or other estate workers. These are almost certainly not the only representatives of contemporary farms or hamlets within the estate of the villa, and at least one other (of higher status?) may have been located on the site of the Witcombe reservoirs lower down the valley. This is suggested by the discovery here in 1859 of a late 2nd-century bronze statuette of the goddess Flora, although there is no other information relating to its context or other associated finds (Clifford 1955, 58).

## 4.4: Context

The Great Witcombe villa lies approximately 5 miles to the south east of Gloucester and less than a mile south of Ermine Street - a major Roman road. This road linked the cantonal and later provincial capital of *Corinium Dobunniorum* (Cirencester) with the colonia at *Glevum* (Gloucester), within the territory of the pre-Roman iron age *Dobunni*. Centred upon the Cotswolds and lower Severn Valley, this was one of the wealthier and most populous tribal groupings in Britain. Epitomised throughout much of the period by numerous hillforts, which cluster particularly upon the Cotswold Hills; power here was evidently becoming more centralised in this region during the final period between the expeditions of Caesar and the Claudian invasion and conquest. Bagendon near Cirencester must have been the pre-eminent *oppidum* of the *Dobunni*, whose power was effectively transferred to the nearby *Corinium* within the succeeding Roman provincial structure. From very early in the history of the new province another focus of power and influence developed at Gloucester, first as a legionary fortress and then as a *colonia* at the end of the 1st century. Continuing fieldwork in both the Cotswold and Severn Valley regions demonstrates a considerable range and density of Romano-British settlement throughout. By the 3rd and 4th centuries this included several other smaller towns, roadside settlements, more diffuse industrial or agriculturally based centres, villa estates, rural temples, and a host of more modest hamlets or farmsteads. Even on the humbler sites the adoption level of a romanised material culture is relatively high, while sites like the Woodchester and Chedworth villas, or the Lydney and Nettleton temples exhibit considerable sophistication and wealth.

The Great Witcombe villa fits comfortably within this context; an establishment representative of the higher echelons of society in the *Civitas Dobunniorum*. It has already been suggested that the villa was built and operated as the residence of a wealthy landowner at the centre of his estates, but who might such a magnate have been?

An analysis of the perceived focus of many villas upon towns suggests that political and administrative considerations were at least as important as marketing advantage in their distribution (Hodder and Millett 1980). In this instance it can be proposed with reasonable confidence that the *colonia* at Gloucester was the regional centre to which Witcombe and its owners owed alliegence. Such families were closely involved with the government and administration of towns from their earliest foundation, as landowning decurions whose origins were normally from among the pre-Roman tribal elites. This was almost certainly the case at Cirencester, but as a *colonia* foundation Gloucester's elite were army veterans, many of whom probably originated from provinces outside Britain and few, if any, will have been of Dobunnic origin. Once integrated into local society through marriage such distictions would become blurred, although until the early 3rd century their status as Roman citizens will have been significant. The foundation of Gloucester dates to the reign of Nerva (AD 96-8), following the army's withdrawal from the legionary fortress there to Wales in the late 70s or early 80s (Hurst 1985). Grants of land were a feature of the settlement of veterans, and while we have no details of this at Gloucester it is reasonable to suggest that the Great Witcombe estate may have originated in this way as part of its *territorium*. It is surely therefore significant that among the finds of a personal nature is a silver ring with 'Eagle and Standards' intaglio, and perhaps also the bone pendant representation of an eagle. As the estate of a Legio II Augusta veteran founded at the end of the 1st century, it is likely that connections with the Army will have been maintained through continued military service by family descendants. Of no less significance however, will have been the family's continuing service and prominence among the government of the *colonia*.

In the 3rd and for much of the 4th century the focus of wealth and investment in Roman Britain shifted from town to country. To an extent this reflects the development and maturity of the province within the Empire, particularly during periods of 3rd-century disruption and instability on the neighbouring Continent, but there were other factors of even greater significance in operation. The decline of urban society, at least within the larger public towns, is now a widely recognised phenomenon in Britain (Reece 1980). This trend is recognised throughout the Empire, and while these places (principally the *civitas* capitals as well as *colonia*) retained an administrative significance, their commercial pre-eminence gave way to a more dispersed pattern of markets with a greater emphasis upon smaller centres, particularly towards the peripheries of the *civitates*. Allied to this was the increasing burden of taxation through the 3rd century, and a change of emphasis by the elite from towns and their buildings and institutions (communal) to the countryside and its institutions (personal), as a means to demonstrate patronage and display (Millett 1990). Effectively, this is reflected by the stagnation and cessation of investment in public urban works on the one hand, and on the other by the expansion and aggrandisement of villas and temples in particular, in the countryside. Here then is the context for building a new and grandiose country house at Witcombe, by a magnate whose political and economic status resided as much in the *colonia* at Gloucester as in his estates, but who now chose the latter as the vehicle for its display.

The original villa at Great Witcombe was an ambitious enterprise; built to a unitary design on a new site in the first half of the 3rd century by a prominent member of *Glevum* society. Unusually, there is no evidence for a predecessor on the site, although one may be suspected elsewhere within the estate. From the foundation of the *colonia* until the early 3rd century the family's principal residence may have been in the town, but with the building of the villa the emphasis must have changed. Elsewhere around Gloucester there was 3rd or 4th-century development of villa sites with earlier origins such as Hucclecote or Dryhill, presumably the foci of similar estates granted originally to veterans. Witcombe's position, style and quality of building suggests its inception by an individual of pre-eminence in local society, a position presumably maintained well into the 4th century. It has few rivals, even in an area notable for 3rd and 4th-century villa development, although the even more palatial later house at Woodchester appears also to have been built to a unified design (Clarke 1982).

In contrast to certain other parts of Britain there is a notable absence of villa development before the 3rd century, in what was one of the wealthier regions of the province. While much of this can be accounted for by the emphasis placed upon towns, particularly in the 2nd century, it was suggested that an influx of foreign capital and landowners into this region, notably from Gaul, could account for subsequent villa development (Branigan 1972 and 1973). This can now be discounted (Smith 1983), their development being seen as part of a much wider phenomena within the Empire, here articulated by a locally based elite. Whatever the factors behind a sparsity of early developed sites, ultimately, the densest concentration of villa establishments is recorded in this part of the province, a pattern into which Witcombe fits comfortably. As further indication of their increasing influence and prestige in local society the owners of this estate may also have taken opportunities, along with others, to endow and encourage the development of local religious shrines and cult centres. The 4th-century *floruit* of temple complexes such as Lydney and Uley surely in part reflects such involvement, and thus give the context for apparent stylistic links in certain items of material culture observed among finds assemblages from all three sites, and probably others.

While it is not possible to directly equate a villa building such as Great Witcombe with productive output, the prosperity of its estate and ownership clearly rested upon agricultural produce and its marketing. It is probably no coincidence that later Roman villa development occurs at a time of observed agricultural innovation and intensification; a phenomenon linked with other social and economic developments affecting the later Roman Empire (Millett 1990, 201-5). Although the evidence is sparse at Witcombe, finds such as the 'corn-dryers' from the latest phases of its use may echo this. A large proportion of the material remains recovered from the site will have originated from its own estate; Oolite, tufa, Lias and Forest Marble stone for buildings and roofs were probably quarried locally, and wood for building, fuel and charcoal, implements, and other uses was readily available. Artifacts or fittings of iron and other metals could well have been manufactured on the estate, as suggested by hearths in the South East Range and the presence of iron slag, but raw materials will have been imported. Finer objects such as jewellery, implements and furnishings of non-ferrous metal, bone, stone, etc., were almost certainly imported from workshops located in the neighbouring towns of Gloucester and Cirencester or from further afield (e.g shale from Purbeck). The Forest of Dean provided materials such as sandstone roof slates and tile, querns and millstones, coal and possibly iron, all of which may have come via Gloucester. Much of Witcombe's pottery and clay tile was probably produced in the vicinity of Gloucester, concievably from kilns owned by the estate, since tile wasters are recorded from the site. Other pottery was imported from Dorset, Oxfordshire and elswhere in the south Midlands, as part of a much wider network of production and supply. Ceramic imports from the Continent, notably samian, were declining by the time the villa was in operation; however, a notable assemblage of vessel glass, much of it from the Rhineland, illustrates better the wealth and range of connections available to the owners of Witcombe. In the same context was the Carrara marble imported from Italy, used both for furniture and to embellish the building interiors. The latter process is illustrated best by wall paintings and mosaic floors, requiring the services of skilled artisans, almost certainly based at Cirencester. Coinage (as copies or official issues), by which so much of this system of production and marketing, and above all its taxation could operate, was plentiful on the site until $c$ AD 380.

By the last quarter of the 4th century there were clear signs of recession and a qualitative decline in the fabric of Roman Britain. These circumstances were part of a more widespread and cumulative breakup of the Empire which affected its western provinces most acutely. This was the context for a fundamental disruption in the occupancy of the Great Witcombe villa building, possibly during the 380s. The final episode of use implies that the villa no longer functioned as a country house but was being adapted for more utilitarian purposes. Even earlier in the 4th century some villas in the region may have been abandoned or downgraded in use as buildings, e.g. Barnsley Park (Webster and Smith 1982), and the type of re-utilization seen at Witcombe can be paralleled elsewhere (e.g. Keynsham, Avon or Rockbourne, Hants.). At Frocester the villa remains were supplemented by timber-framed buildings, and organic-tempered pottery was in use (Gracie and Price 1980); while at the neighbouring shrine at Uley similar pottery and a structural sequence, which may represent conversion and then the rebuilding of a Christian church on the remains of a pagan rural temple, imply activity continuing here into the 6th or 7th centuries (Woodward and Leach 1993).

It is impossible to estimate the duration of the latest occupation at Witcombe and no organic-tempered pottery is recorded here. However, the activity suggests some maintainence of the estate and its operations into the 5th century. Continuity of land use and tenure is likely to have been one of the more enduring elements to survive the break-up of Roman Britain after $c$ AD 400. Many of the material accessories and manifestations of the highly Romanized society of the 4th century may have rapidly fallen away following the break with Rome and the cessation of a tax system which to a large extent drove it, but there is little accompanying evidence for major civil or military disruption, foreign Germanic invasion or natural disasters. The vestiges of a Romanized society may however have persisted for rather longer into the 5th century than purely archaeological evidence will admit (Esmonde Cleary 1989; Millett 1990).

We may never know the fate of Witcombe's former owners, although there is no reason why the building and its estate could not have remained a family possession for several more generations. Did they retreat to the relatively security of a town house within the walls of Gloucester, relocate to another more modest farm, or perhaps re-occupy the villa and continue living there for a time in reduced circumstances? Whatever the exact circumstances, Witcombe and its owners were at the mercy of processes which involved the breakdown of social, administrative and fiscal systems which had evolved over several centuries in imperial Roman Britain. Their effect was most evident upon the institutions, cultural and material manifestations of that society, among them the villas.

Witcombe may have ceased to be a practical residence for the magnate and family who owned it, even before the system which had created and sustained it had collapsed. What almost certainly did not collapse, however, was the aristocratic elite represented by the house and its estate. This was the group who had governed Gloucester and its *territorium* and had strengthened their position and prestige during the years of imperial government. As that system passed away this aristocracy assumed the role of independant governors, in parallel with communities elsewhere, founding the new dynasties and petty kingdoms of post-Roman Britain, based largely perhaps upon the original *civitates*. Such individuals and their new establishments are barely now traceable in the archaeological record, but is there perhaps an echo of their descendants recorded by the Anglo Saxon Chronicle with the fall of Bath, Gloucester and Cirencester following the Battle of Dyrham in AD 577?

# CONSOLIDATED BIBLIOGRAPHY

Allason-Jones, L., and Miket, R., 1984 *The Catalogue of Small Finds from South Shields Roman Fort.* The Society of Antiquaries of Newcastle-Upon-Tyne Monograph Series No.2.

Allen, D.A., 1991 'The Glass' in Holbrook, N. and Bidwell, P. *Roman Finds from Exeter* Exeter Archaeological Report 4

Arveiller-Dulong, V., and Arveiller, J., 1985 *Le Verre d'Epoque Romaine au Musee Archeologique de Strasbourg.* Notes et Documents des Musees de France, 10 Paris.

Avent, R., and Howlett, T., 1980 'Excavations at Roman Long Melford, 1970-1972', *Proceedings of the Suffolk Institute of Archaeology and History* 34, 229-249.

Bedoyere, G., de la, 1993 *Roman Villas and the Countryside,* English Heritage, London

Berger, L., 1960 *Romische Glaser aus Vindonissa,* Veroffentlichungen der Gesellschaft pro Vindonissa, Band 4. Birkhauser Verlag Basel.

Biddle, M., 1967 'Two Flavian Burials from Grange Road Winchester', *Antiquaries Journal,* 47; 224-250

Black, E. W., 1994 'Villa-owners: Romano-British Gentlemen and Officers', *Britannia* 25, 99-110

Boon, G. C., 1963 'Caerleon', *Bulletin of the Board of Celtic Studies* 19, 344-5.

Boon, G. C., 1966 'Roman Window Glass from Wales', *Journal of Glass Studies* 8; 41-5

Boon G. C., 1972-3 'Roman Glass from Caerwent, 1855-1925', *Monmouthshire Antiquary,* 3.ii, 111-123

Boon, G. C., 1974 'Counterfeit coins in Roman Britain', in Casey and Reece 1974, 95-171

Boon, G. C., 1974a *Silchester, The Roman Town of Calleva,* Newton Abbot & London.

Brailsford, J. W., 1962 *Antiquities from Hod Hill in the Durden Collection,* British Museum, London.

Branigan, K., 1972 'Gauls in Gloucestershire?', *Bristol and Gloucestershire Archaeological Society Transactions* 92, 82-95.

Branigan, K., 1977 *The Roman Villa in South West England,* Bradford-on-Avon

Branigan, K., 1977a *Gatcombe Roman Villa,* British Archaeological Reports 44, Oxford.

Branigan, K., and Miles D. (eds.) 1989 *The Economies of Romano-British Villas,* Sheffield.

Brewer, R. J., 1986 'The Beads and Glass Counters', in Zienkiewicz, J. D., *The Legionary Fortress Baths at Caerleon: II, The Finds,* Cardiff; 146-156.

Casey, J. and Reece, R. (eds.) 1974 *Coins and the Archaeologist* British Archaeological Reports 4, Oxford.

Charlesworth, D., 1959 'Roman Glass in Northern Britain', *Archaeologia Aeliana* 4th series, 37, 33-58.

Charlesworth, D., 1967 'The Glass', in Smedley, N. and Oules, E. J., 'A Romano-British Bath-House at Stonham Aspal', *Proceeding of the Suffolk Institute of Archaeology,* 30, 240-1.

Charlesworth, D., 1971 'The Glass', in Rennie, D. M., 'Excavations in the Parsonage Field, Cirencester, 1958', *Transactions of the Bristol and Gloucestershire Archaeological Society,* 90, 84-8.

Charlesworth, D., 1972 'The Glass', in Frere, S. S., *Verulamium Excavations I,* Research Report of the Society of Antiquaries of London, 28, 203-7.

Charlesworth, D., 1975 'Glass', in Hobley, B., '"The Lunt" Roman Fort and Training School for Roman Cavalry, Baginton, Warwickshire', *Transactions of the Birmingham and Warickshire Archaeological Society,* 87, 1-56.

Charlesworth, D., 1978 'The Roman Glass', in Down, A., *Chichester Excavations III,* 267-273.

Charlesworth, D., 1984 'The Glass', in Frere S. S., *Verulamium Excavations III.* Oxford University Committee for Archaeology, 145-173.

Charlesworth, D., 1985 'The Glass', in Nibblet, R., *Sheepen: an Early Roman Industrial site at Camulodunum,* CBA Research Report 57, MF 1:A5-A9, 3:F1-F11, London

Charlesworth, D., and Price, J., 1987 'The Roman Glass', in Green C. S., *Excavations at Poundbury, Dorchester, Dorset 1966-1982 I: The Settlements.* Dorset Natural History and Archaeology Society Monograph 7, 108-9, MF2 E11-F4

Clarke, G., 1979, *The Roman Cemetery at Lankhills.* Winchester Studies 3, Pre-Roman and Roman Winchester Part II

Clarke, G. 1982 'The Roman Villa at Woodchester' *Britannia* 13, 197-288

Clifford, E. M., 1955 'The Roman Villa, Witcombe, Gloucestershire'. *Bristol and Gloucestershire Archaeological Society Transactions* 73, 5-69

Cool, H. E. M., 1990 'Roman Metal Hair Pins from Southern Britain', *Archaeological Journal* 147, 142-182

Cool, H. E. M., 1990 'The Problem of 3rd-Century Drinking Vessels in Britain', *Annales du 11e Congres de l'Association pour l'Histoire de Verre,* 1988, 167-175

Crummy, N., 1983 *The Roman Small Finds from Excavations in Colchester 1971-9* Colchester Archaeological Report No.2

Cunliffe, B. W., 1971 *Excavations at Fishbourne 1961-1969,* Research Report of the Society of Antiquaries of London, 27

Daniels, C., 1968 'A Hoard of Iron and Other Materials from Corbridge', *Archaeologia Aeliana* 4th Series, 46, 115-126

Davey, N., and Ling, R. 1982 *Wall Painting in Roman Britain*, Britannia Monograph Series 3, London

Dearne, M. J., and Brannigan, K., 1995 'The Use of Coal in Roman Britain', *Antiquaries Journal* 75, 71-105

Doppelfeld, O., 1959 'Der Muschelpokal von Koln', *Bonner Jahrbucher* 159, 152-66

Doppelfeld, O., 1975 'Ein farbiger Muschelpokal aus Koln', in *Festschrift fur Gert von der Ostern*, 17-23, Cologne

Dore, J., and Greene, K., 1977 *Roman Pottery Studies in Britain and Beyond* British Archaeological Reports Supp. Series 30, Oxford

Down, A., 1979 *Chichester Excavations 4, The Roman Villas at Chilgrove and Upmorden*

Drury, P. J., 1976 'Braintree: Excavations and Research 1971-6', *Essex Archaeology and History* 8, 1-143

Ellis, S. P., 1995 'Classical reception rooms in Romano-British houses',*Britannia 26, 163-178*

Elmer, G., 1941 'Die Munzpragung der Gallischen Kaiser in Koln, Trier und Mailand' *Bonner Jahrbucher* 146, 1-106

Esmonde Cleary, A. S. 1989 *The Ending of Roman Britain* London

Evans, J., 1996 'Roman Pottery' in Hughes, G. *Excavations at Thornwell Farm, Chepstow 1992* British Archaeological Reports, British Series 244 Oxford

Fowler, E., 1960 'The Origin and Development of the Penannular Brooch in Europe' *Proceedings of the Prehistoric Society* 26, 149-177

Fremersdorf, F., 1959 'Romische Glaser mit Fadenauflage in Koln (Schlangen-fadenglaser und Verwandtes)' *Die Denkmaler des Romischen Koln*, 5, Cologne

Fremersdorf, F., 1961 'Romisches geformtes Glas in Koln, *Die Denkmaler des Romischen Koln*, 6, Cologne

Fremersdorf, F., 1962 'Die Romischen Glaser mit aufgelegten Nuppen in Koln' *Die Denkmaler des Romischen Koln*, 7, Cologne

Fremersdorf, F., 1967 'Die Romischen Glaser mit Schliff, Bemalung und Goldauflagen aus Koln' *Die Denkmaler des Romischen Koln*, 8, Cologne

Fremersdorf, F. and Polonyi-Fremersdorf, E., 1984 'Die Farblosen Glaser der Fruhzeit in Koln 2 und 3 Jahrhundert' *Die Denkmaler des Romischen Koln*, 9, Cologne and Bonn

Fulford, M. G., and Allen J. R. L., 1992 'Iron-Making at the Chesters Villa, Woolaston, Gloucestershire: Survey and Excavation 1987-91' *Britannia* 23, 159-215

Gaffney, C., and Linford, P., 1998 'The Application of Geophysical Techniques at Wroxeter Roman City' *Computer Applications and Quantitative Methods 1997* British Archaeological Reports International Series (in press) Oxford

Gracie, H.S., 1970 'Frocester Court Roman Villa: First Report', *Bristol and Gloucestershire Archaeological Society Transactions*, 89, 15-86

Gracie, H. S., and Price, E. G., 1980 'Frocester Court Roman Villa: Second Report' *Bristol and Gloucestershire Archaeological Society Transactions*, 97, 9-64

Green, H. J. M., 1960 'Roman Godmanchester, Part I, An Early Dwelling', *Proceedings of the Cambridgeshire Archaeological Society*, 53, 8-22

Green, M. J., 1976 *A Corpus of Religious Material from the Civilian areas of Roman Britain*, British Archaeological Reports, British Series 24, Oxford

Green, M. J., 1978 *A Corpus of Small Cult Objects from the Military Areas of Roman Britain*, British Archaeological Reports, British Series 52, Oxford

Guido, M., 1978 *The Glass Beads of the Prehistoric and Roman Periods in Britain and Ireland.* Report of the Research Committee of the Society of Antiquaries of London, 35.

Guido, M., 1979, 'The Glass Beads', in Clarke, G.,1979, 292-4, 297-300

Harcourt, L. V., 1846 'Glass and Earthenware and Ornaments Discovered near Chilgrove in Sussex', *Archaeologia,* 21, 312-7

Harden, D. B., 1947 'The Glass', in Hawkes, C. F. C., and Hull, M. R., *Camulodunum, First Report on the Excavations at Colchester 1930-1939.* Research Reports of the Society of Antiquaries of London, 14, 287-307

Harden, D. B., 1958 'Four Roman Glasses from Hauxton Mill Cambridge, 1870', in Liversidge, J., 'Roman Discoveries from Hauxton' *Proceedings of the Cambridge Antiquarian Society,* 51, 1958, Appendix 1, 12-16

Harden, D. B., 1961 'Domestic Window Glass: Roman, Saxon and Medieval', in Jope, E. M. (ed.), *Studies in Building History: Essays in Recognition of the Work of B.H. St J. O'Neil*, 39-63, London

Harden, D. B., 1962 'Glass in Roman York', in *An Inventory of the Historical Monuments in the City of York, 1, Ebvracvm*. Royal Commission on Historical Monuments, 136-41.

Harden, D. B., 1963/4 'The Glass', in Gould, J., 'Excavations at Wall (Staffordshire) 1961-3 on the Site of the Early Roman Forts and of the Late Roman Defences', *Transactions of the Lichfield and South Staffordshire Archaeological and Historical society*, 5; 41.

Harden, D. B., 1967 'The Glass Jug', in Biddle M., 1967, 238-40

Harden, D. B., 1968a 'The Glass', in Hanworth, R., 'The Roman Villa at Rapsley, Ewhurst', *Surrey Archaeological Collections,* 65, 1-70

Harden, D. B., 1968b 'Glass', in Brodribb A. C. C., Hands, A. R., and Walker D. R. *Excavations at Shakenoak, I;* 74-81

Harden, D. B., 1974 'Window Glass from the Romano-British Bath-house at Garden Hill, Hartfield, Sussex', *Antiquaries Journal,* 47, 280-1

## CONSOLIDATED BIBLIOGRAPHY

Harden, D. B., 1975 'The Glass', in Cunliffe B., *Excavations at Porchester Castle I, Roman*, Report of the Research Committee of the Society of Antiquaries of London, 32, 368-74

Harden, D. B., 1975/6 'Fragments of Glass', in Kenyon, K. M., 'Excavations at Viroconium in Insula 9, 1952-3', *Transactions of the Shropshire Archaeological Society*, 55, 5-75

Harden, D. B., 1979 'Glass Vessels', in Clarke G., 1979, 209-220

Harden, D. B., and Green, C., 1978 'A Late Roman Grave-Group from the Minories, Aldgate', in Bird, J., Chapman, H. and Clark, J., (eds.) *Collectanea Londiniensia;* 163-175

Harden, D. B., Hellenkemper, H., Painter, K. and Whitehouse, D., 1987 *Glass of the Caesars*, Olivetti

Harden, D. B., and Price, J., 1971 'The Glass', in Cunliffe B. W. 1971, *Excavations at Fishbourne 1961-1969, ii: The Finds.* Reports of the Research Committee of the Society of Antiquaries of London 27, 317-374

Hawkes, C. F. C. and Hull, M. R., 1947 *Camulodunum*, Reports of the Research Committee of the Society of Antiquaries of London 14

Heighway, C. M., 1983 *The East and North Gates of Gloucester* Western Archaeological Trust, Excavation Report 4, Bristol

Henderson, J., 1980 'Some new Evidence for Iron Age Glass-Working in Britain', *Antiquity* 56; 60-1

Hingley, R., 1989 *Rural Settlements in Roman Britain*, London

Hodder, I. R. and Millett, M., 1980 'Romano-British Villas and Towns: a systematic analysis' *World Archaeology* 12 (1), 69-76

Howe, M. D., Perrin J. R. and Mackreth,D.F. 1980 *Roman Pottery from the Nene Valley, a guide*, Peterborough City Museum Occ. Paper 2

Hull, M. R., 1958 *Roman Colchester*. Report of the Research Committee of the Society of Antiquaries of London, 20

Hurst, H. R., 1985 *Kingsholm* Gloucester Archaeological Reports, Vol.1.

Isings, C., 1957 *Roman Glass from Dated Finds*, Groningen.

Isings, C., 1971 'Roman Glass in Limburg', *Archaeologica Traiectina*, 9. Groningen

King, A. C. and Potter, T. W., 1990 'A new domestic building facade from Roman Britain' Journal of Roman Archaeology 3, 195-204

Lawson, A. J., 1976 'Shale and Jet Objects from Silchester', *Archaeologia* 105, 241-275.

Lyne, M. A. B. and Jefferies, R.S., 1979 *The Alice Holt/Farnham Roman Pottery Industry* C.B.A. Research Report 30

Lysons, S., 1819 'Account of the Remains of a Roman Villa discovered in the Parish of Great Witcombe in the County of Gloucester' *Archaeologia* 19, 178-184

McWhirr, A., 1981 *Roman Gloucestershire* Gloucester

McWhirr, A., 1986 *Houses in Roman Cirencester*, Cirencester Excavation Reports III.

Manning, W. H., 1985 *Catalogue of the Romano-British Tools, Fittings and Weapons in the British Museum*, British Museum, London.

Miles, D., 1986 *Archaeology at Barton Court Farm, Abingdon, Oxon*, C.B.A. Research Report 50, London.

Millett, M., 1990 *The Romanization of Britain*, Cambridge

Neal, D. S., 1977 'Witcombe Roman Villa: A Reconstruction', in Apted,M.R., Gilyard-Beer,R. and Saunders, A.D. (eds.) *Ancient Monuments and their Interpretation*, 27-40. London

Neal, D. S., Wardle, A. and Hunn, J., 1990 *Excavation on the Iron Age, Roman and Medieval settlements at Gorhambury, St.Albans*. London

Newstead, R., 1914 'The Roman Cemetery in the Infirmary Field, Chester', *Annals of Archaeology and Anthropology*, 6, 121-167.

Orton, C. R., 1975 'Quantitative Pottery Studies' *Scietific Archaeology*, 16, 30-35

Orton, C. R., 1989 'An introduction to the quantification of assemblages of pottery' in *Journal of Roman Pottery Studies* 2, 94-7, Oxford

Oswald, F. and Price, T. D., 1920 *An Introduction to the Study of Terra Sigillata*, London

Peacock, D. P. S. (ed.), 1977 *Pottery and Early Commerce: Characterisation and Trade in Roman and Later Ceramics* London

Peacock, D. P. S. and Williams, D. F., 1986 *Amphorae and the Roman Economy*, London

Price, J., 1979 'The Glass', in Gracie, H S, and Price, E G, 1979; 9-64

Price, J., 1980 'The Roman Glass', in Lambrick, G., 'Excavations in Park Street, Towcester, 1963-8', *Northamptonshire Archaeology*, 15; 35-118

Price, J., 1982a 'The Glass', in Webster, G. and Smith, L., 1982, 174-185

Price, J., 1982b 'The Roman Glass', in Leach, P., *Ilchester Volume 1, Excavations 1974-5*, 227-232, Western Archaeological Trust Excavation Report 3, Bristol

Price, J., 1986 'Vessels of Glass', in Miles D, (ed.), 1986, IV.8.15

Price, J., 1987a .'The Roman Glass', in Frere, S. S., 'Brandon Camp, Herefordshire', *Britannia* 18, 71-76

Price, J., 1987b 'Glass from Felmongers, Harlow in Essex. A Dated Deposit of Vessel Glass found in an Antonine Pit', *Annales du 10e Congres de l'Association Internationale pour l'Histoire du Verre*, 185-206

Price, J., 1989 'Glass', in Stead I. M. and Rigby V., *Verulamium, the King Harry Lane Site*, English Heritage Archaeological Report 12; 40-50

Price, J., 1990 'Glass', in Wilmott, T., 'Excavations in the Middle Walbrook Valley, City of London, 1927-60', *London and Middlesex Archaeological Society Special Paper* 13; 153-167

Price, J., and Cool, H. E. M., 1984 'Glass from the Excavations of 1974-76', in Brown A. E. and Woodfield C., 'Excavations at Towcester, Northamptonshire: The Alchester Road Suburb'. *Northamptonshire Archaeology* 18, 115-124

Price, J., and Cool, H. E. M., 1985 'Glass', in Hurst H. R., 1985, 41-54

Rahtz, P. and Greenfield, E., 1978 *Excavations at Chew Valley Lake, Somerset* Department of the Environment Archaeological Reports 8, HMSO, London

Reece, R. M., 1972 'A short survey of the Roman coins found on fourteen sites in Britain' *Britannia* 3, 269-76

Reece, R. M., 1979 'Zur Auswertung und Interpretation romisher Fundmunzen aus Siedlungen' in *Studien zu Fundmunzen der Antike*, I, 175-95, Berlin

Reece, R. M., 1980 'Town and Country: the end of Roman Britain' *World Archaeology* 12 (1), 77-92

Reece, R. M., 1989 'Coins and Villas' in Brannigan & Miles (eds.) 1989, 34-41

Reece, R.M., 1995 'Site finds in Roman Britain', *Britannia* 26, 179-206

RIC Mattingly, Sydenham, Sutherland & Carson, 1923 *Roman Imperial Coinage*, London.

Ricken, H., 1948 *Die Bilderschusseln der romichen Topfer von Rheinzabern, Tafelband*, Bonn.

Ricken, H. and Fischer, C., 1963 *Die Bilderschusseln der romichen Topfer von Rheinzabern, Textband*, Bonn

Riha, E., 1979 *Die romischen Fibeln aus Augst und Kaiseraugst Forschungen in Augst Band* 3, Basel

Robinson, H. S., 1959 *The Athenian Agora*, V, Princeton

Rogers, G. B., 1974 *Poteries sigillees de la Gaule centrale, Gallia*, Suppl.XXVIII

RCHME, 1976 *Iron Age and Romano-British Monuments in the Gloucestershire Cotswolds*, Royal Commission on Historical Monuments (England), London.

Skilbeck, C. O., 1923 'Notes on the Discovery of a Roman Burial at Radnage, Bucks', *Antiquaries Journal* 3, 334-337

Smith, J. T., 1978 'Villas as a key to social structure', in Todd, M., 1978, 149-56

Smith, J. T., 1983 'Flight of Capital or Flight of Fancy?' *Oxford Journal of. Archaeology* 2 (2), 239-46

Stead, I. M., 1980 *Rudston Roman Villa*, Yorkshire Archaeological Society, Leeds

Sumner, H., 1924 *Excavations at East Grimstead, Wiltshire*. London

Symonds, R. P., 1992 *Rhenish Wares. Fine Dark Coloured Pottery from Gaul and Germany*, Oxford University Committee for Archaeology, Monograph 23, Oxford

Tabor, R. *Geophysical Survey at Chedworth Roman Villa, Gloucestershire* Birmingham University Field Archaeology Unit Report No. 363

Thorpe, W. A., 1935 *English Glass*, London

Todd, M., (ed.), 1968 *The Roman Fort at Great Casterton, Rutland*, Nottingham

Todd, M., (ed.), 1978 *Studies in the Romano-British Villa*, Leicester

Todd, M., 1989 'Villa and Fundus', in Branigan and Miles (eds.) 1989, 14-20

Tomalin, D. J., 1987 *Roman Wight: A Guide Catalogue to "The Island of Vectis, very near to Britannia"*

Tomber, R. and Williams, D. F., 1986 'Late Roman Amphorae in Britain', *Journal of Roman Pottery Studies* 1, 42-54, Oxford.

Trow, S. D., 1987 'Excavation at Ditches Hillfort, North Cerney, Gloucestershire, 1982-3', *Bristol and Gloucestershire Archaeological Society Transactions* 105,

Von Boeselager, D., 1989 'Zur Datierung der Glaser aus Zwei Grabern an der Luxemburger Strasse in Koln', *Kolner Jahrbuch fur Vor-und Fruhgeschichte* 22, 25-35

Watts, L. and Leach, P., 1996 *Henley Wood, Temples and Cemetery Excavations 1962-69*, C.B.A. Research Report No. 99

Webster, G., 1981, 'The Excavation of a Romano-British Rural Establishment at Barnsley Park, Gloucestershire: Part I', *Bristol and Gloucestershire Archaeological Society Transactions* 99, 21-78

Webster, G., 1982 'The Small Finds', in Webster, G. and Smith, L., 1982

Webster, G. and Smith, L., 1982 'The Excavation of a Romano-British Rural Establishment at Barnsley Park, Gloucestershire, 1961-1979, Part II', *Bristol and Gloucestershire Archaeological Society Transactions* 100, 65-189

Webster, G., et. al. 1985 'The Excavation of a Romano-British Rural Establishment at Barnsley Park, Gloucestershire, 1961-1979, Part III', *Bristol and Gloucestershire Archaeological Society Transactions* 103, 73-100

Webster, P. V., 1976 'Severn Valley Ware: a Preliminary Study' *Bristol and Gloucestershire Archaeological Society Transactions* 94, 18-46

Webster, P. V., 1977 'Severn Valley Ware on the Antonine Frontier' in Dore and Greene 1977, 163-176

Webster, P. V., 1993 'The Post-Fortress Coarsewares, Severn Valley Ware' in Manning, W.H. (ed), 1993 *Report on the excavations at Usk 1965-76, The Roman Pottery*, 285-294, Cardiff

Wheeler, R. E. M. and Wheeler, T. V., 1932 *Report on the Excavation of the Prehistoric, Roman and Post-Roman Site in Lydney Park, Gloucestershire*, Research Report of the Society of Antiquaries of London, 9, Oxford

Whiting, W., 1925 'The Roman Cemeteries at Ospringe', *Archaeologia Cantiana*, 37; 83-96

Williams, D. F., 1977 'The Romano-British Black Burnished Ware Industry; an essay on characterisation by heavy mineral analysis' in Peacock (ed.), 1977, 163-220

Williams, J. H., 1972 'Roman Building Materials in South West England' *Bristol and Gloucestershire Archaeological Society Transactions*, 90, 95-119

Woodward, A. and Leach, P., 1993 *The Uley Shrines, Excavation of a ritual complex on West Hill, Uley, Gloucestershire* English Heritage Archaeological Report 17

Young, C. J., 1977 *The Roman Pottery Industry of the Oxfordshire Region* British Archaeological Reports 43, Oxford

www.ingramcontent.com/pod-product-compliance
Lightning Source LLC
Chambersburg PA
CBHW050941010526

44108CB00060B/2841